The American Passport in Turkey

DEMOCRACY, CITIZENSHIP, AND CONSTITUTIONALISM

Rogers M. Smith and Mary L. Dudziak, Series Editors

The American Passport in Turkey

National Citizenship in the Age of Transnationalism

Özlem Altan-Olcay *and* Evren Balta

PENN

UNIVERSITY OF PENNSYLVANIA PRESS

PHILADELPHIA

Published by
University of Pennsylvania Press
Philadelphia, Pennsylvania 19104-4112
www.upenn.edu/pennpress

Printed in the United States of America
on acid-free paper

10 9 8 7 6 5 4 3 2 1

Library of Congress Cataloging-in-Publication Data

Names: Altan-Olcay, Özlem, author. | Balta, Evren, author.
Title: The American passport in Turkey : national citizenship in the age of transnationalism / Özlem Altan-Olcay and Evren Balta.
Other titles: Democracy, citizenship, and constitutionalism.
Description: 1st edition. | Philadelphia : University of Pennsylvania Press, [2020] | Series: Democracy, citizenship, and constitutionalism | Includes bibliographical references and index.
Identifiers: LCCN 2019034847 | ISBN 978–0-8122–5215–6 (hardcover)
Subjects: LCSH: Citizenship—United States. | Americans—Turkey. | Dual nationality—Turkey. | Dual nationality—United States. | Turks—United States. | Transnationalism—Social aspects.
Classification: LCC JK1759 .A42 2020 | DDC 323.6089/130561—dc23
LC record available at https://lccn.loc.gov/2019034847

For Defne Paker
and
Efe Yağmur Olcay

Contents

Abbreviations

ABCFM	American Board of Commissioners for Foreign Missions
AKP	Justice and Development Party
CDC	Centers for Disease Control and Prevention
CEDAW	Committee on the Elimination of Discrimination against Women
CENTO	Central Treaty Organization
CHP	Republican People's Party
DP	Democrat Party
HDP	People's Democratic Party
METU	Middle East Technical University
NATO	North Atlantic Treaty Organization

Introduction

Meanings and Values of American Citizenship in a Transnational World

On 24 August 2013, Turkish Bloomberg published a story online about the trend among Turkish women of giving birth in the United States. The manager of a health tourism and international education company, part of whose business catered to this group, estimated that around 450 women went to the United States for this purpose every year, spending around $13 million. He also added that this trend was growing as much in China, Russia, and several Middle Eastern countries. When probed about the motivation, before giving a variety of misconstrued expectations, he said: "[In this way] the child will become a U.S. citizen upon birth and will have the right to remain a U.S. citizen their entire life" (Bloomberg HT 24 August 2013). Apparently, these mothers-to-be, who are permanently settled in Turkey, imagine U.S. citizenship as offering their children something beyond their own citizenship status, regardless of whether the children end up living in the United States in the future. What does this story tell us? What does it mean to be a U.S. citizen in Turkey? What does it signify to be a U.S. citizen outside of the United States? What do the allure and privileges of U.S. citizenship in Turkey tell us about U.S. global power and its connections with local politics? What do the transnational meanings and values attached to U.S. citizenship signal about the transformation of the institution of citizenship?

People can give diverse answers to these questions. When a mother tells us that she wants to protect her daughter's modern, secular upbringing through U.S. citizenship, this aspiration lies atop an iceberg of Turkish national history, whose early republican legacy half of the country's population considers to be under threat. For her, U.S. citizenship is a form of insurance for her daughter given Turkey's unknown future. When a Turkish American citizen describes how he can make more credible claims of national belonging (because he returned to Turkey) and a cosmopolitan Western identity (because he lived in the United States and can always go back because he has U.S. citizenship), this says something about the popular identification of the West with the United States, a remnant of the political and cultural history between the two countries. When a natural-born U.S. citizen describes with enthusiasm the upward mobility that he has experienced since moving to Turkey, it signals a need to investigate what it is about the status of U.S. citizenship and "Americanness" that makes it a valuable asset outside of the United States. These stories and others show the many ways in which imaginaries about and the practices and experiences of U.S. citizenship outside of the United States are inherently connected to everyday experiences of economic opportunity and political unpredictability in Turkey and beyond. They reflect a history of conflicted relations between the non-West and the West, its echoes in cultural battles around questions of identity, and life in transnational spaces. More important, they elicit questions about the unequal meanings, practices, and values attached to national citizenship in transnational spaces.

This book explores the diverse meanings and values that various actors attribute to U.S. citizenship, actors who possess or seek to obtain U.S. citizenship while residing in Turkey. It is based on interviews with families who obtain U.S. citizenship for their children by giving birth in the United States, Turkish citizens who receive green cards and U.S. citizenship for themselves through naturalization but choose to return to and reside in Turkey, and natural-born U.S. citizens who have settled in Turkey during their adulthood. We propose that these meanings provide a unique vantage point to study locally situated political and economic tensions, inequalities, and struggles as well as the everyday workings of U.S. hegemony in the world. Through their narratives, we shed light on how U.S. citizenship is imagined, experienced, and practiced in a setting where everyday life is marked by unequal opportunities, brought about by the consolidation of economic liberalism on the one hand and more recently impacted by the convergence of national, regional, and transnational political unpredictability on the other. We argue that there are highly relevant questions to be explored in these diverse accounts of living in Turkey and the United States, experiences of U.S. and Turkish citizenship, in connection with individual subjectivities.

This book suggests that the transnational meanings and values of U.S. citizenship are ultimately connected to U.S. global power. Having U.S. citizenship outside the United States brings with it a set of symbolic meanings that are articulated in negotiations of identity. U.S. citizenship is also recognized outside the United States because of its strategic advantages compared to most citizenships. People who live in a region where most inhabitants have only limited options to escape political crisis and life-threatening situations may see their U.S. citizenship as insurance, a guarantee for safe passage to what they perceive to be a stable, liberal democracy. This is a transnational value that needs to be recognized. Or, in times of economic downturn and crisis in the United States, U.S. citizens can seamlessly pass across national borders, looking for work elsewhere while being able to reasonably expect that they will not experience much downward mobility. These diverse meanings and values of U.S. citizenship, which signify unequal transnational opportunities and symbolic recognition, give clues about the everyday workings of U.S. global power.

We also believe that the hierarchical meanings and values emerging from diverse experiences with, practices of, and imaginaries about U.S. citizenship reveal the need to rethink our conceptualizations of citizenship in the contemporary world. The values and meanings associated with national citizenship regimes transgress state borders, overlap with one another, and create new frontiers. These meanings and values are distinct and do not always necessarily mirror the experiences of those situated within the official borders of a single citizenship regime. In other words, we need to think about citizenship as an institution, an experience, and a set of practices unfolding in transnational spaces. In this book, we recognize the persistent relations of inequality between states and emphasize the need to locate the diverse meanings and values of citizenship in people's experiences, both inside and outside of countries of origin.

Broadly, this book makes three arguments. First, we propose that the privileges that people associate with U.S. citizenship in countries like Turkey provide a unique vantage point from which to explore the everyday workings of locally specific political polarization, social hierarchies, and cultural contestations. These privileges also give important clues about the long-term power of the United States in the region where Turkey is located, beyond its foreign policy interventions. The American empire persists at the intersection of the history of U.S. foreign policy, U.S. geopolitical prowess, *and* people's experiences of privilege with and desires for U.S. citizenship outside of the United

States. These citizens, current and aspiring, spread across the world, create "the American third world" (Altan 2006a): a new kind of empire of transnational Americans living outside the United States. This is an empire that extends beyond the official borders of the United States and is configured in the seemingly apolitical, everyday practices of American subjects as they fashion their agencies in social realms and cultural contestations ostensibly unrelated to U.S. geopolitical power.

Second, U.S. citizenship, whether the holder is born or naturalized into it, combines a unique set of values and meanings. It plays a powerful role in individuals' identity negotiations between national belonging and transnational aspirations. It enables people to forge creative combinations of subject positions, precisely because they are situated outside of the United States. The allure of U.S. citizenship is also strategic, located in the exit options that it generates in case of crises, the geographical mobility its passport facilitates, and the upward mobility it enables. The status of U.S. citizenship enables individuals to make sense of and reconfigure positions in political and economic conundrums in transnational spaces.

Finally, these U.S. citizens beyond the borders of the United States reveal the need to rethink the transformation of the institution of citizenship. We argue that we need to take into account the ways in which diverse individual claims and aspirations, in tandem with unequal proliferation of state powers, unfold in transnational spaces. The book argues that national citizenship continues to matter, but now does so in ways that cannot be captured by a sole focus on domestic state-citizen relations. We need to consider how people imagine, experience, and strategize around their citizenship status against a background of macropolitical circumstances beyond their choosing and not necessarily confined to the official state borders of their citizenship regimes. An increasingly transnationalized world does not necessarily mean a decrease in the significance of national citizenship. National citizenship still matters greatly for ordering inequalities, but now in transnational spaces.

Current and Aspiring Citizens of the United States: A Word on Method and Context

We study U.S. citizenship in Turkey through a total of 110 semi-structured interviews with three groups of people who have different relations to U.S.

citizenship. Together they allow us to map the diverse meanings and values attached to U.S. citizenship outside of the United States—ranging from those who imagine what U.S. citizenship means, through those who experience the advantages of this status alongside and in comparison with Turkish citizenship, to those whose U.S. citizenship coincides more unequivocally with "being American." These subjects are parents who do not have U.S. citizenship themselves but traveled to give birth to their children in the United States so that the latter had U.S. citizenship from birth; Turkish citizens by birth who have lived in the United States long enough to obtain a green card or U.S. citizenship; and U.S. citizens who are permanently settled in Turkey. Exploring their personal journeys—which extend to but also go beyond Turkey and the United States—we seek to understand the variety of ways in which actual people imagine, practice and experience U.S. citizenship in Turkey.

The stories we tell in this book are also stories of an increasingly polarized country: a country where scores of urbanites have been socialized into thinking of Turkey as a Western country whereas the current political authorities frequently deploy a rhetoric portraying connections to the West as "a betrayal of the Turkish nation." Studies focusing on Turkey and its relations with the West in general and with the United States, in particular, do so from a macro-political perspective. In contrast, we emphasize the importance of highlighting everyday experiences and narratives that make sense of them, and connecting these to the macro-political context. Individuals strategize at the intersection of institutions that regulate citizenship, political contexts that affect their lives, and individual resources, which are always unequal. By turning our gaze to actual people and their everyday experiences in contemporary Turkey, we uncover how certain citizenships can become an important tool in managing diverse insecurities.

This research has a very personal starting point for us. We are both middle-class Turkish mothers who previously resided in the United States for close to a decade during our doctoral studies before returning to Turkey after graduation. Evren moved from the United States to Turkey while she was pregnant whereas Özlem gave birth several years after moving to Turkey. When Evren made the decision to return to Turkey while four months pregnant, many around her questioned her judgment. Friends and acquaintances asked her repeatedly why she did not stay in the United States a bit longer to give birth to her daughter Defne there instead. When Özlem was pregnant, she frequently encountered a different variation of this question. Was she going to go back the United States to give birth since she had so many ties there and knew the place inside out? The answer was negative: Her son Efe Yağmur was also born in Turkey. On the one hand, these questions evoked guilt about not having made the "right" choice for our children. On the other hand, as social scientists deeply interested in questions of micro politics of belonging and everyday strategizing, we began to think about what these insistent questions mean. Why do people think that it is a good idea to travel thousands of miles in the later stages of pregnancy, spending tens of thousands of dollars in the process, taking on health risks for ourselves and the unborn child, especially during a period when the support of one's family and social network is of paramount importance? What do these questions say about experiences with the Turkish context as well aspirations regarding U.S. citizenship?

It was with these in mind that we initially began the research with interviews with forty parents who had given birth in the United States to acquire U.S. citizenship for their children. We contacted our interviewees, mostly mothers, through different points of entry into the field: There were individuals who had experienced this among our own acquaintances; others we reached through the schools where our children were enrolled; we found online blogs that some women write about their experiences; and our initial contacts led us to more people to interview. Three categories emerged at the intersection of familiarity with the United States and economic power. The first group comprised couples with at least one that had previously lived in the United States and was a high-level professional or business owner. This group not only had significant economic resources but also in-depth familiarity with the workings of everyday life in the United States. The second group was also made up of high-level professionals with substantial income and wealth. However, unlike the first group, their familiarity with the United States was limited to short-term visits for pleasure or business. Nevertheless, they could claim knowledge of and affinity with what they often referred to as "the American way of life." The third group was the smallest of the three: Even though they too had visited the United States briefly and claimed cultural affinity, their financial means were more limited. All interviews, which on average lasted between one and two hours, covered the parents' motivations for and interpretations of their children's citizenship status, the intricacies of the journey itself and the ways in which parents were raising their children in Turkey.

We conducted these interviews in 2012 and at the beginning of 2013, a time in Turkish political history when the governing Justice and Development Party (Adalet ve Kalkınma Partisi, AKP) had begun alienating the liberal and secular middle classes, accusing them of being elitist. Its grip on political power was rising as it had successfully neutralized the military, a move desired by many, although the party then moved on to intimidate and repress opposition groups as well as to encroach on the independence of the judiciary. This was a time when the overwhelming sentiment among Turkey's secular urban middle and upper classes was a fear that the early republican values of secularism and Western modernity were being damaged, along with a sense of a loss of stable life trajectories and sociocultural privileges.

This first group of interviewees belonged to those sections of Turkish society who were increasingly anxious about the possibility that the quality of their lives and their domestic status could decline. This anxiety had pushed them to strategize for their children's future in case their predictions about Turkey's worsening ties with the West, rising authoritarianism and desecularization would come true. They told us stories of their own upbringings and the insecurities that they felt in the contemporary context. Many described the longing they had for the freedom they had experienced when they lived in the United States or had observed about everyday life during their visits there. When people talked about their desires for individual freedom and a predictable political setting, these comments were intricately connected to apprehensions about the Turkish context. They also signified a sense of loss: These groups, regardless of their income and wealth, were brought up with an inherent sense of high social status because they had shared in the hegemonic narrative of Turkey as a nation that is part of the West (Altan-Olcay and Balta 2016). At this juncture, however, they felt that this narrative was losing credibility, along with their historically assumed social and cultural identities and privileges associated with them. In the end, because they did not feel capable of doing much to change the political affairs of the country, they used their individual resources to take precautions for their children's future. Hence, for them, U.S. citizenship was a "gift" to their children (Balta and Altan-Olcay 2016) that represented expanded future possibilities and acted as a signifier of how the parents wanted to raise them. More important, people perceived it as a crucial precaution for the children if the parents' premonitions about becoming the new minority in Turkey reached a point where they felt threatened.

As our interviews accumulated, patterns began to emerge: among others, anxieties about future risks, the motivation to protect children from such risks, and U.S. citizenship as possible insurance. The narratives we heard revealed imaginaries about and expectations of U.S. citizenship by people who themselves do not have the status (or plan to acquire it). However, it also became clear that these conversations were largely about the unknown future experiences of the children. At the time we conducted this first group of interviews, all the children whose parents we talked to were under the age of sixteen. We had little insight into what the children's experiences and perceptions were concerning U.S. citizenship. With this in mind, we expanded our scope to ask a more inclusive question about how U.S. citizenship is experienced outside the United States, particularly in Turkey. Over the course of 2014 and 2015, we conducted interviews with two additional groups of actors: U.S. citizens by birth who had come to settle in Turkey during their adulthood and Turkish citizens who had become naturalized in the United States but returned to Turkey.

Our second group of interviewees included thirty-six U.S. citizens who were permanently settled in Turkey. This group had rich experiences with transnational mobility, career choices, and more intimate reasons, such as marriage, that took them outside the United States. In contacting this group, we also used various networks, such as acquaintances, institutional affiliations, personal blogs, and expatriate lists, in order to achieve diversity across gender, profession, age, and duration of stay. This group was also the most diverse in terms of socioeconomic origins. The stories of their familial backgrounds, upbringings, the schools they attended, and the options they had after graduating from college clearly revealed a wide range of socioeconomic opportunities in the United States. We asked them to describe their upbringing in the United States, the choices that led them eventually to Turkey, their experiences of the transition to and living in Turkey, and their personal interpretations of privileges and ambivalences of "being American." Often we saw that, for this group, Turkey was not the only place outside of the United States in which they had lived, as many had also stayed in other countries in Europe, the Middle East, and the Far East, allowing us to tap into rich accounts of being transnationalized Americans with experiences of privilege in comparison with the citizens of various countries, including but not limited to Turkey.

These were actors who were natural-born U.S. citizens, socialized thoroughly in their country of origin, but now continuing their lives in Turkey.

Thus, the meanings and values they associated with U.S. citizenship were informed deeply by their identification with "Americanness." Their narratives revealed complicated issues of national belonging, however: Having lived in Turkey—and, for several, other countries in the developing world—they had seen firsthand the historical impact of U.S. foreign policy around the world. They could also compare the more consumerist everyday life in the United States with the significantly narrower range of choices outside. These experiences invariably produced discomfort about what it meant to be American. Yet at the same time, being recognized as an American almost always turned into various personal experiences of privilege. When individuals talked about the latter, some found themselves expressing patriotic pride. These experiences of privilege encompassed more lucrative jobs, interesting career paths, and elevated social status. They signaled the symbolic recognition that being an American elicited and how it could translate into upward mobility that was not available to the same degree if they had stayed in the United States. Once again, however, these were complicated processes, with people's ethnic and racial backgrounds as well as gender and sexuality playing significant roles in the outcome. Ultimately, this group's narratives documented the conditions under which U.S. citizenship and nationality come to be associated with one another and produce upward social mobility outside the United States.

Finally, we interviewed thirty-four individuals of Turkish birth who held a green card or U.S. citizenship. They had obtained their status mainly through long-term stay in the United States (as students and later for work-related reasons), the diversity lottery, or spousal/familial connections. At the time of the interviews, most of this group had returned to and decided to permanently settle in Turkey. We also conducted interviews with a small number of individuals who were still living in the United States but were entertaining, to different degrees, the option of returning to Turkey in the near future. These individuals were thus "hyphenated American citizens:" They had grown up in Turkey, some up to college age, some up to the point where they began graduate studies, and almost all into their twenties. Many had lived in the United States for at least a decade. Now back in Turkey permanently or visiting frequently, they had a distinct comparative perspective on Turkish and U.S. citizenship. We asked them about their life trajectories, their move to the United States and back to Turkey, their motivations for and experiences with obtaining the green card and/or U.S. citizenship, and how they currently lived with their dual citizenship in and outside the United States and Turkey, including the benefits that they gained and the ambivalences they experienced.

On the one hand, this group, more than any other, provided us with colorful stories about the strategic advantages of U.S. citizenship for crossing nation-state borders compared to Turkish citizenship. Furthermore, their dual citizenship status worked for them in a unique way: When they decided to go back to Turkey, they could utilize their Turkish upbringing and familiarity with Turkey to find jobs, while using their green card or U.S. citizenship to push for more lucrative, higher-status positions. Furthermore, the status of U.S. citizenship meant that the move to Turkey did not have to be permanent; they could circulate between Turkey and the United States if necessary. On the other hand, their stories were never only about the strategic advantages of having dual citizenship. Rather, U.S. citizenship also signified for them a cosmopolitan cultural disposition and confirmed their aspirations to belong to a transnational network of mobile actors. In other words, these actors also saw their U.S. citizenship in terms of political belonging. They often tied their U.S. citizenship status to personal dispositions, which they felt were more in tune with what they described as the American culture and which made them feel alienated in contemporary Turkey. Yet, their narratives were rife with ambivalences and contradictions as they tried to juggle their simultaneous cultural affinities with the United States and Turkey.

This group included the secular middle and upper classes as in the group of parents. Their narratives resonated with the first group's but enriched them with actual experiences of U.S. citizenship. In these narratives, we could see the dominance of fears about the political future of Turkey in conjunction with economic opportunities, and frequent references to possession of U.S. citizenship to explain transnational identities and to retain distance from contemporary hegemonic political discourses in Turkey. Interestingly, however, the group also included middle-class individuals who defined themselves as conservative and had political identifications with the AKP in government. These individuals also found something alluring in what they referred to as "American culture." Even when they spoke harshly against U.S. foreign policy in the Middle East, their personal stories also revealed a fascination with values like individual freedom and cultural tolerance. For them, their experiences of religious tolerance in the United States stood out as the major attraction of the so-called American culture. Such stories revealed intense and diverse meanings attributed to America from the outside. The American dream with its promises of individual freedom and (various types of) multiculturalism spoke to desires and self-perceptions of cosmopolitanism. However, there was almost always a hesitation in these statements: Almost immediately after defining themselves using adjectives such as cosmopolitan, transnational, and multicultural, people often felt the need to assert that they belonged in Turkey. U.S. citizenship carried intense symbolic meaning, but one that needed to be constantly explained and defended as the actors went about their lives in Turkey. They were never "Turkish Turkish" nor "American American," as one of them put it.

Overall, what linked these latter two groups—despite their ethnic, national, and religious differences—was their American citizenship and the ways in which Americanness and social class positions became mutually constitutive of each other *outside* the United States. For many of the Turkish Americans, their access to U.S. citizenship had become a possibility because of their middle- or upper-class origins in Turkey, although there was also a small group with working-class backgrounds. As for Americans who permanently settled in Turkey, being an American outside the United States often resulted in a variety of privileges, regardless of their original socioeconomic backgrounds. Their narratives suggested the emergence of an American transnational class whose privileges are intricately connected to being outside the United States. This book is also about the shaping of this new class of transnational Americans and the values they attach to U.S. citizenship.

Although we do rely on the rich narratives of our interviewees to organize our discussion of concepts such as transnational and global as well as the United States, America, and Americanness, we are theoretically inspired by debates in citizenship and migration studies. We do not use these terms interchangeably but rather they denote specific lenses through which experiences of strategizing, belonging, and mobility are interpreted. When we sift through our material, one thing becomes quite evident: When people talk about the U.S. or the U.S. citizenship, this is often an allusion to very material relationships that individuals establish with the state through the official institution of citizenship. We retain this logic in our own thinking and use the concept of U.S. citizenship thematically to discuss material circumstances that it enables. When people discuss *American* citizenship, these narratives either focus solely on cultural identifications of what it means to be an American or straddle ambiguous connections between identity and privilege. We build on these to open the diverse ways in which citizenship connotes more than national origin. We emphasize that while the geopolitical power of the U.S. is to be traced within the very material inequalities between states, we need to always make a connection between this power and the transnational imaginaries of America, as Grewal suggests (2005).

In the interviews, the differences between *global* and *transnational* are harder to decipher: People use multiple words to assert their positions with respect to their birth citizenships and build individualized identity narratives. They can use the terms "global citizenship," "transnational citizenship," or "cosmopolitan citizenship" interchangeably, while also arguing some national contexts are more open to multicultural belonging. In describing state level power inequalities, we use "global," "bilateral," or "international" depending on what level of relations are under consideration. We find in these everyday narratives traces of a history of diverse usages of the concept of the transnational, ranging from advocacy networks to capitalist classes, civil society to wars, cultural connections to migrant flows (Appadurai 1996; Faist 2000; Glick Schiller 1997; Glick Schiller, Basch and Szanton Blanc 1995; Grewal 2005; Kivisto 2003; Portes 1999, Sklair 2001; Urry 2000). Faist conceptualizes "transnational social space" as a way of thinking about the multilayered actors and flows involved in border crossing and boundary breaking processes. He proposes it as a conceptual tool through which to explore the creation of new social spaces across borders as people traverse them, retain a multiplicity of social ties and respond to structural circumstances defined by markets as well as states (Faist 2000). He emphasizes the importance of looking at impact not only through the lens of individual lives, but also attending to the changes in the very institutions and inequalities people navigate (Faist 2010, 2016). Following this suggestion, we consider the navigation that is happening between the U.S. and the Turkish state borders a transnational practice, a border crossing that generates a new social space where both the actors and their citizenship status acquire new meanings.

We also rely on Grewal's usage of "transnational America" to indicate how American citizenship, practices, and imaginaries around it create an America beyond the borders of the United States. This transnational America is indicative and productive of social hierarchies elsewhere, as well as identity narratives, which claim to transcend the nation while being informed by it (Grewal 2005). Thus, throughout the text when we use the concept transnational, this usage deliberately focuses on individuals' practices and imaginaries around America and American citizenship without losing sight of the fact that these practices are never divorced from state powers and state-level power relations (Faist 2010; Faist and Kivisto 2010; Grewal 2005). Overall, we aim to examine international, transnational, and global scales as sites through which individual interactions can change existing social orders and create new ones (Go and Lawson 2017, 27). We move away from analyses in which individual narratives are assumed to be completely structured through macro-level processes. Instead we adopt a form of methodological relationalism that starts from the constitutive relations between "inside" and "outside" and treat the national, transnational and global as scales rather than discrete units of analysis (Go and Lawson 2017, 28). We show how forms of citizenship are created as individuals interact with institutions and navigate, reproduce and reshape scales.

Of course, state-level processes were an integral part of the context in which our interviewees lived, strategized, and talked with us. In the summer of 2013, around the time we finished our interviews with the parents, Turkey experienced its own wave of popular protests, following in the footsteps of the Arab Uprisings. What started out as a small, localized demonstration against increasing encroachment on public space and the shopping mallization of Istanbul quickly spread to many cities to become a massive mobilization against the government's increasingly authoritarian tendencies. After a euphoric couple of months, however, the protests were crushed and the government's repressive measures against opposition groups took a suffocating turn. It was in this context that we conducted interviews with the second and third groups during the course of 2014 and 2015. Scenarios about what could go worse were becoming more tangible and more plausible while people were also witnessing the ramifications of the Syrian refugee crisis in the city's everyday life. The tragedy of hundreds of thousands of Syrian refugees whose livelihoods depended on the whims of the Turkish state reminded people of the civil war and ISIS violence next door and made questions of free mobility across borders a more immediate concern. These observations sharpened our interviewees' perceptions of and experiences with life in the United States, the status of U.S. citizenship, and what it means to an American or a Turkish national.

The arguments we make are necessarily limited to the groups of people whose stories we captured against the sociopolitical background in which they conducted their lives. In other words, we do not claim to make generalizations about a specific population or the entire Global South. However, our arguments about the meanings and values of U.S. citizenship in transnational contexts are also enriched to the extent that we were able to delve deeply into the experiences of our interviewees in Turkey, the United States, and anywhere else they might have lived. Ours is a quest to document the nature of a process that may provide important insights into the workings of U.S. citizenship in conjunction with U.S. global power elsewhere. This is an intermediate, limited generalization that offers a way to trace processes in people's narratives of everyday experiences (Payne and Williams 2005). This level of generalization is also reflexive, guided by our own situatedness (Harding 1995): We, as researchers, are also part of the web of relations that cross borders, but we retain painstaking awareness of them. This is a web of relations that includes mobilities, imaginaries, desires, and experiences of "other" lives in a context defined by a history of state formation in Turkey, the Turkish state's shifting geopolitical positioning, and relationship with the U.S. global power.

American Culture and the American Empire in the Middle East: New Trajectories

What are the various ways in which America is imagined outside of the U.S.? How are these imaginations informed by local political and sociocultural contestations? What do these processes say about American cultural power? Answers to such questions have been located at the intersection of postcolonial studies, which explore the enduring influence of "the West" in newly formed nation-states, and in studies of "the American empire." In dialogue with this literature, we are especially interested in understanding the lure of U.S. citizenship, its uncertainties, and the privileged experiences it entails in a context where U.S. power has been visibly present.

Postcolonial studies show us how "the West" became the object of multiple, ambivalent discourses during and after modern nation-state formation in the twentieth century. On the one hand, the West signified the intruder, the one whose unequal power resulted in experiences of colonization. On the other hand, in the establishment of postcolonial nation-states, the need to reckon with this power was realized in institutional continuities, discourses of modernization, dynamic contestations about what cultural practices were required for achieving modernization, and how these would sit with claims of cultural authenticity (Blom and Stepputat, 2001; Krishna, 1992; Ludden, 1992). These are histories in which the nationalist elite reacted to *and* adopted colonial powers' discursive contrasts between the "civilized," "rational," "enlightened" "Western" and its "Eastern" other. These dichotomies were also complicit in discourses of who truly belonged as a citizen in the new, modern nation-state and who did not (Adas 1989; Chatterjee 1993; Mamdani 1996). Often, those who were able to fashion themselves through discourses of modernization were the groups that successfully claimed the position of "desirable citizens" as opposed to those in need of being "modernized," "educated," and "civilized."

As the new nationalist elite sought to simultaneously define their cultural authenticity and catch up with Western powers, they also engaged in producing homogenized and selective definitions of "the West." These debates did not necessarily only occur at the level of the political leadership either. On the contrary, meanings of "the West," "Western," and "modern" became central to larger cultural processes and contestations. Westernized dispositions and an intimate knowledge of the workings of former colonial powers became particularly central to the urban classes' self-definitions through a wide variety of cultural and consumption practices that continue today (Altan-Olcay 2008; Babb 2001; Colonna 1997; de Koning 2006; Öncü 1999; Peterson 2011; Pink 2009; Üstüner and Holt 2010). In other words, questions of Western identity have figured across a widespread terrain and they have always been conflicted. While the locally adopted imaginaries of the West have become central to individualized claims of value, legitimacy, and distinction during the twentieth century, anxieties surrounding questions of "authenticity," in both the new nation-states and the West, have also turned them into continuous struggles (Bhabha 1997; Chakrabarty 1997; Chatterjee 1989 and 1993). These processes, we know, speak to both the local politics of modernization and the enduring power of former colonial powers in these contexts.

Over time, and especially in the second half of the twentieth century, for parts of the world where U.S. state power was increasingly felt, "the West" began to be associated more strongly with the United States itself. To that end, American cultural power—its production, dissemination, reception, and re-appropriation—became paramount in everyday politics both inside and outside of the United States (Berghahn 2001; Little 2008; McAlister 2001; Saunders 2000). Grewal argues that studying the American nation as well as U.S. state power in contemporary global politics requires more than readings of U.S. foreign policy or domestic politics. It necessitates looking into what America means, as well as into the construction of American subjects beyond U.S. borders. She makes the case that constellations of consumer citizenship as symbolized in "the American dream" and discourses of multiculturalism have produced diverse notions of America, circulated among and translated across networks of the upper and middle classes in postcolonial contexts, and immigrant and diaspora communities. Accordingly, this dream extends far beyond the borders of the country to "many who have never lived in or visited the United States" (Grewal 2005, 206). She argues that this is the fundamental global power of the United States, generated at the intersection of geopolitics, neoliberalism, and the biopolitical performances of the so-called American dream (Grewal 2005).

In Turkey as well as the Middle East at large, the American dream has been associated with privilege, modernity, and transnationality in complex ways. For instance, American-style education has played a role in making locally specific class and status claims (Altan-Olcay 2008 and 2012; Anderson 2011; Miller-Idriss and Hanauer 2011). In general, local adaptations of U.S. consumption patterns have played ambivalent but powerful roles in creating social distinctions (de Koning 2006; Kuppinger 2000; Üstüner and Holt 2010). The meanings that "Americanized" consumption patterns and cultural practices carry around the world have almost always been classed processes. For most populations, it would be safe to say that U.S. geopolitical power can evoke nationalist reactions, often also encouraged by populist governments. The upper and middle classes, with more access to Westernized institutions, education systems, and cultural products, are more likely to associate "American" with cosmopolitanism and transnationality, although this tendency also rests on their precarious ability to separate their own cultural dispositions from negative connotations of U.S. political power in the world (Altan-Olcay 2008 and 2009b).

Notions of American culture circulate globally in diverse and unexpected ways. Edwards (2015), for instance, discusses the ways in which American cultural products are appropriated in the Middle East at the same time as they are stripped of their links to the United States. Building a theorization of endless circulation, he traces these processes of appropriation and reappropriation to show that the result is often cultural products whose meanings may not be readily recognizable in or translatable back to the United States (Edwards 2015). He invokes the possibility of the fragility of U.S. "soft" power given this explosion of meaning production outside U.S. borders.

We want to ask a related but different question of circulation: What happens if we think about the global diffusion and transformation of "American culture" together with the historical roles it has played in organizing social stratification elsewhere? Here we follow in the footsteps of Bourdieu (1984, 1986, 1987, 1989) and contemporary studies of social class. We look at individualized strategies of identity-making (Bottero 2004; Devine et al. 2005; Savage 2000), and the ways individuals claim distinction through the embodiment of American cultural practices and consumption patterns (Katz-Gerro 2002; Lamont and Molnár 2002; Lawler 2005; Le Roux et al. 2008; Savage, Bagnall and Longhurst 2001). We suggest that, in a world where "American culture" is more widespread and more available in the form of consumption patterns and lifestyle choices, the contribution it makes to people's individualized classification struggles inevitably declines. This signals that the cosmopolitan middle and upper classes in locations such as Turkey need to invent new strategies to assert Westernized identities before claiming local distinctions on that basis. For those who can access it, U.S. citizenship becomes just that. It is a status that brings privilege outside the United States for various groups, in conjunction with the U.S. government's global power. For these groups, cultural affinity with the U.S. is no longer enough to assert contextually specific stratifications, so they seek U.S. citizenship. This is an example where U.S. "soft" power actually continues to work, not only through unequal processes of globalized cultural production and dissemination, but also by offering a globally privileged citizenship and the feeling of security associated with it *despite* increasingly negative perceptions of the U.S. government.

There is a second contextual element that contributes to the workings of U.S. power through desires for and privileges associated with U.S. citizenship. This phenomenon is occurring in an era when market economies are being consolidated around the world. Economies are liberalizing and paving the way for transnational cultural access, globally shared consumption patterns, and border-crossing mobility for more privileged segments of populations everywhere (Elliott and Urry 2010). In much of the world, however, and contrary to expectations, economic liberalization has not been accompanied by political liberalization. In fact, in Turkey, along with numerous nation-states in Eastern Europe, the Middle East, and Latin America, it has often been each state's ability to monopolize political power that has made possible the consolidation of market economies and economic deregulation despite popular resistance. Histories of state repression and neoliberalization in these places are also intricately connected to the history of successive U.S. governments' geostrategic alliances, regional presence, and interventions (Migdal 2014; Yom 2015), complicating the "values" associated with American culture (Altan-Olcay 2008). In the current context—following popular uprisings against authoritarianism, corruption and social injustice (Bellin 2012; Lynch 2014)—things have taken a turn for the worse in several countries, including Turkey (Bozarslan 2015; Heydemann and Lender 2013; Prashad 2012).

This is the setting. On the one hand, U.S. cultural practices and products are more desirable, accessible, and globally recognizable, mostly due to the transnationalization of market economies. On the other hand, U.S. foreign policy continues to wreak havoc across the world, contributing to local and regional dynamics that lead to rising authoritarianism and political unpredictability. As a result, anti-Americanism is on the rise, also with the encouragement of populist governments. Yet it is in this context that we argue that U.S. citizenship embodies durable claims of distinction and might provide protection from the whims of authoritarian politics in a way that access to and socialization in Western institutions cannot. The narratives of our interviewees show that U.S. citizens can make claims of transnationality and cosmopolitanism while also achieving higher socioeconomic status. U.S. citizenship can offer official protection against rising nationalist and authoritarian tendencies, provide access to the global protection of the U.S. state, and allow mobility in a transnational space *despite* overwhelmingly negative popular sentiments about the exercise of U.S. global power (Krastev 2004). People value and desire U.S. citizenship because it enables more seamless border-crossing than passports of most citizenship regimes in the Global South. It allows easier escape from political and economic crises, and its recognizability protects against downward social mobility.

These desires and perceptions elicit the need to think about U.S. citizenship's ability to provide unequal transnational opportunities and symbolic recognition at the individual level. The privileges that people associate with U.S. citizenship in places like Turkey are indeed indicative of workings of U.S. power, at the intersection of geopolitics and biopolitics (Grewal 2005). This includes not only the weight of the U.S. government's foreign policy and the global recognizability of U.S. cultural products, but it also manifests itself in the symbolic recognition and privileges that U.S. citizenship generates across the world. U.S. citizens create a new kind of empire whose borders and state-citizen relations do not map neatly onto recognizable political territories. This is a fragmented imperial state, whose power manifests itself in the ability to have, protect, and create recognized and privileged extraterritorial citizens, and retain desires for membership across the world (Isin 2015).

Transnationalizing Citizenship?

The 1990s witnessed the flourishing of a literature discussing, in addition to the concept of transnational citizenship, notions such as "global citizenship" and "cosmopolitan citizenship" (Appadurai 1996; Falk 1994; Hannerz 1996). Hannerz's classical formulation of "transnational communities" is useful for describing how such communities can be formed without permanent relocation across nation-state borders (Hannerz 1996, 89, 98). These networks can develop around common educational experiences, occupations, and kinship and friendship (Hannerz 1996), not limited to places of birth or residence. They can also emerge from market exchanges and the ease of access to cultural production elsewhere (Appadurai 1996). These studies showed that transnational practices and acts of citizenship (Isin 2008) are without doubt on the rise, and true for diverse groups of people: immigrants retaining connections with countries of origin (Fitzgerald 2009; Glick Schiller 1999; Levitt 2003; Portes 1996), advocacy networks (Keck and Sikkink 1998; Sikkink 2002) and the career-motivated relocations of professionals in multinationals (Robinson and Harris 2000; Sklair 2001; van der Pijl 1998) among others. In the 1990s, these actors and their experiences appeared to suggest multiple paths for postnational lives in a world of shared cosmopolitan meanings.

A second aspect of this transnationalization has been advance of the universal human rights discourses. The Westphalian conception of citizenship has been based on the assertion of attributing a citizenship status to everyone and has depended on the mutual recognition of these statuses by states, although it has never prescribed content in terms of rights or political participation (Bauböck 2018). However, over time, normative and widespread acceptance of the universality of human rights has begun to fill out the ultrathin conception of citizenship, one that is neutral with regard to the nature of political regimes (Balibar 2004; Bauböck 1994; Faist 2009; Soysal 1994; Bauböck 2018). This process has also suggested possibilities for expanding of noncitizen rights and the dilution of nation-state-based identities (Joppke 2010 and 2018; Soysal 1994; Spiro 2007). In a world where rights are relatively divorced from citizenship status, people can act as citizens and become rightfully recognized members of a society even when they do not hold its official citizenship (Bosniak 2006; Vora 2013). They can access rights, based on the recognition of their personhood and their residence in host societies while attaching identity meanings to their countries of origin (Soysal 1994). They can also assert transnational identities, loyalties and engage in political actions, which are not limited to singular nation-states of birth (Bauböck 2007; Brubaker 1989; Fitzgerald 2004; Smith 2003 and 2007; Soysal 2012).

During the same period, these transformations have caused many scholars to argue that the value of national membership and national citizenship has decreased (Spiro 2007; Soysal 1994). Spiro, in fact, has said, "when everyone is American, no one is," in order to argue that U.S. citizenship as a source of national identity and its ability to draw distinct boundaries around who an American is weakening (Spiro 2008, 52). This is the case, he argued, not only because what is considered "American" is adopted by many around the world, but also because U.S. citizens have multiple sources for defining their allegiances and identities. More recently, however, he has also built a connection between the status of dual citizenship and individual rights to autonomy and freedom of association, thereby emphasizing that access to dual citizenship for immigrants is a human right (Spiro 2016). He has also argued that that dual citizenship is in the interest of nation-states and strengthens state-based connections, even though, in the long run, it will likely undermine the intensity of national identities, hollowing out the state from within and accelerating a postnational world (Spiro 2016, 131–132). As a result, intensification of access to dual citizenship will, over time, contribute to the "decoupling of the citizenship status from actual parameters of community" (Spiro 2016, 134).

Against this background of transnational identities, practices, and the growing acceptance of the framework of universal human rights, however, there is also a wind of change: Populist nationalist rhetoric is spreading across the world, accompanied by, at the very least, intense policy debates on "protecting" borders and collective identities (from the "encroaching immigrants") (Brown 2017). It is in this world of contradictory pulls of transnational aspirations and renationalizing tendencies that Bauböck has observed that while citizenship as an institution is in decline, demand for Western passports seems to be on the rise (2018). How can we understand these evolving contradictions and tensions?

Transnational citizenship itself denotes a situation in which borders between nation-states become more and more porous in a world of global connectedness (Castells 2000). And yet, despite this image of mobile populations, nation-state borders are still barriers to most, providing seamless transit only to actors with the "right" passports, the "right" class positions, and the "right" cultural capital (Balibar 2004). The ease of mobility across borders, as Elliott and Urry (2010, 79) have argued, has become essential to membership in an increasingly transnational world. This is a world in which, although increasing opportunities for mobility emancipate certain groups from territorial constraints, majorities do not have similar chances (Beck 2008; Bauman 1988). While we do not normatively juxtapose locality and mobility to social hierarchies, we suggest that unequal visa requirements that privilege citizens from rich democracies create a new kind of global stratification (Mau 2010). The more "privileged" passports mean that their holders can change residence flexibly and take for granted minimal stigmatization wherever they live.

In other words, U.S. citizenship is not the only citizenship that offers chances of geographical mobility, protection against economic and political risks, transnational possibilities for upward status and class mobility, as well as symbolic recognition of belonging in the West. At the time of the interviews and the few years that has passed since then, Turkey has continued its downward political spiral. The election of Donald Trump in the U.S. has also been raising questions about how safe and predictable the so-called American system, about which many of our interviewees talked, will remain. In the current atmosphere, anecdotal evidence and newspaper reporting indicates that U.S. citizenship is not the only status that is valued. Turkish Jewish citizens are applying for Israeli and Spanish citizenships, based on ancestral ties. The descendants of Turkish migrants from Bulgaria, who arrived in Turkey in different waves from Bulgaria, are applying for Bulgarian citizenship in such numbers that there are rumors that the government offices and archives, from which applicants need to collect documents, have ground to a halt in the face of demand. Those with more means are buying up property in places like Greece, Spain, Portugal, and Malta to obtain residence and mobility rights in the EU. Although official figures are hard to come by, the intensity of demand can be seen in the emergence of legal consultancy and international real estate firms that provide services to these groups. These stories do not necessarily indicate a decline in the value of U.S. citizenship, as evidenced, for instance, by the few interviewees who had more than two passports and said that they would retain only the U.S. citizenship if push comes to shove. Yet they show the diverse ways in which individuals strategize to offset what they see as a decline in their primary citizenships, given the means at their disposal. As political and economic circumstances shift in Turkey as well as abroad, people's perceptions of national citizenships and the strategies they develop also change.

What doesn't change, however, is that transnationalization of identities, rights and even meanings attributed to citizenship does not necessarily mean a decline of the institution of national citizenship. We need to consider the unequal opportunities that national citizenship regimes offer in transnational spaces. We suggest that these discussions can be enriched if we take into account the continuous inequalities between citizenship regimes *together with* unequal possibilities for transnationalization at the level of individual actors. It is these overlapping inequalities that signal the persistent importance of national citizenships, albeit in a different manner.

Hierarchies of Citizenship in Transnational Spaces

Ayelet Shachar (2009) has famously argued that not all citizenships are equal in terms of the opportunities they provide to their holders, and that they can be thought of as property in a broad manner. She points to the fact that certain citizenships are more valuable than others because of the role they play in determining people's positions in a globally unequal distribution of security and opportunity. These systemic inequalities (Shachar 2007) are all the more problematic because they are bequeathed on people through the arbitrariness of birthright citizenship (Shachar and Hirschl 2007), outside of the control of actual people. The question for us is how individuals attempt or desire to navigate these conditions of inequality between citizenship regimes, drawing also on inequalities within citizenship regimes.

We show that inequalities between citizenship regimes crystallize the tensions between one's feeling of belonging and the instrumental values of official citizenship status, the latter being an outcome of economic and political hierarchies within the state system. Whereas states at the top of these hierarchies provide more opportunities to their members, those at the bottom provide fewer. Our contention is that these unequal opportunities are not restricted to life chances within the nation-states, but also manifest themselves in terms of freedom to travel, to settle and live *elsewhere*. As a result, life chances of individuals are increasingly determined not only by the socioeconomic hierarchies in which they are situated nationally, but also by unequal transnationalizing opportunities attached to particular citizenship regimes. In other words, by focusing on the transnational value of the U.S. citizenship, we emphasize how global sorting of citizenship rights interacts with domestic hierarchies and how actors on the ground negotiate this dual inequality.

Studying actual experiences with and desires for U.S. citizenship provides a unique opportunity to understand how this negotiation happens in the everyday. This book shows that the transnational meanings and values attached to U.S. citizenship are strikingly different from those that could be evoked at the national level. Our three groups all repeated with different levels of intensity the assertions that the U.S. passport gives its holder an exit option in case of crises, facilitates a greater degree of geographical mobility in general, and the status associated with it enables upward mobility in the developing world. They shared stories of how their status elevated once outside the U.S. and repeated in different ways the protection they expected to receive from the U.S. government globally. These experiences and expectations of U.S. citizenship can also be perceived as what Joppke (2010, 161–162) calls "*light citizenship,*" one that "confer[s] many transnational rights without obligations and with a cultural content that requires belonging not to a particular national culture but to universal values."

Yet there is more: These narratives also show how conflicted these processes are and how they entail much more than clear calculations of cost and benefit. By approaching values and meanings attached to citizenship regimes from the vantage point of transnational experiences with and aspirations of U.S. citizenship, we rescale questions identity and juxtapose them with individual motivations for improving status outside the borders of the United States. U.S. citizenship enables people to make creative combinations of subject positions and offers these advantages mostly *because* they are situated outside the United States. This is thus a transnationalized U.S. citizenship, established and re-established each moment people actively imagine and/or experience privileges in connection to their passports. U.S. citizenship manifests its hierarchical power not in the United States, but when its holders move outside. The unfolding of these hierarchies around U.S. citizenship reveal also the need to rethink the transformation of the institution of citizenship. When values and meanings associated with national citizenship regimes no longer fit within neatly drawn state borders, they also transgress them, produce new boundaries, and construct new hierarchies.

These hierarchies are crystallized especially when we look at debates in dual citizenship. Dual (and even multiple) citizenship is now accepted by a growing number of states, resulting in increasing numbers of people holding more than one passport (Pogonyi 2011; Sejersen 2008; Spiro 2018). Scholars have explained this shift as part of ethno-nationalist strategies to reach out to large diasporas abroad, to maximize remittances, to plant foreign policy satellites abroad, and/or to win elections at home through absentee votes (Joppke 2018, Spiro 2016 and 2018, Harpaz 2018). In other words, as geographical distances shrink and social transactions are no longer confined to territoriality, we also see state structures that position themselves with respect to populations spread beyond official state borders (Joppke 2018, 10). Yet these developments are not necessarily the result only of direct, decipherable motivations on the part of states. Faist et al. explain them in terms of a path-dependent process influenced both by domestic norm changes, such as gender equality and the *jus soli* principle, and relevant international conventions, treaties, and court decisions (Faist, Gerdes and Rieple 2004. Spiro (2016, 13–15) shows that the instances of dual nationality are as old as the concept of nationality. However, in the early models of nationality, subject and claim, rather than citizen and right, were the central notions. Competition between the states was over keeping their subjects, so expatriation represented an intolerable loss of strength. He shows how, over time, states lost their capacity and incentive to suppress the status of dual citizenship because of the intensification of mobility across borders; the universalization of a framework of human rights, which constrains state treatment of individuals; and the mechanization of militaries, rendering manpower less important for state competition in the international system (Spiro 2016). Accordingly, as a result of all these changes, the old notion of loyalty to the sovereign has collapsed and dual citizenship has become more acceptable.

This is a world in which individuals in a growing number of countries are legally free to become a citizen of another country without necessarily giving up their birth citizenship. As the state incentives towards dual citizenship have shifted, so have individual motivations and strategies (Joppke 2018; Spiro 2016 and 2018). One interesting result has been the case of individuals who strategize to overcome the global hierarchy of citizenships through acquiring a "high-value citizenship" of a "first-tier state" (Harpaz 2018). Literature shows such individuals have asymmetric relationships with their two countries, depending on places of residence: An individual may enjoy a wide range of citizenship rights from a country where they do not reside. They may not have to pay taxes or fulfill any of the traditional duties associated with formal membership but they continue to be a member of a second polity while converting it into advantages in the home polity (Benhabib 2007; Harpaz 2010; Harpaz and Mateos 2018).

Examples are numerous: Descendents of European immigrants in Latin America use ancestral connections to access citizenships of countries in the EU (Cook-Martín 2013; Tintori 2011). Citizens of non-EU countries in Europe also do so, making use of shifting borders, especially in Eastern Europe (Neofotistos 2009). Harpaz shows that many, not only from Latin America but also East European countries, apply for a second passport for similar strategic reasons (Harpaz 2018). In these cases, the second nationality is a far less costly alternative than immigration and acts as *compensatory citizenship*, making up for deficits in the original citizenship in terms of opportunities, security, rights, and travel freedom (Harpaz 2010).

Not everyone with whom we have talked had dual citizenship, but the ways in which our interviewees narrated their experiences revealed how hierarchies between citizenship regimes are experienced at the level of the individual. The majority of adult U.S. citizens who have had this status from birth did not express the need or desire for Turkish citizenship, echoing Spiro's observation that additional citizenships bring marginal advantage to those who are citizens of the countries of the Global North (2018). Yet everyone else, whether it is parents who desire a second citizenship for their children even if they do not have one for themselves or Turkish citizens who got naturalized in the U.S., talked about the ways this second citizenship creates expanded opportunities. These narratives resonate with recent discussions on dual citizenship as well as "the instrumental turn" in citizenship granting rules and individual strategies for acquiring additional citizenships (Joppke 2018). They also prove Spiro's assertion about how such strategies among individuals in the Global South stem from existing inequalities and deepen them (2016 and 2018).

In a similar manner, Aihwa Ong's well-known concept of "flexible citizenship" draws attention to how privileged actors across the world strategize to access and combine different sovereignty regimes through the acquisition of multiple passports (Ong 1999 and 2006). She documents this process for the case of Chinese emigrants to the United States and other nation-states, who spread their homes and businesses between multiple countries in an effort to make use of economic opportunities in China while also hedging against its political risks through family members' additional citizenships. Fitzgerald (2009) calls the process whereby emigrants can make use of multiple citizenships "citizenship à la carte." With this conceptualization, he draws attention to how emigrants may have greater leverage to pick and choose from a menu of citizenship rules in order to ensure more favorable combinations of rights and obligations for themselves. These two cases, which look at different groups with divergent resources—Chinese merchant families and Mexican immigrants in the United States—show that conditions of transnationality are largely possible with constellations of multiple citizenships and do not necessarily mean nation-state memberships are becoming less significant (Bauböck 2010; Brøndsted 2008). In these two cases, access to U.S. citizenship enables people to become transnational. In other words, conditions of transnationality derive from the hierarchical ordering of nation-state citizenships.

Joppke has written that states have historically always been strategic in building, changing, and enforcing their citizenship regimes: What is novel today is individuals acting as citizenship strategists (2018). Yet there are also case studies revealing how people do apply for a second citizenship when opportunity presents itself, not because of strategic reasons but rather because of the official recognition that a passport provides for people's identity claims (Pogonyi 2018; Naujoks 2013). We argue that these conditions of transnational connections and new legal possibilities of citizenship signal a need to look closely at the level of individual narratives, paying equal attention to strategic motivations *and* assertions of identity. In other words, there is a second, interrelated way in which national citizenship matters to transnationality: the symbolic recognition attributed to particular citizenships across the world. When the groups we interviewed made claims about being cosmopolitan, multicultural, and transnational, they relied on the power of associations of "the American dream" across the world (Grewal 2005). As natural-born Americans emphasized their own dispositions of inclusiveness, multiculturalism, and hard work, they could make sense of their privileges across the world through individualized but very familiar discourses of what it means to be an American (Grewal 2005). Those who considered U.S. citizenship as insurance against global political risk did not necessarily imagine that the citizenships of other global economic powers like China or Russia would be able do the same thing. Those who sought U.S. citizenship for themselves or for their children also maintained that they could "become" American with U.S. citizenship. Some contrasted this with their experiences in European countries, where they may have experienced familiarity but always felt more like outcasts. Balibar conceptualizes this process for the case of European countries as a kind of apartheid, where immigrants are inside yet still separated from the "real" citizens (Balibar, 2004). For these interviewees, it was the very hope and perception that they could *become* Americans, that *anybody* could become an American, which gave U.S. citizenship a symbolic power and recognition distinct from others. In other words, the hierarchy of national citizenships and passports in a transnational terrain are constituted at the intersection of *strategic values* of geographic mobility, protection from political and economic risk, status and class mobility, *and symbolic meanings* associated with identity and cultural affinity claims. These are dynamic processes, too, shaped with individual practices and narratives, taking their cue from historical experiences and contemporary macropolitical events.

Our argument, therefore, is that we need to engage in discussions that go beyond the permeability of borders, as would be expected from an age of greater transnational mobility. We contend that we need to look at actual experiences, desires, and perceptions that unfold on the ground in response to macropolitical circumstances. Whereas the relevant contemporary debates in citizenship studies make assumptions about individuals' strategic and instrumental motivations against a backdrop of citizenship inequalities, we suggest that there is much to learn from delving into real life experiences. This way it becomes possible to trace the complex interactions between instrumental values and identity meanings associated with citizenship. Through the narratives of the three groups we studied, we refocus the multiplicity of loyalties, allegiances, and identifications that appear to challenge the power of national citizenship, juxtapose them with citizenship strategies they can deploy, and clarify the ways these involve anxiety-ridden, ambivalent, and sometimes even re-nationalizing processes.

National citizenship regimes matter in that they are valued and experienced unequally across borders. These values embody both symbolic significance and strategic thinking on the part of actors located in the Global South. Some citizenships are more likely to signify values such as modernity, multiculturalism, freedom, cosmopolitanism, and being associated with the West, all of which play crucial locally specific roles in identity negotiations. Some citizenships are more likely than others to enable seamless border-crossings, provide safe havens from risk, and offer global protection. They are also more likely to enable individuals to retain and even rise above their class and status positions across borders, building a diverse transnational community whose membership in one polity translates into specific privileges elsewhere (Ong 1999; Friedman 2000). These are processes we can discover precisely because we bring together narratives of three groups with diverse connections to U.S. citizenship, ranging from those who have it from birth to those who are naturalized to those whose non-U.S. parents obtained it for them in hopes of safer futures.

We show how U.S. citizenship can enable the middle and upper classes in Turkey (and possibly elsewhere in the developing world) to transgress the limits of their national citizenship and live as transnational citizens. Yet we need to emphasize that this book is not only a story about Turkey or people who live in Turkey. The United States continues to be the number one immigrant destination in the world, despite the recent rise of anti-immigrant rhetoric (Martin 2017). It is still the center of global cultural production, making numerous cityscapes, artifacts, and images more recognizable as "American" than those from elsewhere (Belmonte 2013; Grewal 2005; Kroes 2002). All of this is on top of a history of the American empire that has made its multilayered presence felt in not only Turkey but numerous locations around the world (Bender 2002 and 2006; Bright and Geyer 2002; McAlister 2001; Thelen 1999; Tyrell 2007). Thus, this is a book about the transnational meanings and values associated with American citizenship and their implications for how we need to refine our thinking of citizenship as an institution, status, and set of practices in the contemporary world.

We look at the ways in which the institution of U.S. citizenship becomes an expression of contextually specific struggles around status and recognition. We also show that U.S. citizenship enables natural-born Americans to become transnational and access privileges unlikely to be available to them inside the United States. U.S. citizenship, therefore, allows us to study individual experiences of social class in transnational spaces. Isin writes on the extent to which the history of imperial power and the institution of national citizenship are integral to one another. Discussing the problems of a historiography that draws a linear trajectory, he suggests that the age of empire has not ended just because we now have bounded nation-states and national citizens (Isin 2015). We follow this suggestion into a terrain that is beyond state intention and interstate relations. We argue that a fuller picture of hierarchical ordering of citizenships and their connections with unequal state powers become possible only if we trace their workings in people's imaginaries, practices, and experiences. This is indeed a new form of imperial citizenship, which responds to state-level processes without being completely subsumed by them. Meanings of U.S. citizenship proliferate, stabilize, and are destabilized as people create, strategize, and assert transnational links and subjectivities around it.

The Story of the Book

In the rest of the book, we follow these groups' narratives, taking up their experiences in separate chapters. Each chapter flows into the next as different actors reveal complex, overlapping motivations and experiences. We trace in their accounts the foundations for diverse identity claims and values attached to U.S. citizenship in Turkey.

In Chapter 1, we set the stage. We use a broad history of state-level relations between Turkey and the United States to construct a cultural history of evolving and diverse perceptions of America in Turkey, and the ways in which these have been part of contestations of hegemonic and alternative claims about "the essence" of the Turkish nation. We draw out the ways in which "the West" and America have become synonymous over time, with a significant impact on individuals' everyday strategies of distinction. We then focus on recent political developments, which reveal a major power shift at the state level, from the set of political actors who identify with early republican notions of Westernism, republicanism, and secular nationalism to those who define Turkishness more around religiosity and connections with the Ottoman past. We begin our portrayal of a political scene where the government has become more exclusionary and deprecating of those groups whose social status is partially derived from their identifications with the West and secularism, a story whose consecutive chapters unfold throughout the book. We also explain Turkey's economic boom of the last decade, which until recently was a magnet for many around the world. We situate the meanings and values attributed to U.S. citizenship in Turkey against this background, carefully emphasizing their diversity. This is a story that seeps into the following chapters as our interviewees narrate their experiences in Turkey and their citizenship statuses. Overall, Chapter 1 aims to develop a more substantial contextualization of the origins of the various groups under discussion, their subjectivities and their positions in current structural circumstances in both local and global terms.

Chapter 2 analyzes the process whereby Turkish citizens residing in Turkey give birth in the United States to obtain U.S. citizenship for their children. We show how this choice emerges at the intersection of the parents' fears of political risk in Turkey, familiarity with the U.S. context, and the ease with which the *jus soli* principle allows them to gain citizenship of a rich, liberal democracy for their children. This case reveals the meanings people who lack U.S. citizenship themselves attribute to it from afar and how they imagine what it could provide for their children who are going to grow up outside of the United States. These actors make strong claims of affinity with the West through their children, whose U.S. passports become a signifier of the kind of socialization to which the latter will be subjected. The transnational meaning of U.S. citizenship, in this sense, is the hope that it signifies for the next generation. Transnational imaginaries regarding the value of U.S. citizenship are also closely interlinked with experiences of Turkish citizenship. Painfully aware of the limited capacities that their primary (Turkish) citizenship has for providing options for protection and exit under unstable circumstances, these groups take precautions for their children by means of U.S. citizenship. It is highly valued because it provides transnational flexibility and exit routes in times of political anxiety. It is akin to an insurance mechanism because it is more readily obtainable than EU citizenship, and because the U.S. polity is expected to retain stability and offer a place for the children with which the families declare cultural affinity. We end this chapter by arguing how these parents' motivations and actions show that citizenship regimes can be differentiated on the basis of their ability to offer seamless exit from unsafe situations and transition to secure havens in times of political risk.

In Chapter 3 we shift gears from the imaginations and hopes of U.S. citizenship to actual U.S. citizens, who have moved in the opposite direction from these parents. We trace the experiences of natural born U.S. citizens, putting to the test the imaginaries of the parents for an unpredictable future. Their stories reveal unexpected advantages of the U.S. citizenship *outside* the United States. Whereas the parents imagine U.S. citizenship as a vehicle of safe passage to the United States in case of a political crisis in Turkey, these people have relocated to Turkey during their adulthood for reasons like education, limited employment opportunities in the United States, career trajectories, and marriage. For this group, their U.S. citizenship and assumptions in Turkey about American cultural upbringing give them distinction. They experience different combinations of upward mobility in Turkey in terms of the jobs they can access, the income they are able to generate, and the social groups they can join. Their stories also reveal intense negotiations of identity, between the national and the transnational, albeit of a different kind. For these groups, U.S. citizenship comes to signify simultaneously national pride and embarrassment because of connections between U.S. geopolitical power and their individual privileges in Turkey. Yet living outside of the United States also allows them to make claims about being a "special" kind of U.S. citizen, one that is more connected and politically more aware. The transnational value of U.S. citizenship for this group is the recognition of what their citizenship evokes and how it facilitates unique privileges in Turkey and wherever else they might have lived, in comparison to their previous lives and opportunities in the United States. Yet these are all complicated processes, as these individuals' ethnic and racial origins as well as gender and sexuality have differentiated impacts on their recognition as "Americans." We also delve into what this recognition means against the popularization of anti-American sentiments and discover a surprising wedge between individual recognition and macropolitical circumstances. This chapter discusses how national citizenship regimes are unequally valued to the extent that their symbolic connotations—often linked to historical power relations between states—translate into divergent class positions for individuals living outside their home countries.

Finally, in Chapter 4 we turn our lens on actors with Turkish citizenship who have lived for extended periods in the United States and have as a result obtained the green card or U.S. citizenship. Most of these people had already moved to Turkey at the time of the interviews, with the remainder planning to do so. This chapter continues the story of the unfolding political crisis in Turkey through the narratives of these groups. For the individuals who returned, the question of why they did so always looms on the horizon, impacting their experiences with the status of dual citizenship. The question of return and the anxieties around it reveal the different experiences between this group and the group in Chapter 3. Nevertheless, in these cases, U.S. citizenship also provides a way to negotiate identities outside the United States. It becomes an expression of membership in a transnational community that is Western-looking while they can still embrace expressions of Turkish patriotism and/or attachment to the cities where they currently live. These identity claims are also linked to what U.S.

citizenship can facilitate outside the borders of the United States and what it can achieve in combination with Turkish citizenship within Turkey. When combined with Turkish citizenship, the U.S. passport allows these actors to escape economic crisis in the United States and carve out higher-status jobs in Turkey. It also makes possibility of circulation between the two countries a realistic one. The chapter concludes with the argument that national citizenship regimes matter in transnational spaces because of their unequal capacity to provide seamless mobility across borders and to lend credibility to individualized descriptions of identity, combined selectively from the local, national and the transnational.

We open our concluding chapter by first describing what has happened in Turkey since 2015, when we finished our interviews. We depict the growing authoritarianism and political unpredictability in the country, heightened anti-American rhetoric, coupled with erratic changes in visa regulations for Turkish citizens governing their (restricted) mobility outside of Turkey as well as into the United States. We discuss the implications of the Trump administration for imageries of rule of law and multiculturalism in the United States as well as the rising tensions between the Turkish and U.S. governments. We also follow the trajectories of some of our interviewees and the choices they have made under these shifting circumstances. Against this backdrop, we assert the need to think about the intersection of individual practices, experiences, and expectations of citizenship statuses in contexts shaped by unequal state-level relations and local political struggles of belonging and privilege. This focus has much to contribute, not only to understanding the variety of transnational meanings and values attributed to U.S. citizenship in Turkey, but also to studying the individualized cultural registers through which strategies are deployed and meanings drawn up with respect to the institution of citizenship.

In this concluding chapter, we also suggest a typology for understanding the persistent importance of national citizenship regimes and inequalities between them in transnational spaces. This typology rests on two dimensions, strategic values and symbolic identity-based meanings attributed to national citizenships. National citizenship status continues to matter in a world of growing transnational connections: It is still this official status that has huge impact on the degree to which people will be exposed to political or economic risks or be able to escape them; the degree to which they will be able to change locations flexibly; and what kind of class and status mobility they can reasonably expect outside their countries of origin. These are the basis for the strategic value of citizenship, which is almost always intertwined with the symbolic meaning of citizenship, the second dimension. People aspire to membership in a country because they assert cultural affinities with it, can make believable claims of belonging once they have the official status, and when they believe their passports can protect them against racism in larger transnational spaces. Overall, we argue that the narratives of these groups are indicative of the need to move beyond existing debates on the relationship between citizenship, transnational citizenship, and inequality. There is much potential in studying the emerging strategic and symbolic values attached to citizenship, beyond conventionally studied local opportunities and obligations, national allegiances, and the complications that migrations bring to these. With our book, we contribute to this quest by conceptualizing the transnational values and meanings of national citizenships. We underline the need for paying closer attention to personal biographies, to what actual people think, imagine, and practice in relation to their citizenship statuses in a world marked by multiple layers of unpredictability, risk, and anxiety.

Chapter 1

Imagining America in Turkey

A Historical Overview

During our research, a staff member at the U.S. consulate in Ankara contacted us. He had heard about our work from the executive of an NGO with whom we had conducted an interview, and he was curious about our findings. He wanted to know if we had any insights about a specific question: How was it that anti-Americanism in Turkey was extremely high even though everyone he came into contact with seemed to want to live in the United States? We did not have an immediate answer, because the people we were studying fell, for the most part, into the group whose desires were captured by the second half of the question. And yet it was a legitimate concern. On the one hand, according to Pew surveys, anti-Americanism in Turkey has increased noticeably in the last two decades (Pew Research Center 2014). On the other hand, the desire to study, work, live in, or just connect with the United States has also increased. This is evidenced not only by the cases of parents giving birth in the United States, but also by a tremendous expansion of American-style private schooling, the continued prestige of old American missionary schools, Turkey's consistent appearance among the top ten countries sending students to the United States (every other country on the list is either a neighbor of the United States or one of the world's most populous countries),[1] the increasing number of professionals finding prestige in working for U.S.-originated international companies, and the very high levels of consumption of American cultural products (Bali 2002; Erkmen 2015).

How can one explain this tension between rising anti-Americanism and the allure of being an American? We suggested a conceptual answer to this puzzle in the introduction: that the American empire's complex workings are to be found in the intersection of U.S. foreign policy and the privileges associated with U.S. citizenship outside of the United States. Some historians have long argued for transnationalizing American history, emphasizing the interconnectedness of the United States to the rest of the world (Bender 2006; Thelen 1999; Tyrrell 2007). This approach does not erase the nation but rather situates it within global power relations, exploring both the impact of the United States on the rest of the world and what this has meant for building the idea of the American nation (Bender 2002 and 2006). The concept of the transnational is also about recognizing that global power configurations encompass more than diplomatic relations between states (Iriye 2002). Grewal's ethnographic work has suggested that as actors and imageries associated with the United States move across borders, they take on diverse meanings and resonate with multiple and contradictory experiences in the world (Grewal 2005). We can trace these multiple contradictory meanings in the flows of American consumer goods and cultural products (Belmonte 2013; Edwards 2015; Kroes 2002; Sharp 2001), as well as the circulation of people—diplomats, missionaries, traders, corporate actors, tourists—and ideas like freedom, modernity, development, and security among others (El-Shakry 2007; McAlister 2001; Rosenberg 1982; Vitalis 2007). These are occasionally connected to interstate relations but not completely so. The so-called American empire emerges as part of this entangled, power-laden global history (Bright and Geyer 2002; Grewal 2005; Perez 2002).

The history of the emergence of diverse implications of America in Turkey falls squarely within this transnational framework. Our objective in this chapter is inspired by these arguments but is more modest. We trace how U.S. citizenship has become a coveted status by documenting how American-Turkish relations have unfolded over the course of the last 150 years. We suggest that history, and how people remember history, matters. The history of bilateral relations between the two countries is not limited to state-level interactions. It also includes everyday encounters between individuals, informed and framed by the macropolitical context. Thus, this chapter canvasses the multilevel interactions between diverse groups of actors. It traces how the rise of American global political, social, and cultural power has been filtered through Turkey's internal dynamics. It contends that these manifold interactions have resulted in the multiple and contradictory meanings of America in Turkey today.

The exertion of U.S. power internationally has too often been guided simultaneously by discourses of security, modernity, and freedom (Kaplan 2009). On the one hand, U.S. state security discourses and strategies have continued throughout the twentieth century, focusing on different enemies at different times, including "radical nationalist leaders," "communists" and "Muslim radicals" among others (Leffler 1992; Little 2008; McAlister 2001). In Turkey, these discourses have been instrumental in consolidating a securitized state, feeding off existing nationalist and state-centric ideologies. Concepts such as freedom and modernity, on the other hand, have also come to signify diverse American efforts to establish market economies and liberal regimes around the world (Rosenberg 1982). These have not always been state-led projects and have involved many non-state actors. In Turkey, these actors and their discourses have overlapped with already existing debates on Turkish "national essence," desires for modernity, and social inequalities expressed in cultural terms. As a result of a history of such multiple, overlapping, and occasionally contradictory practices and discourses, we are now witnessing a simultaneous intensification of desires for U.S. citizenship and imaginations of freedom in the United States *and* popular portrayals of the United States as the source of terrible foreign policies, repression, and violence. The presence of multiple actors with different agendas has created contradictory impressions of America as both the "civilized" and the "corrupt(ing)" West.

These contradictions form the starting point for this chapter, where we describe evolution of United States-Turkey relations over three periods. The first is the late nineteenth-century interaction between the United States and the Ottoman Empire until World War I, initiated by businessmen and Protestant missionaries from the United States. During this period, a positive image of the United States emerged among the Ottoman/Turkish elites, especially compared with that of Europe. For these elites, Europe represented imperial incursions, so they tried to establish good relations with the United States to counter the influence of the British Empire. More important, during this period, U.S. cultural and educational institutions began to take hold in Turkey. The legacy of these educational institutions still heavily impacts the political culture among Turkey's upper and middle classes (Altan 2006a); indeed, many of our interviewees from Turkey had graduated from these institutions.

Second, we focus on the period between the two world wars followed by the Cold War. We document how Turkish political actors reacted positively to the gradual rise of U.S. power globally during this period, continuing to distinguish it from their recent experiences with European imperialism. During the Cold War, the alliance between the two states was consolidated in many realms. However, the Cold War also was a period in which multiple meanings of the United States in Turkey began to emerge. The U.S. government's harshly anticommunist rhetoric, growing intervention in the Middle East and elsewhere, as well as its association with right-wing political parties in Turkey, created intense reactions. This was true especially among urban intellectuals, some of whom were, ironically, graduates of American educational institutions in Turkey. As a result, anti-Americanism became popular in left-wing circles, and it was these groups initially who turned anti-Americanism into an important political force in Turkey.

Finally, we focus on the post-1980s, the time marked by the twilight of the Cold War globally, while a right-wing military coup in Turkey caused another sharp turn in bilateral relations. We discuss how the country's transition to a market economy during the 1980s and 1990s happened in tandem with the rise of new middle and upper classes looking to the United States for definitions of identity. We conclude with an overview of the post-2000s era in Turkey, during which both domestic cultural hierarchies based on discourses of Westernization and modernization are being overhauled, and the Turkish government is becoming increasingly estranged from and isolated in the West. This is the context in which anxieties of belonging are on the rise among the urban secular groups. Now we turn to each period in detail, situating the stories of U.S. citizens in Turkey in this social history.

Traders, Men of God, and New Frontiers for Modernity

One of the dominant themes in American historiography has, until recently, been the idea that the U.S. government did not build empires of the kind European powers did, and that private actors like traders and missionaries mattered much more. Recent debates, however, reveal that these networks did not flourish by themselves. Rather, the U.S. government encouraged commercial and missionary activities, and used diplomacy and even force to achieve access around the world (Bender 2006, 190–191; Rosenberg 1982). By the end of the eighteenth century, for example, while the U.S. government had only two diplomatic missions around the world, it already had thirty-six consulates, responsible for organizing international commercial relations (Bender 2006, 213). Initial contact between the United States and the Ottoman Empire unfolded as part of this pattern.

The first American merchants started trading in Ottoman ports during the late eighteenth century. In the early nineteenth century, missionaries associated with the American Board of Commissioners for Foreign Missions (ABCFM), established in 1806, also began settling in the Ottoman Empire, setting up churches, schools, and hospitals (Yetkiner 2011, 14). The turning point for political relations was the Greek uprising in 1827 when British, French, and Russian naval units destroyed the Ottoman navy, leading the government to request U.S. help in reconstructing it. After the two governments signed a commercial treaty in 1830, an American embassy was established in Istanbul in 1831 along with the first permanent ABCFM mission (Yetkiner 2011). The Ottoman authorities began seeing the U.S. government as a balancing force against European states, and often as an ally.

This new political and economic alliance meant that U.S. missionary and economic activities within the Ottoman Empire were tolerated even more than before (Açıkses and Gür 2009, 102). This was the beginning of a pattern that would continue throughout the twentieth century: As long as the political elite viewed the United States as an ally, they allowed and encouraged cultural and economic exchanges between the two societies, with a significant impact on how America was constructed in the popular imagination. Indeed, during the late nineteenth century, American capitalists were competing with British, French, and German capitalists in Ottoman territory to win concessions.[2] In this competition, the Ottoman authorities again welcomed American capital as a counterbalance to already entrenched French and German financial groups (Ahmad 2011, 83). By 1914, U.S.-Ottoman trade already amounted to $23 million, with U.S. commercial interests in the empire centered on basic goods, tobacco, oil, and railroad construction (Vander Lippe 1993, 33).

The work of the ABCFM and the multiple institutions it set up over decades drew on the heavy involvement of and philanthropic funding by this new generation of American capitalists.[3] Over time, missionary posts throughout the Ottoman Empire began establishing primary and secondary schools as well as seminaries, which would total 450 by the end of World War I (Daniel 1970, 94). In these missionary schools, the objective of proselytizing non-Christians was soon abandoned, while they also had fairly limited success in converting Orthodox Christians. However, many of these missionaries quickly found purpose in "civilizing" and "modernizing" their students, taking a largely secular approach in designing their curriculum (Anderson 2009; Gür 2011). In fact, Robert College, the oldest American institution of higher education outside the United States, and one of the most prestigious schools in Turkey to date, was established in 1863 by a former ABCFM missionary using capital provided by an American businessman and diplomatic negotiations that enabled the school to obtain official permission (Gür 2011; Widmer, 2011). Robert College and comparable institutions in the region followed similar trajectories in combining missionary efforts with U.S. capital and political influence.

The missionaries who established these schools all emphasized in their memoirs their objective of raising generations of moral men who would have the requisite skills for the modern world, and shape their own destinies through their ability and hard work (Altan-Olcay 2008; Anderson 2009; Gür 2011). There were significant differences in the ways these messages of modernity, morality, rationality, and freedom were interpreted by the students, their families, and Turkey's political elite, which paid close attention to them (Gür 2011). On the one hand, as children from poor families became successful after their education in Robert College (and other such institutions in the region), a great deal of public benevolence was attributed to the American civilian presence in the region (Makdisi 2002). In those twilight days of the Ottoman Empire, the Committee of Union and Progress (CUP), which took over the Ottoman government in 1908, also saw the United States presence in a much more favorable light, especially insofar as American finance could reduce the influence of European colonial powers.[4] On the other hand, research indicates that missionary schools and higher education institutions, such as Robert College in Istanbul, Sophia College in Bulgaria, and the Syrian Protestant College (the American University of Beirut), also became places where diverse ethnic minorities were socialized into ideas of nationalism and national independence. On that score, "foreign" schools came under suspicion from the Ottoman government and the Orthodox Christian Churches, which felt the threat of conversion (Danacıoğlu and Temur 2011; Kocabaşoğlu 1989). In fact, revisionist historical writing in Turkey still repeats these suspicions, arguing that these missionary activities and schools "provoked" Christian minorities, especially the Armenians.[5] In this period, the question was already being raised of where "good" modernization ended and the potentially problematic switch to becoming "foreign" began. Similar questions continued throughout the demise of the

Ottoman Empire after World War I and the establishment of the Turkish Republic in 1923. They continue today—albeit in different forms.

This was also the period in which a large number of ethnic Turks emigrated to the United States, benefiting from liberal immigration laws. The U.S. government was explicit in its recognition of naturalized citizens as fully equal members of American society, extending them diplomatic protection overseas as well (Spiro 2016). The U.S. government also signed the Bancroft treaties with various states during this period, initiating a process in which expatriation would eventually become a norm, eroding state expectations of perpetual allegiance and refusal of expatriation and naturalization (Spiro 2016). Although during this period the Ottoman state still held onto the latter principle, the U.S. government's approach to naturalization and the widespread perception of a land of opportunities meant that many from the empire migrated to the United States. Starting from 1880 and up until 1930s, there was a sustained fifty-year period of mass immigration to the United States (Massey 1995, 663). Turkish migration was at its peak between 1900 and 1914 (Karpat 2004, 615).

During this time, people coming from Europe made up 80 percent of all immigrants. Meanwhile hegemonic identity discourses in the United States increasingly defined whiteness and Europeanness as the root of American culture (Massey 1995, 661). Toward the end of the 19th century, the U.S. government began to pass restrictive immigration legislation. Asian immigration was restricted between 1882 and 1917, literacy tests were imposed in 1917, and new "quota laws" were passed in 1921 and 1924. The United States became less accessible to certain populations, limiting who could become an American citizen. But the U.S. government continued to support its citizens on the outside—among them, American missionaries and capitalists in Ottoman Empire, later Turkey. As people crossed the Atlantic either way, the unequal relations between the two states and changing rules of membership in the United States were already having an impact on how people imagined America and experienced being American outside of its borders.

A New Republic, Transnational Encounters, and Local Contestations of Modernity

In 1914, the Ottoman Empire entered World War I on the side of Germany. When the United States joined the Allies and broke off diplomatic relations with Berlin in 1917, Germany began pressuring the Ottoman Empire to sever diplomatic relations with the United States. However, as a result of diplomatic efforts involving well-known American missionaries, the U.S. government did not declare war on the Ottoman Empire (Ahmad 2011, 92).[6] The CUP also tried not to alienate the U.S. government, with its leaders repeatedly stating that American business or philanthropy would not be touched (Vander Lippe 1993, 37). In fact, on the day the government unilaterally abolished the capitulations, the Minister of War, Enver Pasha, made a public visit to Robert College to show the cabinet's support for American activities in the empire. As a result, American educational and medical institutions continued uninterrupted throughout the war, with the former playing an important role in educating the secular, Western-oriented elites of the new republic (Ahmad 2011, 92).

Toward the end of the war, on 8 January 1918, President Woodrow Wilson announced the Fourteen Points, the twelfth of which promised "a secure sovereignty" for the "Turkish portions" of the Ottoman Empire while offering an "opportunity of autonomous development" to the other nationalities of the empire. This often cited principle became the basis of contradictory claims by the Ottoman government and nationalist groups trying to secede from the empire, and even inspired the establishment of a short-lived League of Wilsonian Principles advocating for an American mandate in Istanbul (Gürel 2015). Although the idea was never popular, it was an indication of how, during this period, notable political actors looked to the United States as a less dangerous Western power than its European counterparts (Barlas and Yılmaz 2016; Daniel 1967).

This perception carried over to the military and political cadre that founded the Turkish Republic under the leadership of Mustafa Kemal Atatürk. While they had deep suspicions of the Allied forces, especially the British government, the U.S. government was seen as an outsider and a balance against them (Zürcher 1998, 273). Thus, the Ankara government continued the CUP's position regarding the American schools and medical institutions remaining inside Turkish borders (Freely 2000, 7–8). In 1919, following the armistice, Wilson appointed Admiral Mark Bristol, the commander of the American fleet in the Mediterranean, as high commissioner in Turkey to restore diplomatic and trade relations (Vander Lippe 1993, 43). During his time in office, he concentrated on nonpolitical, humanitarian endeavors, an example of which was the establishment in 1920 of the still-existing American hospital in Istanbul, and on distancing the U.S. government from ongoing conflicts between the Christian population and the new government in Turkey (Mazzari 2011, 127). This pragmatism not only led to the eventual reopening of state level relations (Mazzari 2011, 115) but also contributed to popular associations of U.S. presence in the country with disinterested assistance.

For the United States, however, missionary reporting during World War I, particularly concerning the Armenian question, had created a very negative perception of the Ottoman Empire, Turks, and Turkey. This played a role in the U.S. government's refraining from being a party to the Treaty of Lausanne, with which the Turkish Republic gained international recognition.[7] Lippe (1993, 32) argues that the debate on the ratification of Lausanne became instrumental for U.S. policymakers weighing different models for the postwar world order. On the one hand, there were those who emphasized the "morality and principledness of the American order," focusing on the crimes of the Ottoman state during World War I, against Armenian communities. But there were also those who promoted a more realistic approach, stressing the need to increase U.S. influence in the region (Vander Lippe 1993, 52). This latter opinion, which emphasized the importance of maintaining relations, especially economic, gradually became predominant for the case of Turkey (Armaoğlu 2000). First, at Lausanne, the government of Ankara and the United States signed a separate treaty on 6 August 1923, called the Treaty of Amity and Commerce, which signified U.S. recognition of the new Turkish state in a substantially similar way to the Treaty of Lausanne (Vander Lippe 1993). The Treaty of Amity and Commerce abolished the capitulations; created a new commercial, diplomatic, and legal framework; and addressed U.S. concerns over the protection of missionary and educational schools. Even though it was rejected by the Senate in 1927, the U.S. government worked to get another treaty signed in 1930, as a result of which economic and diplomatic relations were formally established.

This was a time when Turkey's new republican elite were busy configuring a new identity distinct from the Ottoman Empire, despite the obvious continuities (Ahmad 1993; Keyder 2003; Mardin 1997; Parla 1999). Throughout the 1920s and 1930s, Turkish national identity was reconstructed as part of "the civilized West" through the intense writing of a nationalist historiography and literature as well as the implementation of an alphabet change, the building of a secular education system, the introduction of a new dress code for men, and especially, state-level discourse concerning women's elevated place in the new republic (Koçak 2010). As part of this ideology of Westernization and modernization, the leadership of the new republic sought Western-educated individuals, considering them skilled labor, and encouraged people who had migrated to the United States during the war years to return. The government even sent ships from Turkey to the United States to provide free transportation and offered positions in the newly created public offices to those who came (Akçapar 2009a). Yet this was always an ambivalent relationship, as revealed by the nationalist narratives of the era. They argued that Turkey would have to modernize and make itself acceptable as a Western nation-state while not becoming "too Westernized" (Altan-Olcay 2009a; Kadıoğlu 1996). In other words, this new formulation of a Western national identity also reflected apprehensions of the recent history of war with the Western empires.

The new Turkish political elites continued to have a favorable view of the United States during this period, although the U.S. Senate had initially refused to ratify the Treaty of Amity and Commerce. This was primarily because they noted that the U.S. government had not become part of the Allies' secret wartime negotiations and had refused to declare war on Turkey alongside the European powers. Furthermore, many were fascinated by the United States's economic success, something the leadership wanted to emulate (Özoğlu 2011,125). Thus, throughout these early decades, the Turkish government invited American experts as consultants in a wide array of activities, ranging from education to agriculture and from public health to transportation. This approach fit well with the U.S. government's newfound interest in spreading "American culture," advocating the idea that professional expertise, free markets, and private enterprise could bring about economic development (Rosenberg 1982). Although the United States was by no means the only country from which experts were invited, the numbers were still significant (Daniel 1967; Trask 1964). Among these experts—unknown to many Americans—was John Dewey, who wrote a comprehensive report on the development of the Turkish education system, in which he surprisingly moved away from his well-known dedication to democratic education to support a more centralized system in the name of modernization in Turkey (Cole 2014). All these experts had an impact, supporting the image of the United States as a country with the technical expertise necessary for economic development (Rosenberg 1982).

As Smith and Bowman (1988, 439) observe, emerging from World War I, "the massive American industrial economy [was] best poised to expand its control of vacant and not-so-vacant economic spaces around the world.

Indeed, there was little choice except to expand into the world market, if American economic growth was to continue." In line with this observation, during this period, several U.S. companies invested in oil and mineral exploration, attempted to construct railways, and opened factories in Turkey. The beginning of production in Ford's first Turkish factory, for example, excited many, who saw the factory's success in exporting to the Balkans as a sign of Turkey's rapid economic and technological progress (Trask 1964). Although the U.S. State Department played an important role in their selection, these companies and experts were acting in their private capacity, so people, more often than not, saw them as apolitical endeavors (Trask 1964).

American schools established by the ABCFM now had to comply with the requirements of a centralized national education system. The Great Depression of the 1930s also halted their growth because of a sharp decline in funding from abroad. While there had been 450 such schools with 25,000 students during the last days of the Ottoman Empire, by 1939 only a handful remained. While there was a constant pressure to be more "national" due to fears of children becoming "too foreign" (Daniel 1967), the remaining institutions continued to be seen as schools that could be emulated for a better national education system. In the context of rising Turkish nationalism, the schools also began positioning themselves as participants in Turkey's efforts at development (Daniel 1970). For instance, they engaged in a variety of public services, introducing American literature and arts to Turkey's urban scene (Daniel 1967).

Graduates from the remaining schools were becoming important public figures, whether in the state or in the private sector. The prominent positions attained by many former students of Robert College, Sophia College, and the Syrian Protestant College during the end-of-war negotiations, along with their instructors, principals, and presidents, signaled the beginning of a second set of interpretations about what American people and institutions meant. This view continued throughout the twentieth century: Education in and affiliation with these institutions was associated with prospects of leadership and recognition. The two American women's colleges in Istanbul and Izmir prided themselves on producing the kind of graduates the nationalist elite desired: They graduated numerous women who became visible in the public space—both domestically and internationally—through their successful careers while ardently supporting the Kemalist ideology (Childress 2008). The fervor with which they undertook the role of representing "the new, modern Turkish women" was reminiscent of the way the nationalist leadership resolved "the women's question" (Yuval-Davis 1997) in support of their thesis of Turkey being a "Western" nation (Tekeli 1982).

During this time, according to Mazzari (2011, 110), "the old empire was dying and a global power emerging while they danced a strange and delicate *pas de deux* in the first third of the twentieth century." Even though U.S.-Turkish relations at state level remained less visible, there were intense connections established through technocratic exchanges, trade, and American schools. These led to a variety of cultural discourses in which America came to signify "the more benevolent" and "the less dangerous" West. The work of individual Americans, such as diplomats, scientists, tourists, businessmen, and teachers, contributed both to this image in Turkey and to the United States and Turkey's gradual rapprochement (Mazzari 2011, 118). This paved the way for intensified state-level relations during the Cold War, with contradictory impacts on popular perceptions of the United States.

Aspirations for Becoming the "Little America": The 1950s and 1960s

In the late 1930s, the Turkish government signed a number of bilateral agreements responding to rising fascist aggression in the Balkans and the Aegean.[8] Throughout the war, the Turkish government also walked a diplomatic tightrope between Germany, the UK, and the USSR by carefully maintaining its armed nonbelligerent status (Walker 2011, 163–166). It was therefore able to stay out of the war despite increasing pressure to join. It eventually declared war on the Axis powers just eleven weeks before fighting ended in order to become a founding member of the United Nations (Walker 2011, 169).

The most striking result of World War II was the transition of power from Europe, notably the UK, to the United States and the Soviet Union. As the U.S. government gradually replaced British hegemony in the Western world, the Turkish government also intensified efforts to secure U.S. military and diplomatic support. The objectives were manifold: to fend off the Soviet threat to the north, to achieve membership in the Western bloc and to access economic assistance.[9] Meanwhile, the Soviet government was attempting to develop an atomic bomb and refused to withdraw from northern Iran despite prior agreements (Balta Paker 2012a).[10] As the Cold

War intensified, the U.S. government became increasingly involved in Europe and the Middle East, attempting to "secure" countries in the vicinity of the USSR from communism.

The first move in this direction was symbolic. The U.S. government decided to dispatch the battleship *Missouri* to Istanbul, bringing the remains of Turkish ambassador Ertegün, who had died in the United States during the war. Yılmaz (2012, 485) writes that when, in April 1946, the battleship arrived in Istanbul, thousands of people came out to greet it; all the major newspapers continued reporting the event for a week, with some well-known op-ed writers describing the visit as "a strong indicator of the American guarantee in response to [the public's] need for peace and security" (Ahmet Emin Yalman cited in Yılmaz 2012, 485). All major political actors were also present to greet the ship. Prime Minister Saraçoğlu praised American efforts to create a peaceful postwar world order, while President İsmet İnönü addressed the importance of military and economic assistance to Turkey (Yılmaz 2012, 483).

Then, on 12 March 1946, President Harry Truman gave a historic speech before the U.S. Congress, laying out the foundations of the Truman Doctrine that argued that the U.S. government had an obligation to support peoples facing external or internal communist threats (Yılmaz 2012). Although the initial objective of the doctrine was to bolster the Greek government in their fight against communist insurgents and Truman barely mentioned Turkey during the speech, he later overruled objections to including Turkey in the doctrine. The rationale was the proximity of Turkey to the Soviet Union and the potentially disastrous results of a possible Soviet takeover of Turkey (Yılmaz 2012). Following the Truman Doctrine in 1947 was the Marshall Plan, an extensive economic assistance and recovery program for the war-devastated European countries. Under the Marshall Plan, billions of dollars were made available over the next two decades for programs to promote economic recovery, as well as cultural diplomacy, around the world.

Under these conditions, leading Turkish political actors decided that their best chance of winning U.S. government support was to implement a limited democratic reform. After all, the Truman Doctrine had specified that aid to Turkey was premised on progress toward democracy (Yılmaz 2011, 243–244). On 12 July 1947, the same day that the U.S.-Turkish aid agreement was signed in Ankara, President Ismet İnönü announced the country's commitment to democratization and the protection of legitimate opposition parties. This announcement initiated a new chapter in Turkish history. In the 1950 elections, the Republican People's Party (CHP), founded by Atatürk and led by İnönü after the founder's death, lost. The Democrat Party, the conservative and pro-market main opposition party, whose leadership consisted of defectors from the CHP including a former prime minister, won an overwhelming majority of seats in the National Assembly under the leadership of Adnan Menderes. DP ruled throughout the 1950s, winning further elections in 1954 and 1957, until the 1960 military intervention. Throughout this decade, although it had been critical of previous Turkish governments' efforts to become part of the Western alliance, DP also adopted a highly pro-American attitude, finding common ground with the U.S. government in fervent anticommunism.

Given its political leaders' vehement anti-Soviet stance, DP went to great lengths to ensure U.S. support and Turkey's membership in the Western military bloc to the point of sending troops to fight in the Korean War.[11] It also vociferously sought Marshall aid, although Turkey eventually only received a small share of the total assistance provided under the Marshall Plan.[12] Nevertheless, the aid that did arrive was consequential in Turkey's subsequent economic transformation. In the 1950s, the government actively endorsed agricultural production and its modernization through equipment purchased with aid and loans from the U.S. (Er, Korkut, and Er 2003). Coupled with the fortunate weather of the period and the boost in commodity prices because of the Korean War, there was significant economic growth for a few years in the early 1950s.

The U.S. government itself was never limited to ensuring military alliances or economic recovery in Europe. Indeed, the U.S. government saw a serious threat, not only in the economic devastation of Europe, but also in the complacent public opinion and the rising popularity of communism and communist parties among the European intelligentsia. In 1938, the Division of Cultural Relations was established under the tutelage of the U.S. State Department, overseeing international student and faculty exchanges, supporting American schools and libraries, and organizing the distribution of American films and broadcasts (Rosenberg 1982, 204–205). These efforts were also bolstered by the CIA's own covert activities that aimed to familiarize diverse populations with "the American way of life" and to convince them of the existence of an American high culture (Saunders 2000). In the 1940s, the Fulbright Act (1946) and the Smith-Mundt Act (1948) enabled the establishment of a widespread academic fellowship program and broad cultural relations with countries that the U.S. government prioritized (Pakin 2008, 509). The United States Information Service (USIS) was set up under the auspices of the Smith-Mundt Act in 1953, taking over the Fulbright Program, the overseas promotion of American studies and American English language training, and producing content for Voice of America in various countries. The U.S. government also frequently collaborated with foundations such as Ford, Rockefeller, and Carnegie for the same purposes.

All these developments were relevant for Turkey, but in slightly different ways. Internal memos written by USIS officers at the time observed that the country was so adamantly anti-communist that there was really no need to conduct anti-communist propaganda (Örnek 2012, 950). One very well-known speech by President Celal Bayar in 1957, for instance, revealed this pro-U.S. attitude. He addressed cheering crowds saying that he hoped they would make Turkey a "Little America" in thirty years' time (Simpson 1965). Thus, much of the U.S. government efforts became focused not on addressing intellectuals to win them over to capitalism but to developing ties with bureaucrats, technocrats, educators, and other professionals (Örnek 2012). Marshall aid programs provided funding for educational institutions and programs, technocratic aid as well as the more common efforts to introduce American popular culture to Turkey. Örnek suggests that this direction was also due to the popularity of modernization theory among American officials, who saw what was happening in Turkey as a model for the newly emerging independent nation-states: capitalist economic development under the tutelage of authoritarian modernizers (2012, 951). The popularity of this thinking is shown by the fact that the first U.S. cultural attaché outside the Western hemisphere was appointed to the Ankara embassy in 1953.

Throughout the 1950s, the new Turkish government continued to invite U.S. experts to assist in its efforts to boost agricultural production, introduce public sector reform, and establish educational programs and institutions. These technocratic exchanges were so intense that, at one point, all ministries in Turkey had American experts on their payrolls (Örnek 2012, 951). Much of the aid that came into the country along these lines facilitated the building of institutions to introduce American-style organization and management techniques in the public and private sectors (Üsdiken 2011). These included a fully-fledged university in Ankara, the Middle East Technical University (METU), and other institutions in Anatolia, including Erzurum Atatürk University. In all of these endeavors, American experts encountered older bureaucrats and newly emerging Turkish technocrats. These younger generations and the American experts co-produced Orientalist discourses about a generalized mentality of hierarchy, nepotism, resistance to change, and inefficiency as impediments to modernization in Turkey (Keskin Kozat 2011, 196–197). The acceptance of these discourses by the newly emerging professionals in Turkey meant that the politics behind U.S. aid and the institutions it established could be translated into a technocratic language of development and articulated through a nationalist quest for modernization.

On the "cultural front," the U.S. Office of War Information already had an established office in Istanbul (Criss 2011, 285). USIS also expanded into Turkey's major cities, running the Turkish Fulbright program, founded in 1950, arranging for educational and exchange programs between the United States and Turkey, and facilitating the temporary assignment of various eminent American scholars to Turkish universities (Raw 2012, 201). These programs also expedited the formation of American studies and American literature departments in some of Turkey's well-known universities (Pakin 2008). The U.S. State Department was also instrumental in providing lifeline funding to American schools in Turkey.[13] As in other cases, private foundations such as Ford, Rockefeller, and Carnegie also participated. These schools, especially Robert College, produced some of the best-known economic, political, and cultural actors in Turkey, and have been recognized for their production of secular elite culture throughout the twentieth century (Altan 2006a). Even after the government passed a law making it impossible for Robert College to continue as a higher education institution (Freely 2000; Kuran 2002), its high school retained its reputation as the best in Turkey while, alongside METU, Boğaziçi University, the public university established on Robert College's premises, still attracts the highest performing students from around the country. In those decades, students also clustered in newly established American studies and American literature programs, not for ideological reasons but with the objective of getting their education in English and opening alternative career paths for themselves (Pakin 2008, 517). As a result, the idea of an American education connoted among the new generations better opportunities and professional success.

A similar process was happening at the level of popular culture. When the Voice of America launched its Turkish service in 1949, USIS produced its content (Örnek 2012, 948), while the State Department regularly staged

"American Cultural Weeks," sponsoring lectures and concerts (Raw 2012, 201). Jazz players found their way to Turkey as part of the U.S. government's cultural diplomacy efforts (Saunders 2000; Von Eschen 2004), attracting to their concerts members of the Turkish intelligentsia, some of whom had already been educated in the United States or in American schools in Turkey (Gözen 2011). Hollywood movies became more and more dominant. In an effort to avert Soviet influence over artistic production, Turkish regulatory authorities banned movies coming out of communist regimes and promoted American movies instead. They were joined by USIS in Turkey, which censored several American movies before they were shown in Turkey if they were critical of U.S. government policies and arranged for deferred payment of debts to U.S. film distributors (Sarı Karademir 2012, 636–637). As a result, throughout the twentieth century, Turkish moviegoers were exposed primarily to Hollywood movies, producing idealized notions of life in the United States. As the Turkish movie industry also imitated some of the main themes and stylistic choices of Hollywood, these ideas about modern, Western lifestyles in the United States became even further consolidated (Sarı Karademir 2012, 638).

One can see the popularization of positive perceptions of American society and the U.S. government in cartoons of the day, which often portrayed the country as affluent, powerful to the point of omnipotence, and as a lifesaver from communist threats. Yet the same cartoons also reflected suspicions about the problematic connection between U.S. aid and domestic power relations, its reflection of U.S. interests, and the promotion of overly consumerist lifestyles (Erdem 2011). These contradictory depictions signaled that the close relationship between the Turkish and U.S. governments would fail to elicit unanimously positive popular perceptions throughout the Cold War.

Troubled Waters: Rising Anti-Americanism

Although the Turkish government had wished to participate in the Marshall Plan, this soon became one of the major grievances regarding U.S. involvement in Turkey. The Soviet government argued that the plan was a tool to avert impending economic crisis in the United States because it essentially created an outlet for surplus U.S. production in European markets. This criticism found resonance on the Turkish left and intensified their suspicions that the United States had become the new imperial power.

By the mid-1950s, the DP government's economic program, based on free-market policies and agricultural production supported by U.S. aid, had run its course. After an initial economic boom, GDP growth halted by the end of the decade (Keyder 1987). The first sign of economic troubles became visible when the U.S. government pressured its Turkish counterpart to implement a U.S.-IMF-OEEC economic stabilization program in 1958. The program proposed cutting government spending and devaluing the Turkish lira. When it was announced, the opposition accused DP of "blind Americanism" and its party leaders of granting "capitulations" to the Americans (Yılmaz 2011, 253). Widening sectors of society, unhappy with DP's conservatism, pro-Islamic ideology and growing authoritarianism, also saw something to blame in its relationship with the United States. This marked the emergence of a much less benign popular interpretation of the United States in Turkey.

The U.S. military presence in the country (and the region) did not help either. In 1955, a security agreement called the Baghdad Pact was signed between Iran, Iraq, Pakistan, and Turkey, along with the United Kingdom. DP participated actively in efforts in to expand the pact, occasionally even more enthusiastically than the U.S. government would have liked (Sever 1998). In January 1957, President Dwight Eisenhower committed U.S. economic, political, and military support to the Baghdad Pact, promising American economic or military aid to any Middle Eastern country if it was threatened by armed aggression, which would later become known as the Eisenhower Doctrine. Although the Baghdad Pact quickly broke down due to lack of support from major Arab power holders, the Egyptian government's opposition, the Syrian-Egyptian alliance, and Iraq's withdrawal after the 1958 coup, the Eisenhower government signed a bilateral defense cooperation agreement with the three remaining members of the newly named Central Treaty Organization (CENTO) in 1959.[14]

The bilateral defense treaty was highly influenced by the 1957 military coup in Iraq: It included a provision that if there was an armed rebellion against the Turkish regime, the U.S. government could send troops (Yılmaz 2011; 253). The Eisenhower Doctrine promised help to countries threatened with internal as well as external aggression. This fear of an internal enemy resonated deeply with nationalist discourses in Turkey and DP's growing authoritarianism. An Office of Special Warfare, established with the help of the U.S. government, became solely responsible for retaliating against socialist and communist "internal enemies" (Criss 2011, 281). Many political and cultural actors on the left saw this move as entrenching the mentality of a national security state with U.S. government involvement. This perception then turned into anti-Americanism, a language initially adopted by the left in reaction to the right-wing government's fervent anti-communist attitude, but becoming more popular in the years to follow.

The Cuban missile crisis was another incident that contributed to changing winds in Turkey. U.S. nuclear weapons, first deployed in Turkey in 1959, were seen as a symbol of the U.S. government's commitment to Turkey's defense. The Menderes government also saw in their presence a chance to gain more autonomy and bargaining power with the U.S. authorities (Criss 2002). When the U.S. government agreed to dismantle the nuclear warheads in Turkey in exchange for the Soviet government removing its missiles from Cuba, the Turkish government had to face the uncomfortable situation of being treated as a bargaining chip on a par with Cuba, which they saw as a small client state of the Soviet Union. For the Turkish military and political elites, their lack of input in a decision that significantly affected national security opened to question the assumption that they were equal allies with the United States within the NATO system (Güney 2011). These political incidents, together with increasing economic troubles, added tensions to a domestic scene that was already polarized. In 1960, the Turkish military launched a coup, encouraged by the support of Turkey's leftist and liberal intelligentsia and university students. The junta closed DP and the ensuing military tribunals imposed the death penalty on three of DP's leaders, including Adnan Menderes.

Throughout the 1960s, other incidents raised further tensions.[15] One such turning point occured in 1963, when intercommunal violence escalated between Turkish and Greek Cypriots on Cyprus. The Turkish government made known its intention to send troops to the island if the crisis persisted. However, President Lyndon Johnson sent an ultimatum to the Turkish prime minister, İsmet İnönü, warning him that NATO would be under no obligation to protect Turkey if its actions resulted in Soviet aggression.[16] After the so-called Johnson letter was leaked to the public in 1965, there were widespread protests in major Turkish cities against the U.S. government. The Turkish government once again realized that the reliability of U.S. alliance depended on their adherence to U.S. security strategies (Güney 2011, 305–306). Meanwhile Turkish nationalists became overtly critical of U.S. involvement in Turkey (Criss 2002; Güney 2008; Holmes 2014; Türkmen 2009).

Turkish student mobilization intensified throughout the 1960s as they joined their fellow students in Paris, Berkeley, and Berlin in protest against the Vietnam War and U.S. policies in the region (Kürkçü 1998). Leftist student groups held antiwar rallies at all major universities, including institutions like METU and Robert College (Altan-Olcay 2012). Every time a visible U.S. official visited Turkey, students, workers, and leftist political parties organized protests, while fringe groups committed violence. In 1969, Robert Komer, who had served in Vietnam as chief of pacification and had played important roles in the U.S. counterinsurgency program there, was appointed the new ambassador to Turkey. The announcement created an immediate reaction, and when Komer visited METU on 6 January 1969, the students' demonstrations ended with the burning of the car he had arrived in.[17]

Right after the Komer incident, on 16 February 1969, thousands of left-wing students gathered in Beyazıt, Istanbul, to protest against the arrival of the U.S. Sixth Fleet[18] in the Bosporus, shouting anti-United States slogans, calling for an end to U.S. imperialism and for Turkey's full independence. This time Robert College students joined in the protests. The demonstration turned violent when right-wing students backed by the police attacked the demonstrators, chanting *tekbir* (an Islamic Arabic expression meaning God is great). As a result of the clashes, two students died and many more were injured. The protests, however, did not stop. Over the following days, tens of thousands of people demonstrated in Istanbul's Taksim Square against the arrival of the fleet. These protesters saw U.S. power as Janus-faced; the United States was not what it claimed to be. Rather, it seemed more likely to harm those it claimed to protect (Holmes 2014, 72). These protests showed how American soft power was clashing with its ever more interventionist military power.

Decades later, people who were students in the American schools during this period would remember their protests as "a schizophrenic situation whereby [they] did not appreciate the policies of the American administration and at the same time [they] were greatly appreciative of their educational system, of their values as far as debates and liberties are concerned." Although these words were uttered by a former activist at the American University of Beirut, others on the Robert College campus agreed. They would also describe how they became communists and socialists because this school was the only place whose library held Marxist literature so they could actually read the original sources; they praised the difference between their American education and what they perceived as the the closed-mindedness of the Turkish education system (Altan-Olcay 2012). These individual descriptions, reflecting the increasing U.S. government involvement in the region, indicate how diverging perceptions of America were becoming consolidated: a country whose institutions and citizens both represented modernity, civilization, and the desirable West in contrast to Turkish institutions that were more punitive, restrictive, and paternalistic and a country whose government's exorbitant power lay behind the terrible political situation in Turkey. These were also increasingly becoming class-based perceptions: Those who were able to see the "benevolent" side of the United States were mostly those who had access to its institutions, self-designated as apolitical. The more blatant visibility of the U.S. military presence around the world and its hegemonic role in the Cold War meant that the majority of Turkey's population, as well as others around the world, identified the United States as the source of their countries' woes (Criss 2002; Holmes 2014).

The 1970s began with the second military intervention in Turkey's history. In 1971 the military issued a decree demanding that the government take control of the "anarchy" in the country and asserting that the military would exercise its constitutional right to take over if the government failed to do so. The incumbent government resigned and the ensuing military-backed government immediately began a wide-scale repression of left-wing political activists (Ahmad 1993; Zürcher 2004). Yet the 1970s also saw the rise to leadership of Bülent Ecevit, a graduate of Robert College, within the ranks of CHP. Ecevit pushed the party in a more social democratic direction, and the party under his leadership won the general elections in 1973. He was known for his firm belief in Western institutions while opposing U.S. interventionism around the world, a stance that reflected the multiple interpretations of the U.S. presence in the country. Thus, when the U.S. Drug Enforcement Administration demanded that the Turkish government ban opium production in 1971, Ecevit signed a decree allowing the cultivation of poppies for opium in seven provinces in Turkey. Even though the issue would gradually fizzle out, the incident was critical in creating the popular perception that the United States was treating Turkey as a client state (Criss 2002; Güney 2011). Then, again resisting international pressure, Ecevit launched a military incursion into Cyprus in 1974 following the coup d'état orchestrated by the Greek military junta. In 1975, during the Cyprus crisis, the U.S. Congress placed an embargo on transferring military equipment to Turkey; the Turkish government retaliated by suspending all U.S.

military base operations on Turkish territory. This embargo would be lifted in 1978, but the crisis and the temporary falling-out between the two governments fed the anti-American sentiments even more (Criss 2002; Güney 2011).

Overall, the 1970s was a period of political anti-American anti-imperialism (Kadercan 2016). In the widespread popular perception, the United States was an imperial actor, ruling insidiously through patron-client relations by sometimes supporting unpopular domestic political elites. In a context where the discourse of anti-Americanism was widely available and recognizable, political parties frequently accused one another of being covert agents of the U.S. government. Thus cultural and institutional links with the United States both signified privilege and Western modernity *and* aroused suspicion: People who had graduated from American institutions of education, who had social ties and cultural dispositions that could be defined as "Americanized," had to constantly prove that they were true nationalists at heart.

During this period, American cultural dispositions was all it took to establish these precarious distinctions; dual American-Turkish citizenship was not even on the agenda. During the fifty years between 1930 and 1980, immigration levels to the United States were a third below their 1901–1930 average, and the predominance of Europeans among immigrants to the United States came to an end. While an increasing percentage of immigrants came from the Americas, the Middle East contributed the smallest number (Massey 1995, 635). These statistics indicate that the path to citizenship through migration to the United States was more difficult during this period. However, the absence of discussions of American citizenship in Turkey also had to do with structural conditions. In mid-twentieth century, Turkey still prohibited dual citizenship; the U.S. government and court decisions scrupulously limited it, specifying numerous conditions under which American citizens could be denaturalized. This was a world in which majority of states frowned upon and attempted to ban dual citizenship, seeing it as a threat to national sovereignty (Spiro 2016; Harpaz and Mateos, 2018).

The 1970s also saw the weakening of the economy as U.S. aid gradually declined. Turkish public debt rose to new heights, while the program of import substitution industrialization, implemented after agricultural production collapsed, did not generate the expected industrial competitiveness (Keyder 1987). Political violence escalated further as right-wing governments began courting Islamist political movements in an effort to counterbalance what they saw as the rising popularity of leftism, especially on university campuses and urban contexts where student, worker, and Kurdish mobilizations were widespread.

Neoliberalism, Neoconservatism, and Little America Redux?

These political contestations came to an abrupt halt with the 1980 military coup. At the time of the coup, a gradual rapprochement between the United States and the Turkish government was already under way, following the lifting of the arms embargo in 1978. The military, which assumed power in 1980, was openly pro-American and pro-NATO in its foreign policy orientation. This change was consolidated with the election as the prime minister of Turgut Özal, an engineer who had studied for some time in the United States and was well-known for his unwavering pro-market and pro-American stance. The signing of the Defense and Economic Cooperation Agreement and its renewal in 1985 were also indications of this change in direction (Türkmen 2009).

This was also the time when the Cold War was coming to an end. Coinciding with Reagan's and Thatcher's rise to power in the United States and the UK respectively, the end of the Cold War ushered in a new era in which unfettered market forces could rule (Gilpin and Gilpin, 2000). The end of the Cold War also meant that the United States would be the only superpower for a while, as Russia and other former Soviet bloc countries scrambled to make the transition to market liberalism. By 1992, some observers were already declaring an end to history (Fukuyama 1989); that the new wars would be civilizational, not ideological (Huntington 1993); and that this was going to be a unipolar era (Waltz 2000). From this period onward, the core of empire is still the national security state and the military-industrial complex; but now other features come into play, such as the insistence on the inevitability of markets, a tamed definition of multiculturalism that reduces it to consumption of cultural products (Grewal 2005), and the marketing of "American values as global values" (Pieterse 2006). It is an empire constituted through the circulations of goods, people, services, and ideas (Norton 2017, 42).

The rapprochement between the U.S. and the Turkish governments took place in this context. The sudden change in the government's policy orientation led to speculation about whether the United States had orchestrated the coup to bring Turkish foreign policy in line with U.S. government interests. Initially, these arguments were neither openly debated nor officially rejected. However, every nationalist government from then on drew on similar conspiracy theories to gain legitimacy and delegitimize its domestic opponents, while these theories gained impetus, increasingly resonating with the public. Nevertheless, more and more people desired to live in or visit the United States, which was appearing in their living rooms on their new color TVs. America was becoming a widespread cultural icon rather than just a political power. The apparent discrepancy between America as cultural icon and U.S. political power shaped Turkish public opinion. Was the United States an ally or a foe? Was it a symbol of cultural freedom or political oppression? Was it an object of desire or disgust? These contradictory views echoed at every level from then on. After the 1980s, America as image, fantasy, and experience infused Turkish popular culture in unprecedented ways and was appropriated for unexpected purposes (Gross 2000, 380).

This new period also witnessed the growing significance of religious conservative movements around the world, especially in the Middle East, following the success of the 1979 Islamic Revolution in Iran (Little 2008). In later years, various U.S. politicians identified "radical Islam" (and more generally the Middle East) as the new security threat, once again pulling Turkey into the loop of international politics. The Özal government's pro-American stance meant that it fully cooperated with the U.S. government during the first Gulf War, allowing access to Incirlik military base for U.S. combat aircraft, deploying Turkish military forces near the border with Iraq, and complying with the oil embargo on Iraq (Taşpınar 2011). Through these actions the Turkish government was able to insist on its importance as a reliable ally and partner despite the removal of the supposed Soviet threat (Aydin 2009, 127). Ironically, this was also the period of the first wave of state enthusiasm for deepening Turkey's economic and political connections with Russia and China but without breaking ties with the United States.

The two governments' economic cooperation also grew remarkably through the 1990s to the point that, between 1991 and 1997, bilateral trade increased by 70 percent (Türkmen 2009, 113). This economic collaboration worked in tandem with Turkey's rapid transition to a market economy. Governments since the 1980 coup, in collaboration with the business classes and enabled by the junta's constitution, have repressed labor activism, pushed for market liberalization, deregulated finance, privatized state enterprises, and cut back social expenditure (Keyder 2004). After the 1980s, foreign capital poured into the country. There were periodic financial crises, but economic growth continued. There was an export-led growth based on wage repression (Adaman and Keyder 2006; Boratav 1995; Sakallıoğlu and Yeldan 2000). At the same time, market liberalization created unprecedented opportunities for urban educated groups who could find employment in multinational companies and imagine futures less limited by national borders, in terms of both mobility and consumption patterns (Erkmen 2015 and 2018).

We will be turning to these life-worlds in the following chapters. For now, it suffices to say that there were a number of ways in which these classes sought connections with the West, which, more often than not, meant the United States. Starting in the early 1960s and well into the 1970s, large numbers of Turkish nationals had begun to migrate to Western European countries, particularly West Germany (Kirişçi 2002 and 2003). However, this was mainly unskilled labor migration. Since the 1980s, asylum seekers from Turkey have also been heading for Western Europe, initially seeking protection from the consequences of the 1980 coup and later from the increasing violence in the Turkey's southeast (Kirişçi 2002 and 2003). For the urban educated groups, however, migration to Europe was not the most appealing alternative: Their destination increasingly became the United States.

The large-scale privatization of the education system in Turkey resulted in the majority of new schools adopting American-style models in response to the demands of upper-middle-class families (Cinoğlu 2006). During this period, the number of students pursuing undergraduate and graduate degrees in the United States also began to rise. For decades, Turkey has consistently been among the top ten countries sending students to the United States for education, sliding a few places in 2015.[19] There was a large-scale fascination with America, beyond those who sought out its institutions of education: For instance, popular media published many op-ed columnists who wrote series on their visits to the United States. Cities like New York, Miami, and Los Angeles became objects of popular appeal in these narratives (Bali 2002), bolstered by widespread exposure to these cities' landmarks in TV shows and movies. The influx of consumer goods imports prioritized those from the United States (Abic 2012, 255; Leach

2011). Turgut Özal used to fondly repeat Celal Bayar's dream of turning Turkey into a Little America (Mufti 2011). Part of the population seemed to agree as they built various transnational ties with the United States, and more and more people began to settle in the United States, a process we detail in Chapter 4.

This mobility and migration coincided with more visible reporting in the media as early as the 2000s on how to obtain a green card or U.S. citizenship (Bali 2012, 284–286). These popular discussions reflected the shift in the United States, where several Supreme Court decisions have set a precedent for the necessity of individual consent in the loss of U.S. citizenship (Aleinikoff 2000; Spiro 2016). They also reflected the official recognition of dual citizenship in Turkey: Since 1981, the Turkish nationality act no longer blocks dual citizenship, and since 2009 has explicitly guaranteed Turkish citizens' right to hold multiple citizenships (Keyman and İçduygu, 2003).[20] Furthermore, the principle of birthright citizenship means that everyone born in the United States has a right to U.S. citizenship, regardless of the status of the parents. These official shifts coincided with the intense bilateral relations between the two states and the popular appeal of American cultural products.

While market liberalism was in full swing, what was known in the 1970s as the "Turkish-Islamic synthesis" also became consolidated as one government after another adopted policies that introduced Sunni Islam more openly and forcefully into the public sphere, partly in an effort to curb leftist opposition to neoliberalism and partly to control the impact of the 1979 revolution in Iran (Özkan 2015). While early versions of Islamist parties were shut down by the Constitutional Court, the atmosphere of relative political liberalism meant that they could become alternatives to the Kemalist modernization paradigm that had dominated the political scene since the 1920s. In 1994, the predecessor to AKP, the Refah Party, won municipal elections in major cities and went on to become the senior partner of the center-right coalition government following the 1995 general elections. However, on 28 February 1997, the National Security Council, then very powerful and predominantly controlled by the higher echelons of the military, issued a strongly worded declaration warning against the rise of radical Islam in the country and accusing the coalition government of aiding and abetting this process (Gülalp 1999). The statement precipitated a series of events that led to the fall of the government. A succession of coalition governments between 1997 and 2002 failed to address Turkey's economic problems and that failure, compounded by the economic meltdown of 2001, exacerbated the discontent with existing political parties and what was perceived as the trenchant state elite. Born out of the remnants of Refah Party, AKP won a majority of the seats in the first national election it contested in 2002 (Özel 2003; Çarkoglu 2002; Müftüler-Baç 2003). It has continued to hold power as a single-party government since then.

Initially, AKP was perceived as a democratic force because of its ability to represent previously excluded groups such as Kurds and pious Muslims. It was also persistent in its attempt to join the European Union (EU), citing the EU's inclusionary and democratic practices (Balta Paker 2012b; Özer 2016). AKP thus adopted an openly pro-EU and pro-Western attitude, promising democratization and economic development, which challenged its negative image as an Islamist party (Balta Paker 2012b). The government's initial reforms significantly reduced the military's role in domestic politics and granted cultural, educational, and linguistic rights (albeit very limited) for Kurds (Balta Paker 2005). In the late 1990s and early 2000s, political actors within AKP, the U.S. government, and political scientists in both countries were enthusiastically discussing the new Turkish model as an example of democratization for the rest of the Middle East: Here was a moderate Islamic political party that still played by the rules of the game, and promoted both economic and political liberalism within the constraints of the "domestic culture" (Keyman 2007).[21] People talked about Turkey as a "success story with a growing economy, a functioning democracy, a strong government, a relatively good governance compared to other Middle Eastern governments, and a capitalist system which respected the principles of property rights and open markets" (Taşpınar 2011, 12). Moreover, the government had pledged to align its foreign policy with that of NATO (Taşpınar 2011). However, it has to be also noted that the promotion of so-called moderate Islamic actors as the way to move forward with democratization elicited negative responses from the secular segments of society, which often began voicing the objection that, had it not been for the support of the U.S. government, AKP would have not survived politically (Öniş 2012).

The enthusiastic support that the U.S. government initially gave to AKP began to decline after the 2011 Arab revolts, and especially the Syrian crisis. From then on, official U.S. circles began seeing what was happening in Turkey as an "Islamist axis shift" (Taşpınar 2011, 11). During the 2003

U.S.-led invasion of Iraq, the Turkish parliament rejected a government proposal to allow foreign troops to deploy in Turkey and for Turkish troops fight in Iraq (Güney 2008, 479).[22] On 4 July 2003, U.S. soldiers arrested eleven Turkish Special Forces officers in Sulaymaniya, Iraq. The Turkish soldiers were taken from their headquarters and questioned under the suspicion of planning to assassinate a local Kurdish politician. Pictures showing the officers hooded and handcuffed were regarded as a national insult by the media and by the wider Turkish public, creating an extraordinary reaction against the United States. The upsurge in anti-American sentiment (Grigoriadis 2010, 58; Güney 2008, 480) reflected a merging of two radically different ideological stances—secular and Islamist, Kemalist and pro-AKP—in that both sides blamed U.S. government policies for what was wrong in Turkey, but for contrasting reasons.

Popular cultural productions intensified this rhetoric. In particular, a movie called *Kurtlar Vadisi: Irak* (Valley of the Wolves: Iraq), a spin-off from a proto-fascist TV series, depicted a fictionalized version of the detention of the Turkish officials in Iraq in which a single Turkish officer took revenge on the American soldiers who had put sacks on their heads before bringing peace to Iraq, something that U.S. troops had been unable to achieve. The movie became one of Turkey's highest-grossing movies in its opening weekend (Güney 2008, 483). Meanwhile, a book called *Metal Storm* portrayed a fictionalized war between the Turkish and U.S. armies in Iraq, the invasion of Turkey by U.S. troops, and the successful retaliation by a Turkish spy in Washington and New York. This book also rapidly became a best seller (Güney 2008, 483). There is also a palpable trend, which our American interviewees also noted, of conspiracy theories dominating mainstream thought (Türkmen 2009). These theories include the idea that the U.S. government is always the cause of one woe or another in Turkey, with the choice of problem changing to the point of absurdity from one person to another depending on their ideological stance.

According to Taşpınar (2011, 14), this phenomenon indicates that resentment of U.S. foreign policy, once primarily a limited, left-wing opinion, has gained traction during the 2000s as part of a new, more defiant strategic orientation. Turkey's foreign policy was now accompanied by an increasingly nationalist discourse that attracted people from various ideological positions demanding more international respect. High-level political actors in Turkey also resorted to a language of anti-American nationalism, asserting that nobody had the right to tell them what to do, emphasizing the rise of the non-Western world, and questioning the sustainability of the United States' global primacy (Güney 2008, 479–480; Kardaş 2011, 33).[23]

In 2008 the U.S. mortgage crisis erupted, and financial crisis spread globally. In the following years, the capacity and willingness of the United States (or EU countries) to sustain the international order weakened. The U.S. government, which had almost unilaterally guaranteed the maintenance of the international order in the post-Cold War era, proclaimed a policy of retrenchment under the Obama presidency (Brooks, Ikenberry, and Wohlforth 2012). As Kardaş (2011) argues, an intense debate also surfaced about the role of U.S. leadership in the global economic and financial order after the 2008 mortgage crisis. Many of our interviewees mentioned the effects of this crisis in their life trajectories. U.S. citizens born and raised in the United States began considering jobs abroad as the U.S. job market shrank, while Turkish Americans who experienced greater competition and insecurity in the United States chose to return to Turkey. Under these conditions, Turkey provided a more hospitable environment for business within its less competitive market environment and offered more secure working conditions. During this period Turkey's commitment to Western norms and democracy was not yet open to question. Both Turks and Americans who relocated there wished to play a role in the country's political and economic future and wanted to take advantage of these opportunities. Their optimism concerning the future of the country encouraged them to settle in Turkey.

However, this hope was short-lived. On the international front, Turkey's assertive and daring foreign policy became more difficult to sustain. Since 2011, the most problematic issue between Turkey and the United States is the future of Syria and Iraq, specifically the Kurdish question in both countries. As Kurds have become the major U.S. ally in these countries, Turkish suspicions about U.S. intentions have intensified (Gunter 2015). As AKP began to face serious external and internal challenges, an exclusionary populism has gradually surfaced domestically (Kaya 2015). Notions like "the American among us" or "the supporters of the West" have been transformed into "the traitors among us." As AKP kept winning elections even though domestic and international opposition also grew, its leader, Recep Tayyip Erdoğan, increasingly tightened his grip on the party; the checks and balances of the political system were undermined both through legal reforms and informal practices. The coup attempt on 15 July

2016 was the most recent in a chain of developments that deepened historical fault lines, even though overwhelming majority of the Turkish society opposed the coup.[24]

The urban secular middle- and upper-middle classes identified with a Western republican Turkey, while the more religious conservative groups were divided among themselves about AKP rule. In this context, various groups began considering how welcome they were in their own country and what they could do to secure the future for themselves and their children. Given that our interviewees' experiences, desires, and fears respond to and are shaped by these macropolitical circumstances, we will discuss political shifts in Turkey and the Turkish government's foreign policies, including its relationship with the U.S. government, in more detail in the coming chapters.

Conclusion

This chapter has looked at the various ways America has historically manifested itself in Turkey. This history shows that imaginations of America are sieved through local political and sociocultural debates and informed by the unfolding course of U.S. global power. First, we have suggested that historical and contemporary perceptions of America are integral to a history of modern Turkish nation-state formation, within which the West has become the object of multiple and ambivalent discourses. These discourses have continued throughout the twentieth century: "The West" has signified the impostor, constantly reminding the Turkish political elites and citizens of a lack respect for them, but at the same time political actors have sought constantly to establish institutional links with the West, increasingly the United States, and individuals have strategized to access institutions and cultural practices they perceived as American. This is a history of anxious desires for Western modernity and U.S. power, where biopolitical performances intersect with geopolitics (Grewal 2005).

The manifestion of U.S. power in Turkey has significantly changed in the last two centuries; these shifts and continuities are an important backdrop to the multiplicity of ways in which America is imagined and experienced today. There have been roughly three stages of the American empire as seen through the lens of Turkish politics. The first stage began in the nineteenth century with the arrival of American merchants and missionaries in the Ottoman lands and ended around 1917 when newly reelected

President Wilson reversed his campaign theme of staying out of the European conflict and declared war against Germany. This period sowed the seeds of the long-lasting impact of the United States: American missionary institutions came to be associated with benevolence, modernity, and progress. The fact that U.S. government had refrained from directly intervening in either the domestic or foreign policies of the Ottoman Empire, and opened its borders to large-scale migration from around the world, gave rise to the impression among Turkish political actors and the public of a powerful state that could remain apolitical, noninterventionist, and mainly interested in humanitarian and technical assistance and cultural dialogue.

The second stage, which initiated the rise of U.S. global power, started after World War I, but took decades to bear fruit. Initially coming to a halt during the 1930s, with the near-collapse of the U.S. economic system and a new restrictive approach to immigration, U.S. power was cemented by the eventual victory in World War II. By its end, U.S. power already stretched throughout Europe, reaching the borders of the Soviet empire. During the Cold War, U.S. aid, military, and corporations became dominant forces in conflict patterns and socioeconomic changes in many countries. As the U.S. government established its geopolitical control, U.S.-based cultural products also expanded their reach, proliferating discourses about the "American way of life" in contextually specific ways, beyond U.S. borders. Situated within this reach, in Turkey, the U.S. government aid and political/military interventions began to impact domestic power struggles for years to come. The concept of the West became synonymous with America and Americans, creating contradictory discourses: The popular appeal of American culture was obvious, and many looked to American institutions of education for upward mobility. However, this was also the period in which anti-Americanism gradually took hold, pulling perceptions of what the United States stands for in different directions.

The transition from the second stage to the third stage of the American empire came slowly and culminated in the post–Cold War period. The central aspect of this third stage has been the rise of a hybrid formation of U.S. geopolitical power, hegemonic discourses of market inevitability, and the now global reach of cultural products and models emanating from the U.S. (Grewal 2005; Pieterse 2004 and 2006). This was the period in which diverse affinities with the U.S. became sources of domestic distinction: In the case of Turkey, American-style education was highly sought-after, people traveled to the United States for tourism and for higher degrees, and some settled there. However, as America went global and American cultural and consumer products opened to wider public consumption, something else began to happen: Familiarity with American culture or education in American-style institutions was no longer enough assert status distinction in Turkey. Ironically, Spiro's observation "when everyone is American, no one is" was playing out in a different way, creating the conditions under which the upwardly mobile actors began seeking other institutional links with America (Spiro, 2008, 52).

This "insufficiency" coincided with the global move toward the acceptance of dual citizenship, as we discussed earlier (Aleinikoff 2000; Keyman and İçduygu 2003; Harpaz 2018; Spiro 2016). Thus, for those who could live in the United States for extended periods, obtaining green cards and U.S.-Turkish citizenship became more significant in status claims when these individuals returned to Turkey. American citizens from birth who came to Turkey during the market boom also experienced upward status mobility, resonating with the perception of their "authentic" Americanness. Nonimmigrants could give birth in the United States and obtain dual citizenship for their children as a result. As natural-born and naturalized Americans traveled outside of the United States and Turkish families came back to Turkey with children who had American citizenship, they became part of transnational networks that expanded the borders of the United States. This deterritorialization of citizenship is reminiscent of discussions in citizenship studies, which contrast the Greek and Roman models and see in the Roman imperial model a state strategy to pacify and integrate peoples of newly conquered lands (Balot 2017; Joppke 2018). Yet the key difference in the stories in this book is the absence of clear state intent. The American empire becomes what it is in the everyday strategies of various groups who respond to macropolitical contexts, threats and opportunities not of their choosing.

As we have emphasized, the experiences, practices and desires people express reflect more than strategic and instrumentalist thinking. These citizenship discourses are also part of anxious and ambivalent identity claims. In Turkey, throughout the twentieth century, being modernized, educated, and civilized has become synonymous with the "desirable citizen." The locally adopted imaginaries of the West have become central to individualized claims of value, legitimacy, and distinction within this history of nation-building and the coeval unfolding of Turkish-U.S. state-level relations. However, this desirable citizen has constantly needed to prove authenticity. As the so-called American way of life is becoming more global, anti-Americanism is also becoming a global feature. Thus, in the case of Turkey, claims of distinction based on cultural and institutional links with the United States often have to fend off growing anti-Americanist accusations. Today the United States has become ever more present in the minds of ordinary Turkish citizens as either a yardstick or a counterpoint, or both. It serves as a model for emulation and rejection simultaneously.

In public opinion surveys, for example, Turkish people overwhelmingly disapprove of U.S. government policies in the Middle East, give very low approval ratings of U.S. presidents, and dislike the spread of "American culture and values." Pew Research Center (2014) results indicate that Turkish people have a very poor image of the United States: In the 2014 survey, only 19 percent offered favorable opinions of the United States. There is also an overwhelmingly negative view of NATO at 79 percent (Pew 2014). These are not anomalous results either: Since the Second Gulf War began in 2003, popular opinion seems to have become increasingly negative (Pew 2014). Yet the same opinion polls also indicate that Turkish people sympathize with American democratic values and businesses, while the majority see no problem with having American neighbors (Güney 2008, 482). Indeed, in a 2001 opinion survey, when people were asked which country was Turkey's best friend in international relations, the United States came first. Paradoxically, when the question was reversed and people were asked which country was Turkey's number one enemy, the United States ranked second (Gürel 2017).

This is the geopolitical context that interacts with practices and production of multiple American(ized) subjects, who do not neatly overlap with national borders and cannot be demarcated along the lines of political versus apolitical or the political elite versus the rest. This multiplicity indeed resonates with the divergence in the meanings of the United States/America in Turkey to which these surveys results allude. The question that guides us in the rest of the book is the following: What if we change the scope of these questions on perceptions of the United States and explore how America is imagined outside of the United States by looking at American subjects themselves? What if we explore America through the personal biographies of people who desire or have access to the status of U.S. citizenship outside of the United States, in Turkey?

We argue that we need to pay closer attention to the contextually and historically specific meanings of America for actual people. Postcolonial studies show us that empires become what they are not only through the overt intent displayed at state level, but the ways in which a range of ordinary actors from the colonizing officer to the colonized people live in the everyday. Timothy Mitchell (1988) has urged us to study the state as an effect: Rather than conceptualizing politics in terms of states imposing their will on the people, he proposes studying the multifaceted techniques through which power works. Similarly, our suggestion is to trace the workings of the American empire in the life stories and strategies of individuals. These everyday actions respond to power relations beyond individual control, meanwhile blurring the boundaries between imperial subject groups empires attempt to neatly decipher (Bhabha 1997; Mamdani 1996). People's desires, anxieties, and subjectivities tell us rich stories of encounters with power, fleshing out how the political categories we take for granted, such as citizenship, are never fully stabilized.

It is with this intention that we focus on individuals' narratives and contend that different groups' experiences with and imaginations about U.S. citizenship in Turkey can tell us more about transnational imaginaries of America, their implication in domestically specific power struggles, and the cultural registers through which people make sense of U.S. citizenship in particular and citizenship as an institution in general. These stories are shaped at the intersection of local and global inequalities in a world defined by transnational connections.

Chapter 2

Imagining U.S. Citizenship

Risk Societies and Calculating Mothers

> *I spent so much money and energy to get pregnant. Things did not go smoothly after I got pregnant, either. There was a risk of miscarriage. . . . There were all kinds of risks, but I decided to give birth in the United States anyway. I thought I should do it for my daughter's future, even though it was risky. I thought that was the best thing that I could do for my daughter. It was the best gift I could give her.*

When Zeynep decided to give birth in the United States in order to acquire a second passport for her daughter, her gynecologist, considering her delivery to be high-risk, warned her against traveling. Nevertheless, the mother-to-be flew more than 5,000 miles to the United States, where she had few connections, stayed in a hotel by herself for the last months of her pregnancy, and spent thousands of dollars before leaving the country one week after she gave birth. She quit her high-profile job in advertising for this purpose, not knowing whether she would be able to return to her career after such a long break. Two years later, still a homemaker, she explained to us why she had taken "all kinds of risks," defining her efforts and the outcome of U.S. citizenship as a gift for her daughter. Her story is representative of hundreds of women who plan such journeys from Turkey to the United States during the later stages of their pregnancy.

The practice of giving birth in the United States to ensure that children have U.S. citizenship from birth is not restricted to Turkey. Although there is no statistical information documenting numbers over the years or ranking countries with respect to the popularity of the practice, there is anecdotal evidence of similar trends among well-to-do families from countries such as China, South Korea, India, and Mexico, as well. According to data from the Centers for Disease Control and Prevention (CDC), out of the United States's foreign-born population in 2015, 51.1 percent came from Latin America, 30.6 percent from Asia, and only 11.1 percent from Europe. Extrapolating from these figures, we suggest that the practice might be more common in Asian and Latin American countries. There is also a visible growth of news reporting on the phenomenon in the United States, with estimates of anywhere from 30,000 to 60,000 such births every year (cf. Kessler 2015; Medina 2011; Sheehan 2015; Popina 2018). Some reports describe so-called maternity homes that house and care for such tourists in the later stages of their pregnancy; hotels whose clientele is almost completely made up of long-term guests, staying there for the purpose of giving birth to their children in the United States; health tourism companies navigating the blurred terrain between legality and illegality when they organize birth packages for pregnant women from around the world; and police officers raiding these places and shutting them down (Lewin 2015; Medina 2011; Popina 2018). The tone of this coverage usually carries a whiff of scandal because it is connected to domestic immigration debates in which the conservative right has produced a discourse about undocumented immigrants abusing U.S. resources, giving birth in the country, and "anchoring" their stay through their babies.

The fact that this group has no plans to stay in the United States refutes the premise of these debates and begets other questions, however. Why do mothers make this risky journey during a period when they most need the support of their social network? What do the motivations of this particular group of women who give birth to U.S. citizens and raise them in Turkey reveal about the meaning and value of (U.S.) national citizenship in the contemporary world? How are discourses and practices of motherhood in transnational spaces connected to individual experiences and narratives of belonging and identity?

In the previous chapter, we left the genealogy of American-Turkish relations and cultural connections at a point when there was a significant growth of anti-American sentiment, voiced both at the government level and in popular discourse. This turn signified both the AKP government's domestic populism and its increasing political distance from the Western hemisphere. However, the full transition to a market economy that Turkey made in the post-1980 period has also expanded an already large urban and secular-oriented population—these are the new professional classes with middle to high income levels. These actors have benefited from internationally recognized higher education institutions in Turkey as well as, increasingly, universities in the United States (Altan-Olcay 2008; Öncü 1999; Üstel and Caymaz 2009). Because of their education and especially their language skills, they have become desirable employees in globally connected sectors of the economy, expanding because of the consolidation of market economy in Turkey (Emrence 2008; Erkmen 2018). At the juncture of relatively high economic capital and access to transnational networks, these groups have also developed tastes, consumption habits, and cultural affinities (Bali 2002; Erkmen 2015 and 2018; Karademir Hazır 2014; Öncü 1999; Üstüner and Holt 2010) that resemble, in their Western orientation, their counterparts in many countries in the developing world (de Koning 2006; Myers and Kent 2004; Ong 2006; O'Dougherty 2002).

The parents that we interviewed, mostly mothers, predominantly belonged to these classes that fully endorse historical narratives of Turkey as a Western country. They often used terms such as Western, modern, or secular to identify who they were.[1] Most had grown up in middle-class households, while a large group had been educated in foreign-language schools and/or English-language universities in Turkey. While some had taken their undergraduate degrees in the United States, a larger group had lived in the United States as graduate students or expatriate workers because of their positions in international companies. They are, therefore, "glocally entangled" (Lan 2014) mothers (and fathers): While permanently settled in Turkey at the time of the interviews, they all retain ties to the United States through their cultural upbringing, contemporary consumption patterns, and frequent travels. Overall, they belong to a segment of society that has enjoyed high social status and relative economic security through their educational achievements, jobs, and, in a majority of cases, high incomes.

Yet in the last decade, these groups have been experiencing or fearing a decline in their position in Turkish society—whether this has to do with their perceived social status as members of the urban, secular middle classes or their political capability and their sense of control and predictability with respect to the Turkish political system. This fear of loss has increased their anxieties for their children's future and led them to choose to give birth in the United States. In this chapter, we follow their journeys and trace in their thinking how the status of U.S. citizenship is imagined from afar. Parents who themselves are not U.S. citizens but give birth to U.S. citizens who will grow up in Turkey offer clues about the unique way in which the American empire transcends the borders of the United States through imaginations about U.S. citizenship. This practice also complicates the notion of national citizenship in a transnationalized world.

National Citizenship Through Transnational Chains of Status and Privilege

The number of Turkish citizens obtaining U.S. citizenship by birthplace over the past ten years has increased from around one thousand to around fifteen hundred per year. Almost half of them permanently reside in Turkey, suggesting that up to half of their mothers may have been in the United States just to give birth.[2] There is little reliable information on the exact numbers. Nevertheless, we have found numerous tourism companies that advertise "birth packages" in the United States and blogs where women who have given birth there share information with their readers. At the very least, this testifies to a visible tendency among Turkey's upper-and upper-middle income groups to consider the possibility of acquiring U.S. citizenship for their children.

Overall, data from the CDC indicate that in 1970 only 4.7 percent of total births in the United States were in the foreign-born population, but this increased to 7.9 percent in 1990 and 13.5 percent in 2015.[3] It has to be noted that it is difficult to estimate how many of these births represent mothers who were in the country just to give birth since it is impossible to know how many women were undocumented migrants at the time. Regarding Turkish mothers who give birth in the United States before returning to Turkey, our estimate is around 500–700 per year, which is minuscule compared with the annual number of births in the United States or Turkey. However, the number's significance becomes more apparent when compared with the pool from which it comes. This practice is necessarily possible only for a small segment of the population that has (at the very least) above-average financial means, some familiarity with the U.S. context, and enough transnational connections to pull off such a complicated endeavor. And this number needs to be assessed with respect to a smaller portion of this group that is pregnant at any given time. In any case, the phenomenon encourages inquiry about what meanings these families attribute to U.S. citizenship from outside of the United States.

These parents were able to obtain U.S. citizenship for their children without necessarily immigrating to the United States because changes to citizenship laws in both countries have made it possible for these mothers to obtain multiple citizenships for their children (Aleinikoff 2000, Keyman and Icduygu 2003; Spiro 2016). Not only do both states now recognize dual citizenship, but the jus *soli* principle also guarantees U.S. citizenship for everyone born in the United States. Thus children born in the United States become citizens without their families being obliged to live there for extended periods, in contrast with the nationality acts of other rich liberal democracies, which have more stringent residence requirements. This indicates why the United States might be significantly more attractive for families seeking guarantees for their children's future.

Once the families made this decision, many interviewees told us that they chose destinations where they would give birth and stay for extended periods of time based on their degree of familiarity, whether they had friends and family in these locations, the kind of environment they were seeking, and their expectations of current and future costs. Among the interviewees, Miami, Los Angeles, Boston, New Jersey, and New York were the most popular. Decisions about location were also tied to the cities' health-care facilities. Recent decades have witnessed the emergence of an international medical tourism sector, within which a group of companies, with bases in both Turkey and the United States, have started offering concierge services to pregnant women and their families. Such companies offer "birth packages" that include detailed information about living experiences in several locations along with differentiated costs of living and medical care. One such company's packages contain, for instance, choices among nine different states, several hospitals, and various types of accommodation. The cost ranges from $22,000 to $60,000 USD.[4]

Among our interviewees, however, very few had utilized the services of such companies because most were already familiar with the United States. Some couples did extensive Internet research about which hospitals were most likely to be accommodating toward foreigners and which doctors were more likely to accept such patients. They mobilized transnational networks that included friends and family in the United States or their doctors in Turkey, who contacted colleagues in the United States. When there were alternatives, they finalized their decision after inspecting facilities in the

United States. Those with more limited means usually opted to stay with acquaintances, who also helped with the search for hospitals and doctors. Some arranged for housing from Turkey through online real estate listings, while others started out with temporary hotel accommodation until they found longer-term housing.

Although some were disappointed with the health system, everybody talked in great detail about how wonderful the U.S. bureaucracy was. Once the children were born, navigating it ended up being much more straightforward than they had feared. They received birth certificates in the hospitals and further official documents, such as Social Security numbers, from local government offices, with no questions asked. Just days after the birth, parents, or often just the father, applied in person at a federal government office and paid to get the child's passport, usually choosing expedited service. Soon enough—some told us as early as five days later—the passports arrived. During this time, the parents also went to the Turkish embassy to register their child as born in the United States in order to obtain a Turkish ID card upon returning to Turkey. We also encountered a couple of cases where the parents decided to not apply for Turkish citizenship for their children at all. The majority returned to Turkey within weeks of the birth, although a few stayed longer because of health-related complications.

The key in this chain of events involving transnational markets of tourism, health services, and real estate and resulting in U.S. citizenship for the children is that the families *returned.* These parents neither intended to live in the United States permanently nor knew whether their children would do so. After returning, the children would, over time, become acquainted with their citizenship status and be exposed to the United States through their parents' cultural orientations, their own schooling, and visits there. However, the adults resumed their lives as usual. Thus, to repeat our earlier question: Why did the parents, but especially the mothers, go through all this trouble?

Risk Societies and Exit Strategies

When Zeynep, whose story opened this chapter, talked about taking "all kinds of risks," she was describing a calculation she had made. She had weighed the physical and emotional risks of traveling during pregnancy, giving birth in a country where she was not residing permanently and where she would have a very limited social support system, and traveling back the same long route with an infant, against her larger experience of living in Turkey and fearing for the political future of the country. This theme repeated itself throughout the interviews, with parents often juxtaposing their fears about the future of Turkey with their desires for their children.

"I want to raise a child who is independent and is able to take care of himself. This is true for wherever he lives in the world, in Turkey or in the States or anywhere else in the world. What is important is that he has the freedom to make his own decisions, and in doing so, not be constrained by the rules of this country," Ayşe, a professional working in the finance sector, commented. Her use of words like "independence," "ability to take care of oneself," "ability to live anywhere" (that is, have the chance to adapt) were repeated in almost every interview. Such descriptions were reminiscent both of feminist conceptualizations of "the ideology of intensive mothering" (Hays 1996), which advises mothers to expend exorbitant time, energy, and money to ensure children's success in life, *and* of neoliberal individualism, obliging individuals to manage the self, avoid calculable risks, and improve one's life circumstances through informed decision-making (Beck 1992; Reich 2014; Vincent and Ball 2007). The literature on middle-class norms of mothering, predominantly in advanced capitalist societies of the West, tells us that mothers are increasingly held responsible for risk management and life-planning for their children (Ekinsmyth 2014). Wilson and Yochim (2015) have called this "mamapreneurialism," arguing that this instrumentalized web of affective labor feeds a cruel optimism, channeling mothers' efforts into the very systems that guarantee neoliberal precarity. This process is anxiety-laden, and mothers feel intense pressure to seek out the best possible opportunities for their children, even before they are born (Shirani, Henwood, and Coltart 2011).

However, Ayşe's words were not only concerned with raising a child who could make his own decisions toward a successful life; she also wanted to ensure that he would have the opportunity to live in places where his decisions would be respected and where he would not be constrained "by the rules of this country." This is where the difference in this particular, contextually specific strategy of intensive mothering emerges. These parents wanted to raise flexible, adaptive, and autonomous adults, a goal recognized both in discourses of intensive mothering and neoliberal individualism. However, in their discussion of individual freedom, there was always an additional component. All the mothers we interviewed were increasingly concerned that the current government in Turkey was challenging their self-defined identities as modern, Western and secular citizens of (and women in) Turkey, and feared that the opportunities provided as part of these identities may be lost one day.

Political Change and Unpredictability

We conducted the interviews with the parents over the course of 2012 and 2013. These years marked the beginning of the consolidation of AKP rule. Since 2007, a number of developments have contributed to the party's growing hegemony. First, in 2010, there was a referendum to change clauses of the constitution introduced after the 1980 military coup. During the campaign for this referendum, segments of the liberal intelligentsia joined the AKP's own supporters in backing the proposed changes, seeing them as a first step toward removing authoritarian tendencies ingrained in the political system since 1980. Embedded in the changes passed was a structural transformation of the Supreme Council of Judges and Prosecutors, the institution responsible for deciding tenure and appointments in the court system (Bali 2010). This enabled the government to exercise more power over the selection of judges to this council, leading many in the opposition to fear that the government was protecting, promoting, and increasing the number of judges and public prosecutors with clear ideological affinities to AKP (Esen and Gumuscu 2016).

Second, the same year, when a newspaper reported that parts of the military leadership were planning to take over the government, a series of investigations began. Popularly known as the *Balyoz* and *Ergenokon* court cases, the trials lasted for two years and diminished the military establishment's political power, with the long-term imprisonment of high-ranking officers found guilty of conspiring against the government. Yet the trials were not limited to the military: A wider range of civilians were found guilty of conspiring to overthrow the AKP government (Balta Paker and Akca 2012). Although the trials were initially applauded for demilitarizing the political scene, many began to question their legitimacy as they began to include vociferous critics of AKP (Meyersson and Rodrik 2014). During this period, the number of court cases where critics of the government were accused of slandering various political leaders also increased exponentially. Eventually the country witnessed a political consolidation in which both the military and certain civilian political actors were being effectively sidelined through the instrumentalization of the legal system by the governing party. As of 2019, the Balyoz and Ergenekon court cases have collapsed completely, with all the charges against the military officers dropped and the jailed officers released after very long periods of imprisonment. Occasionally referencing these developments, our interviewees often displayed a palpable loss of trust in the legal system. They constantly brought up and contrasted their perception of the rule of law in the West with their experiences in Turkey. Many repeated to us, unaware of other interviewees' similar descriptions, that Turkey was not Switzerland; that one could not trust the rules to work in the way they should. One of the few mothers who asked us to not tape the interview because she was afraid that it could be used against her and her family if it accidentally found its way into the public realm, explained her anxiety about Turkey in the following way:

> This country is always full of unknowns. You cannot simply say this is how things are. You cannot plan for the future. You know the situation in education; the college entrance exams are changing every day. The same is true for military service. We, even adults, fear for our lives, for our tomorrows. Our children have a long life ahead of them, so our worries about them are much more intense. We don't know what they will encounter in the future. U.S. citizenship is security. In this country, we have injustice everywhere. Nobody gets what they deserve. It is not like we are living in a country where there is rule of law. . . . We have given them the chance to escape if they want to. This is a huge opportunity.

Educating Children on Shifting Sands

This fear for the future also had to do with a sense of unpredictability: not knowing whether the parents' plans for their children's future would work, if their investments in education would pan out, and so on. One predominant policy area where many felt insecure and ideologically unprotected was the national education system. Over the twelve years preceding our interviews,[5] thirteen major changes were made to the national education system (Aktaş Salman 2013), a very visible outcome of which was the growing emphasis on Sunni Islam within the core curricula at all grade levels. Historically, Turkey's national education system has always included limited religious education, since the early republican leadership saw secularism as a political doctrine to delegitimize religion's interference in the affairs of the state (Özek 1962) but not the reverse. The state took it upon itself to establish the necessary institutions and legal framework to control expressions of Islam in the public space (Parla 1992; Davison 1998; Tarhanlı 1993). Religion classes were removed from the state school curriculum in 1940 but reintroduced in 1949 as electives with a centrally determined content. These classes remained as electives until the 1980 coup.

After the 1980 coup, the military officers devised a new state strategy to socialize Turkish youth away from leftism, one that was frequently referred to as the "Turkish-Islamic synthesis." Religion classes were made compulsory for all students from the fourth grade until the end of high school. Research on the content and experience of these classes shows that, for twenty years or so after their inception, these classes remained peripheral within overall curricula and national exam systems and were more about reinforcing Turkish nationalism than Islam (Altan 2006b). However, in recent years, building on this existing structure, there has been significant change in both the content and quantity of religion courses. Since 2012, religious celebrations have been officially included in school calendars and multiple elective courses on Islam have been centrally introduced (Kaya 2016, 9). Although they are officially electives, in many cases students end up having to choose one or more of these classes because schools do not have the necessary infrastructure to offer numerous options. Throughout this period, textbooks have been rewritten to increase the emphasis on Islam, to the point that one can now find religious references even in science textbooks (Türkmen 2009; Altinyelken-Kosar, Cayir, and Agirdar 2015, 478). Another relevant transformation concerns the status and the number of religious-track high schools (İmam Hatip), originally established to educate clerics to be employed in the state-run mosque system. After 2009, a series of legal and policy maneuvers have led to an explosion in their numbers. They have become alternatives to state secular schools and, in many districts, the only options for families.[6] Finally wearing the headscarf, which has been allowed at the university level since 2011, was permitted in 2014 at K-12 schools, as well.

These policy changes have amplified the anxieties of the secular groups that the parents we talked to come from (Altan-Olcay and Balta 2016). Although they acknowledged that they had not had an immediate impact on their lives because they sent their children to internationally oriented private schools, they still feared that a time could come when this strategy would not suffice. One successful pastry shop owner, who ardently described herself and her family as Turkish, following in the footsteps of Mustafa Kemal Atatürk, said that she wanted her son to grow up Turkish, defending the modern Western principles on which the country was established. She was trying to achieve this by paying close attention to his schooling but, she continued: "I will raise him as an Atatürk supporter, I will raise him as . . . someone who appreciates his culture. But how will I be sure that the school he ends up going to is not a Gülen school?[7] There are obvious brainwashing possibilities in Turkey. They can do that. And for that reason alone, I can end up having to leave Turkey. I panic every time I think about this." As Merve's words suggest, our interviewees felt that the changes in the school system could presage a future in which their own socialization would make them feel unwelcome in Turkey. The threat of having their lifestyles and cultural norms delegitimized weighed on their minds. In this conception, the newly rising, so-called Islamic classes threatened to take over enrollment in Turkey's prestigious schools and commandeer its businesses. A U.S. passport thus emerged as a distinct strategy to manage this unknown, anxiety-laden future for their children.

"Modern Women," "White Turks," and Anxieties of Belonging

Yet another realm of increased conservative policies and attempted policy change has been women's rights. The 1990s and early 2000s saw intense feminist activism and collaborations, with the result that the original reservations the Turkish government placed on CEDAW, the Convention on the Elimination of All Forms of Discrimination Against Women, an international treaty adopted by the United Nations in 1979, were lifted in 1999; and new, more progressive civil and penal codes were adopted in 2002 and 2004, respectively. Through these shifts, some of the legal bases of gender inequality both at home and in the public space were removed (Fisher Onar and Müftüler-Baç 2011). However, as the AKP resorted to a more conservative and authoritarian path, a concerted effort by AKP MPs to introduce legislation that once again reduced women's control over their bodies and reinforced a direct link between women's sexuality and "family honor" has begun.

These legislative proposals, which could not be passed due to widespread protests, include criminalizing adultery, reducing rape sentences if the rapist agrees to marry the rape survivor, and legalizing polygamy. Other changes were successfully introduced: The Ministry of Women and Family became the Ministry of Family and Social Policies while the Women's Directorate, originally assigned with the task of achieving gender equality through state action, was subsumed within it—effectively relegating women's rights to the familial realm (Alnıaçık and Üstübici 2012). Abortion options have been restricted in practice. Transformations in the welfare system have reduced institutional services for children and the elderly by paying family members for care, which effectively designates women, such as mothers and grandmothers, as the "ideal" caregivers (Kılıç 2010; Yazıcı 2012). These changes are also linked to women's persistently low labor force participation rates. In March 2017, women's labor force participation was only 30 percent while women's employment rate was 27.5 percent despite consistent economic growth in recent decades.[8]

While our interviewees did not talk much about the macroeconomic environment in which they worked or used to work or the legal changes, almost all expressed a longing for the ideals of the early republican period, when the political leadership had expanded women's rights. They contrasted Mustafa Kemal Atatürk's emphasis on women's education, employment, and public presence to AKP members' well-publicized discourses on women. Some mentioned political actors who encouraged women to give birth to more and more children, declared that women and men were not equal (because they were not the same), and argued that women's main duty in life was motherhood. The literature on the early republican period shows that women's rights were introduced in somewhat limited ways in relation to their successful fulfillment of familial obligations (Altan-Olcay 2009; Arat 1994). Nevertheless, our interviewees' anxious descriptions reflect a noticeable shift and cannot be written off as mere nostalgia for a period that was not as emancipatory as they painted it. There is an expansion in official declarations that emphasize women's "natural" duties at home and in the family. A lot has been written in recent years about these public declarations, which pit "honorable" women against those who are not; "honor" being defined in terms of marital status, sexuality, and so on (Acar and Altunok 2013). Such discourses also differentiate between "good" mothers who raise "good," "pious" citizens, respectful of "customs"; and mothers whose child-rearing practices are considered questionable, or women who choose not to have children at all (Cindoğlu and Ünal, 2017; Coşar and Yeğenoğlu 2011; Kandiyoti 2015). All this fed the women interviewees' sense that their personal freedoms may be under attack.

These concerns were more intensified for daughters. As Banu, a part-time life coach who had given birth to her daughter in the United States, put it: "I am an independent woman; I want to live freely. I really don't like the restrictions on individual freedoms." She then explained her desire to make sure her daughter's freedoms would be protected. According to her, anyone who had a daughter should consider obtaining U.S. citizenship as an exit option because in the future "their daughter's freedom may be taken away; maybe she will be banned from the streets; maybe she will be harassed by the public police." When we asked whether they would recommend this practice to others, another told us: "If they are going to have a baby girl, they should definitely go for it. The status of women in this society is so unclear." In other words, U.S. citizenship was an exit option for the daughters if women's status continued to deteriorate.

However strategic these calculations sounded, they were almost always laden with descriptions of U.S. citizenship as a hope with which the families attempted to alleviate their fears about the future of Turkey and their children in it. Many described a sense of disbelief that the rug might be pulled from underneath them. They could not believe that the country where they grew up, went to school, had their families and careers, and had always felt a sense of status and privilege as "modern Turkish women" was transforming so radically that the political and social system that afforded them these opportunities might be completely overturned. Zehra explained to us that, as a divorced woman who led a free-spirited life, consumed alcohol, and dated men, she feared for her and her daughter's future. She wondered whether one day she would wake up to find her door marked, Nazi style. She expressed her frustration: "I am very angry with this government, those who elected them, what we are living through. Our freedoms, women's rights, the republican system—we got them without having to strive for them. And now we are going to lose them because they have not been internalized." Many interviewees shared Zehra's anxiety. This fear concerned the possibility that there might come a time when they would no longer be considered legitimate citizens of their country.

Such gendered declarations on the part of AKP's leadership are often also embedded within populist discourses against the so-called white Turks (Fisher Onar and Müftüler-Baç 2011; Kandiyoti 2015), casting doubt on the supposed "Turkishness" of urban, secular, Westernized social groups (Kaya 2015). AKP's policies and high-ranking members' increasingly derogatory speeches about white Turks, claiming to speak in the name of the downtrodden and the ordinary, made the parents even more anxious and pessimistic about the future, regardless of their gender: "I have a particular social and political perspective. But I feel I am more and more in the minority. We cannot do anything collectively, it seems. But the opposite side has a very programmed, planned project. . . . I really do not expect things to get better in the next ten years." Banu's words reflected a sense of misrecognition, in addition to desires for individual freedoms and a predictable political setting. "Becoming the new minority" meant that, even though they defined themselves as Turkish and their home as Turkey, the interviewees were not sure whether their personal dispositions made them welcome anymore. They were worried that there might come a time when the Turkish context was no longer a "safe home" (Yuval-Davis 2009) or even a place for whose future they could have reasonably stable expectations.

One mother remarked, "OK, we are not considering things like [changing countries], but then this is not Switzerland. Today something happens; the next day something else. We never know what the future holds. I guess I see this as life insurance [for my child]." In other words, the increased pressure of maternal responsibility and increased unpredictably in the Turkish political system obligated parents to calculate risks and manage opportunities individually in search of a better life for children. Their strategies were reminiscent of Beck's (1992) argument that contemporary societies have become increasingly engrossed with risk. His conceptualization of the risk society depicts individuals' increased preoccupation with an unknowable future and their calculated actions to try to mitigate perceptions of risk. Yet, because collective mechanisms of insurance to mitigate individually felt risks are largely evaporating, the ethos of our time is that an increased sense of risk goes hand in hand with individualization, which assumes agency to shape one's destiny through individual choice rather than through social collaboration (Vincent and Ball 2007, 1074).

Grewal discusses the popularity of the discourse of "security moms" in the United States, in terms of an articulation between nationalist politics of security and idealization of motherhood for female citizens. She suggests that the discourse becomes an integral part of the American empire precisely because it reinscribes the work of the state through women's bodies and actions (Grewal 2006). In our case, women were feeling unsafe *because of* the government, no longer sure whether the state recognized them as part of the nation and/or their motherhood as desirable. Thus, the children's U.S. citizenship is akin to an individualized insurance policy in response to anxieties about the future of Turkey as well as these families' own sense of belonging to it (Balta and Altan-Olcay 2017). U.S. citizenship has this very specific value in Turkey, because it is an insurance that enables exit or "withdrawal from membership," in Hirschman's words, if the political system transforms so radically that their children are no longer welcome (1970). As Banu put it, parents did this because building channels for exit seemed more plausible than attempting to correct the relationship (Hirschman 1970). In this sense, U.S. citizenship facilitates a different kind of a relationship with the Turkish state in a situation of perceived potential vulnerability.

Global, Mobile, and Flexible Citizens of the United States

The stories we have told so far have been about the ways the parents experienced their belonging in Turkey and felt anxious about their children's future. The parents envisioned that their children would be able leave Turkey primarily because they would be traveling on U.S. rather than Turkish passports. When they talked about expanding the options available to their children, they underscored the importance of U.S. citizenship for their children's geographical mobility. However, the benefits of the U.S. passport are not only limited to providing an exit opportunity from an unpredictable political system. There was more in their stories, which also raised complex questions of identity. While asserting their children's Turkish citizenship, these parents were actively making decisions that contradicted the nationalist paradigm. They often also described their desire to raise their children as "global citizens" while simultaneously struggling with the tensions between these descriptions, their own conceptualization of belonging in Turkey, and the Americanness of their children. Ideas around the U.S. passport both facilitate and at some moments resolve tensions around multiple layers of belonging (Yuval-Davis 2009).

Many interviewees used the phrase global citizenship in explaining their aspirations for their children. When we asked what they meant by this phrase, their descriptions revolved around flexibility, openness, and an ability to live and work anywhere. Their practices resonated with Ong's (1999) conceptualization of "flexible citizenship." Ong discusses the ways in which mobile managers, technocrats, and professionals aim to sidestep and benefit from different nation-state regimes because they can simultaneously locate their families, work, and investment in a variety of sites. These actors, through their sites of residence and work, acquire multiple residency permits and passports in order to attain flexibility for themselves in their encounters with national regulations (Ong 1999). In this particular case, institutionalizing these claims for children means that they could flexibly change locations if the parents' fears about the future of the country did materialize.

The mothers identified this flexibility first in terms of how much easier it is to travel with a U.S. than a Turkish passport. For instance, Selin, who was a finance manager in a global firm, said: "This passport gives them global mobility. I did not get U.S. citizenship for my children; they became citizens of the world. Wherever they go, doors will be wide open for them." Her expectations were justified in the sense that Mau (2010) has shown that a new kind of global stratification is occurring with respect to people's unequal abilities to cross borders. According to a recent global survey of passports, only three other passports outranks the U.S. passport in terms of ease of travel, while the Turkish passport ranks seventy-sixth.[9] Several interviewees also saw a significant advantage in the global protection that U.S. embassies extend to U.S. citizens abroad. They believed that, through the acquisition of U.S. citizenship, their children could become thoroughly transnational citizens whose rights would be protected by U.S. consulates, which was proof of the strength of both the U.S. passport and U.S. global power. One said, "in my child's passport, there is actually a statement saying that the U.S. state will support their citizens everywhere. In other words, if you are in a country other than the United States and register yourself with the embassy, the U.S. state stands behind you in any potential problem, from health-related issues to robbery."

Such calculations were not solely strategic, as the interviewees also attributed symbolic meanings to their children's U.S. passports: They felt that they encountered a poor reception when they went abroad while using Turkish passports, especially in Europe and the United States, the very places with which they identified most. As one put it, "Both my husband and I travel abroad frequently, to the U.S., to Europe . . . Every time [we] wait in line for visas, have to prepare files of documents for the application, etc. . . . These still get to me. I am constantly irritated that I am treated like a second-class citizen." Even though they described themselves as global citizens who had the necessary multicultural dispositions to live, work, and thrive anywhere, their self-descriptions did not mean much when they went outside Turkey with passports that immediately identified them as "third-world nationals." In this sense, they believed that not only would U.S. citizenship give their children a much-desired international mobility, but it would ensure their membership in a network of global citizens. Elliott and Urry (2010, 79) argue that international mobility is the signifier of membership in global networks. They argue that restrictions to movement are akin to "symbolic death." Our interviewees echoed this argument each time they brought up the contrasts between their self-perception and their experiences in seeking visas and crossing borders, especially in Europe and the United States. Thus, they wanted to provide their children with this practical ease of geographical mobility and the symbolic recognition that comes with it.

In this sense, U.S. citizenship signifies to the outside world more than an American identity. U.S. citizenship's transnational value, for this group of people, lay in its power to align the way they expected their children to define themselves with the treatment the latter would receive abroad. Yet these transnational ties did not completely erase the question of the national, a tension to which we now turn.

Raising U.S. Citizens in Turkey: More Questions of Identity

Many times, we heard the the phrase "this is not Switzerland," but people were not going to Switzerland or other European countries to obtain a second citizenship for their children. They were choosing the United States, for strategic but also significant symbolic, identity-based reasons.

A main reason for this choice is the differences in requirements for accessing a second citizenship. As the aspiration for a second citizenship has grown since the 2000s among the educated middle classes of Turkey, European citizenship has taken a restrictive turn, reversing the liberalizing trend of the 1980s and 1990s (Joppke 2008). Joppke shows that while in the 1980s and the 1990s many European nations made citizenship a legal entitlement for second- and third-generation immigrants, eased naturalization requirements, and tolerated dual citizenships (with some exceptions), in the last two decades citizenship status in Europe has been increasingly restricted. This process has taken the form of revoking unconditional *jus soli* citizenship, restricting access to citizenship through marriage, tying citizenship more firmly to state-defined notions of national identity, and ethnicizing citizenship by strengthening ties with expatriate communities abroad (Joppke 2008, 4–7). Consequently, European citizenship has become less accessible while at the same time this inaccessibility politicized through discourses that justify its availability only to "the deserving." Compared with the transformation of the European citizenship regulations, U.S. citizenship regulations have remained, until recently, more accessible and liberal—at least in the eyes of Turkish citizens.

The story does not stop with these unequal barriers, however. While these parents expected that their children could live anywhere in the world with their U.S. passports, more often than not, the destination they had in mind was the United States. The stories we heard almost always circled back to the United States as *the* place to which children could safely escape to in case of problems in Turkey. The choice of the U.S. passport was indicative of their imaginations of the United States. The interviewees frequently described a "mentality" and a sense of freedom that they associated with everyday life in the United States. They asserted their own affinity with this mentality and explained that this reflected how they raised their own children. But these expressions always swung between their affinity with the American system and their assertions of Turkishness, complicating the relationship between membership, identity, and national boundary.

As the quotation with which we began this chapter reveals, women sometimes found themselves justifying their decisions to go against medical advice. In some cases, the decision required negotiations with spouses. Sevgi explained to us that her husband was reluctant at first, but she was adamant to go through with the plan because she wanted to offer her child the chance of a life in the United States:

> It was my decision to give birth in the U.S. My husband thought it would be difficult. But if I am willing to do it, why shouldn't he be? We had enough money to finance the trip. . . . When you have a child, you want her to have the best of everything. . . . Obviously, this depends on your opportunities and your resources. My mother used to tell us that she had sacrificed everything for us. I needed to do the same thing to be a good mother. But, unlike my mother, I have lived in the U.S., and I know how life is there. So, I feel the need to provide that life to my daughter.

In other words, the U.S. emerged as the first choice for mothers as a result of their own experiences. Many offered stories of freedom and a sense of future possibilities, including those of belonging, when they talked about their lives in the United States. In contrast, even when they admitted that they felt more affinity with "European cultures," they were convinced that the chances of their children feeling "at home" in the United States would be higher than in Europe, should they choose to continue their lives outside of Turkey. This is also related to the stories of Turkish immigrants living in Europe circulating in popular discourse. Although the families we interviewed do not share the class origins of majority of Turkish immigrants to Europe, their recollections of being *recognized* as a Turk as a tourist or professional in European countries emphasized for them the discriminatory cultural and social practices faced by Turkish immigrants. Some told us stories of people who were incredulous when they learned that our interviewees were from Turkey and expressed disbelief with statements such as "you don't look (or talk) like a Turk." In these brief encounters, their class origins protected them from being identified and treated as "an immigrant Turk." However, they also were reminded of the possibilities of discrimination that they could face if their children decided to live in Europe, even when they held the citizenship of the country in question.

Like this interviewee, most mothers we interviewed equated this difficult journey with doing the best they possibly could for their children. Most of them felt a burning sense of personal responsibility because they thought this particular lifetime opportunity was available only if they made the right decisions before birth. It has to be said that both parents felt the same drive in most cases, with only a few mothers having to negotiate with and convince more reluctant fathers-to-be. In such rare cases, they used the "motherhood card," arguing that not providing their children with the best possible opportunities to maximize their potential would be "bad mothering."

In many cases, fathers were already willing or had even raised the idea in the first place. This was especially the case when the father had studied or worked in the United States. Many mothers stated that their husbands felt anxious about their children having only a Turkish passport based on their own or friends' experiences of inferiority in the United States. One high-level banker, Şebnem, who at the time we spoke was preparing to go to the United States to give birth to her second child, told us that she frequently thought about the exodus from Iran in the aftermath of the 1979 Islamic Revolution. She knew many Iranians in California from their days of living there and some of their stories of hardship had inspired her to get

U.S. citizenship for her children so that they would not be treated as refugees if they had to leave Turkey. She explained that her husband "has several MD friends. They are frantically trying to get the green card. I mean will they work on their careers or this? So much trouble. I wanted my son to have this chance." According to this narrative, U.S. citizenship and the legal protection it provides would allow her son to make the move from Turkey to the United States as seamlessly as possible. He would be able to concentrate on building his life and career without having to worry about legal and bureaucratic hurdles. The expectation was that the children are more likely to be accepted as Americans with official citizenship status than would be the case in Europe. It was this expectation through which the desired status of American citizenship became a conduit for the American dream abroad (Grewal 2005).

Becoming American: Desires, Norms, Subjectivities

Parents hoped that U.S. citizenship would enable their children to thrive in the American system because they would already have been brought up according to its norms. One interviewee said: "My mentality is very close to theirs, my work ethic, way of life. . . . They are always functional, rational. They are very direct and open. Even when they are firing someone, they are open about the reasons. That's what I do in my work, as well. They do not have backstage stuff going on. I am a very direct person, and so is my husband. That's why we have internalized America." Another described daily life in the following way: "Not everyone on the street may have in-depth knowledge about what is going on in the world, but the way they greet you in the street, that civilized attitude alone is enough. You can walk in the shortest shorts in the street; go out in your bikini. No one would care." The "civilized attitude" that this interviewee described was a recurring theme in many interviews. Some talked about the cultural practice of affording people their space and freedom; others mentioned friendliness toward strangers.

Based on these experiences, people often assumed that the United States could be the final destination in case the children needed to leave Turkey permanently. Elif, who received a graduate degree in the United States before relocating to Turkey, stated: "When I lived in the States, my life was fast, active, and fun. I worked and studied . . . I did everything [I wanted to do]. Later I said to myself, this must be freedom. I was free there; unlike

I am here. Of course, you do everything by choice; getting married, having children, raising a family. . . . I chose these. But then I never had that sense of utter freedom that I had felt there; it was different." These images were partly a fantasized understanding of the United States, depicting pockets of upper- and upper-middle-class experiences in cosmopolitan urban centers but not always noting the vast inequalities in the country or the differences in cultural practices often tied to them. This is not to say that the interviewees were unaware of difficulties of life in the United States: Many also talked about them. Yet it was because of this imagery of freedom and choice that these mothers were giving birth in the United States. Their experiences and expectations spoke to the complex ways in which they identified simultaneously with the United States and Turkey, placing their hopes on the former for their children in case things went seriously wrong in the latter.

Everyone talked about the "American system," which they believed gave U.S. citizens security and stability because the rules were reliable. According to their narratives, this system retained a sense of comfort in everyday life because everyone respected the rules and one another. This led several people to two conclusions: First, things worked so people trusted them to work, which created a virtuous circle. Second, if you had the right work ethic, you could make it in the United States. "If you are not looking for ways to abuse this system, you make it one way or another. You can live your life in good circumstances because the American society and the American legal system have established a setting where, excuse the language, even an idiot can survive, can live securely." As we argued at the beginning of this chapter, these actors belong to a relatively privileged segment of Turkish society. Yet the U.S. passport for their children and its association with life in the United States with predictability, the rule of law, and rewards for a work ethic provided them with a sense of security should their status and rights be taken away in Turkey. Their children, they hoped, would make it in the United States, because they were legal and legitimate members of the society. In other words, U.S. citizenship institutionalized for their children a variety of identity characteristics they saw in themselves.

In the introduction, we opened up a debate about whether the value of U.S. citizenship as a meaningful indicator of membership in the United States and its power for building a national community are declining because the international spread of English and the recognizability of U.S. cultural and political practices around the world makes potential immigrants into Americans even before they arrive in the United States (Spiro

2008). We connected this debate to others that explored the possible emergence of a new global order premised on transnational citizenship at the intersection of plural authorities, rights regimes that transcend borders, migrations, mobilities, and multiple allegiances (Balibar 2004; Bauböck 1994 and 2007; Faist 2009; Soysal 1994; Spiro 2007).

Drawing on these discussions, we suggest that U.S. citizenship carries unexpected and intense meanings for people located outside U.S. borders. These narratives reveal a different take on the importance of national citizenship in a transnational world. U.S. citizenship is remarkably valuable for these individuals because they feel that their affinities with America will be consolidated for their children, who can only become true members of the U.S. polity if they are citizens. The fact that they are doing it from afar also indicates how the American nation is extending beyond the borders of the United States: These parents are raising U.S. citizens in Turkey based on both their self-dispositions toward what they define as Western values and their imaginations of future lives for their children in the United States.

Remaining Turkish: Overlapping Identity Frames

However, these descriptions of how they would raise their children almost always had a secondary component. Their children had U.S. citizenship; they were going to instill in them values such as multiculturalism, equality, modernity, respect for others, and the rule of law, all of which they saw as lying at the core of life in the United States. Yet they were also Turkish, and these values were part of their definition of themselves and their children as Turkish citizens. Seda, who had spent her high school years in Europe and her college years in the United States, told us that she still tears up when Turkey's national anthem plays and that she gets upset when her children make fun of her: "We have a beautiful country, nothing in the world compares to it. I am so saddened that we are destroying it piece by piece." Or as Emel put it, "I am Turkish, my husband is Turkish, and I love Turkey. I am an ardent supporter of Atatürk's Turkey. I will raise my son as a Turk. My husband comes from eastern Turkey;[10] so for him any other option is impossible anyway. His mother tells me that when he was a little boy, he did not ask for toys but wanted *baklava*! I suppose the culture is in my son's genes, as well. But I do not know where Turkey is going." A Jewish Turkish woman whose family had tried living in Tel Aviv for ten years before returning to Turkey told us, "You can never uproot yourself. Life here, the sight of the Bosporus, the smell of bread in the morning, . . . There is so much that ties us here." While she wanted her children to be both transnational and U.S. citizens, she could not imagine not instilling in them her sense of local cultural values. Aydan, a banker who gave birth to both her children in the United States, assisted by the fact that half her family was already there and had U.S. citizenship, told us that when it came time to choose a school for her daughter, they decided to send her to a private but Turkish school:

> We considered international schools. But then we went ahead and found a regular private school. I mean we are living in Turkey after all. The children will need to learn traditions and culture of Turkey. I mean she needs to know what April 23, May 19 is. She will have to have an idea of what Şeker Bayramı is.[11] I mean we did think hard about it because we had given birth to her in the States; we want her to have a chance outside Turkey, etc. But then she cannot grow up here, knowing only Easter, can she? She would be too isolated.

When we asked our interviewees whether they emphasized the children's "Americanness" at home, they typically answered that the children knew they had U.S. citizenship but still saw themselves primarily as Turkish—whose upbringing combined Western norms with cultural proximity to Turkey. In these instances, they conceptualized being an American in terms of an institutional link with the U.S. state and being Turkish as a cultural tie, but one whose definition might be shifting even as we spoke. As for Americanness, in these moments, the cultural traits they associated with being an American were almost always translated into a language of Western values, cosmopolitanism, and openness, de-emphasizing nationality and distanced from what they saw as wrong with American society and politics (Altan-Olcay 2008). These narratives revealed not only the transformations in the connection between citizenship and national belonging, a process which Spiro has delineated (Spiro 2007 and 2016). They also exemplified the ways in which these parents negotiated issues of cultural belonging, mobility, and opportunity through their children's citizenship(s).

These stories reveal the need to take seriously the premise of transnational citizenship scholars, that people increasingly have multiple identities, memberships, and loyalties, no longer attached to singular nation-states

(Bakker 2010; Bauböck 2007; Brubaker 1989; Fitzgerald 2004; Smith 2007; Spiro 2007; Rumelili, Keyman, and İşyar 2011). However, we also want to suggest that this is not because citizenship is necessarily becoming less national or more transnational. Rather, these (predominantly) women interviewees are "emotional subjects" who negotiate the power relations of citizenship governance (Ho 2009, 789) in attempting to secure their children's future. Their stories shed light on how intensive mothering can become intertwined with experiences of citizenship as political and emotional status (Ho 2009), how different political subjectivities are cultivated across spaces and scales of citizenship (Staehelli 2003), and how these subjectivities are still negotiated in tandem with formal citizenship status (Joppke 2007).

Yuval-Davis reminds us that citizenship is multilayered; it involves complicated negotiations of belonging, security, and legal and political recognition (Yuval-Davis 2009). These women were simultaneously reproducing and disrupting hegemonic notions of motherhood and citizenship. When they emphasized their allegiance to raising modern Turkish citizens, they resorted to familiar discourses of mothers as reproducers of the nation (Yuval-Davis 1997). Yet when they expressed their desires for their children to have U.S. citizenship and talked anxiously about the narrowing possibilities for modern citizenship in Turkey, they complicated the terrain of national citizenship. Their desires for their children to be born American, determination to raise them as simultaneously Turkish, transnational, global and West-bound, and their fears about the future of Turkey create a complex story of belonging in which the parts do not always hang together. This is not an erasure of national belonging, but it is a story of transnational aspirations, resolved through hierarchies of national citizenship regimes, in this case Turkey and the United States, with their associated experiences and imaginaries, as well as others which could have been targeted but are not.

Imaginations of U.S. Citizenship from Afar

Citizenship is traditionally conceptualized as a status that links individuals to territorially defined nation-states, through either their parents' nationality or their birthplace. Alternatives to these state-centric models of citizenship, such as postnational citizenship (Soysal 1994), flexible citizenship

(Ong 1999), or transnational citizenship (Spiro 2007), have already challenged this traditional linkage between citizenship and national territory. Accordingly, the diversity of formal or informal activities individuals engage in with respect to multiple nation-states mean that citizens and citizenship need to be discussed in terms of practices organized around both scale and territory (Staeheli, Marshall, and Maynard 2016).

These parents's narratives reveal the need to think about citizenship as a "constellation" in which individuals can be linked to several political entities at the same time (Bauböck 2010). These citizenship constellations, we suggest, are almost always emotionally laden processes that can involve a great deal of imagination from afar. If, as Yuval-Davis suggests, citizenship and belonging can be conceptualized in terms of feeling at "home" and feeling "safe" among other things (Yuval-Davis 2009), these women were at home, where they continued to reside but no longer felt safe. Thus, their anxieties of belonging played a pivotal role in their aspirations to acquire second citizenship for their children—specifically U.S. citizenship. The mothers saw in U.S. citizenship a prized entitlement because they imagined it opening up for their children a world of possibilities, predominantly a safe and seamless exit from Turkey if the worst happened. In a world where one's transnational opportunities for mobility are necessarily linked to one's passport (Bauman 1988; Beck 2008; Mau 2010), these mothers' strategies signal how people experience citizenship in new ways. While emotional attachments, simultaneous feelings of anxiety and hope, and experiences of political rights and opportunities continue to be attached to national citizenship regimes, they have now become entangled in fluid practices that spread across borders (Ho 2008).

These mothers are thus enterprising *and* emotional subjects who, based on their unequal resources, strategize to acquire U.S. citizenship for their children to alleviate the uncertainties and risks that they believe their children might face in the future. The narratives we explored in this chapter complicate the usual links that hegemonic nation-state projects establish between citizenship and motherhood, where mothers are given the duty of producing and raising the next generation of citizens and demarcating the boundaries of the nation (Yuval-Davis 1997). As these Turkish parents raise U.S. citizens in Turkey, the U.S. nation also transcends the borders of the United States itself. As they are inspired by the possibilities that U.S. citizenship offers for the future of their children, the American empire extends its power through these imaginations. Imaginations of opportunities in the

United States, the U.S. political system, and U.S. power in transnational spaces are contrasted with anxiety-provoking experiences in Turkey. These contrasts provoke desires, influencing the conduct of these parents, their emotional and political relations with the Turkish state, and create individualized "glocal entanglements" (Lan 2014) with the U.S. state. As a result, we have a situation in which national citizenship regimes still matter precisely because they are unequal in their ability to sustain transnational aspirations. U.S. citizenship symbolizes for these parents their children's inclusion in this de-territorialized but bounded community.

However, these are still just imaginations. At the time we conducted our interviews, the children who held U.S. passports were all under the age of sixteen. Many were attending foreign-language schools and had had many encounters with the United States through travel, language training, summer schools, and American au pairs. Nevertheless, all the families continued to reside in Turkey and almost no one expressed a desire to apply for U.S. citizenship through their children. Instead, this practice was all about aspirations for the children's future, a future that has not yet arrived. This raises further questions: To what extent are these imaginations truly a possibility and what are their limits in actual experience? Is the United States always a safe haven, a place of refuge from risk? Can anyone make it there? What actually happens when U.S. citizens travel and live in places other than the United States? Are there other values and meanings that these parental imaginations cannot reveal? These are questions that have become even more pronounced in the few years following our interviews with the parents. In the next two chapters, we turn to these questions in the narratives of U.S. citizens and Turkish-American citizens who reside in Turkey. We extend the ways in which U.S. citizenship is imagined and experienced by complicating notions of risk and security and focusing more on the multifaceted relationship between citizenship and inequality.

Chapter 3

Transnationalized Americans

Stories of Moving Up in the World

Ethan was a thirty-two-year-old man who had moved to Turkey about five years before we met. After college in the United States, he had followed in the footsteps of his teacher parents, taught for a few years at an inner-city school, and then decided that he wanted a change. In the depths of the economic crisis in the United States, it did not seem to him likely that he could find more interesting work that could guarantee regular payment of student loans. He told us that it was then he realized he had this "magic ticket to go anywhere in the world, get a job anywhere around the world, and make better money than a lot of people that you meet." As he put it, "I'm nobody special where I'm from, but because I'm an American, there is a big market for teaching English abroad." He did not even need language teaching qualifications to get most of these jobs.

He went first to Southeast Asia, stayed there for a couple of years, and then came to Turkey because it was closer to Europe, where he traveled frequently; the lifestyle was amenable; and he had a lot of job options with respectable salaries to choose from. He worked in private English-language schools for the first few years. In between, he also tutored children whose families sought an immersion experience for them, played in a band, auditioned for commercials and television shows, and at the time we spoke was working at an international company as an in-house editor. He reflected on his life in the following words:

> Had I stayed in the States, I would have had more debt and I'd probably be less happy in my job. I probably wouldn't feel as

> upwardly mobile as I am here because I am a rare person here and I can do strange things. . . . I think about my life here in Istanbul like a game of *Grand Theft Auto*. . . . When you start the game, you're staying in the most terrible apartment and you're doing terrible jobs. But with hard work . . . you improve your situation. I don't know if I would feel the same way in America.

In the previous chapter, we documented how middle- and upper-middle-class parents in Turkey *imagined* U.S. citizenship as a status that would provide security for their children in the face of their perceptions of escalating political risk in Turkey. These stories were indicative of both the strategic values attributed to the United States from afar and their anxieties about being located in Turkey. That is, U.S. citizenship had greater power to provide security than its Turkish counterpart. Juxtaposing Ethan's narrative onto these stories from the previous chapter leads to several questions: How is U.S. citizenship actually experienced inside and outside the United States? How do we make sense of natural-born U.S. citizens who move to or stay in Turkey during their adulthood against a backdrop where Turkish citizens express their fears of political repression and where there is a documented rise in anti-American attitudes? What do their stories confirm, refute, and add to the imaginaries we opened up in Chapter 2?

In this chapter, we trace the experiences of U.S. citizens born and raised in the United States from the moment they make the decision to move abroad through the time they come to, and settle in, Turkey. First, we focus on the value of U.S. citizenship as it facilitates various privileges, ranging from geographical mobility through status recognition to upward socio-economic mobility, as they move from the United States, where economic opportunities are restricted and competition is high, to a place where as U.S. citizens they become rare "assets." We then explore their self-described identities as American citizens living outside of the United States and the ways they distinguish themselves as such from the majority of Americans who remain in the United States as well as the majority of Turkish society. We suggest that U.S. citizenship is not only unequal in its ability to enable mobility and exit from politically risky situations, it is also unequal in its ability to create conditions for upward mobility *outside* of the United States.

Because the U.S. government does not collect systematic census information on American citizens who live temporarily or permanently outside the United States, estimates vary widely from anywhere between 2.2 to 6.8

million (Costanzo and Klekowski von Koppenfels 2013). What we know of emigrants' motivations and identity negotiations comes from limited research in migration studies (Klekowski von Koppenfels 2014). These studies show that U.S. citizens tend to move abroad for employment, marriage, or education. In addition, there is evidence about the importance of cheaper living costs for American retirees living south of the U.S. border and a more liberal political scene to the north (Croucher 2007 and 2012; Dixon, Murray, and Gelatti 2006; Hardwick 2009 and 2010; Rojas, LeBlanc, and Sunil 2014; Sunil, Rojas, and Bradley 2007). Klekowski von Koppenfels calls "accidental migrants" those who settle in countries they travel to for short-term contracts and/or education because their employment contracts are prolonged, they land unexpected job opportunities, and/or meet a partner (2014).

One of the key differences between this group, whose members move from the United States to Turkey during their adulthood, from the other two groups, Turkish parents and Turkish-American citizens, was that they were more likely to be "recognized" as "authentic Americans" because of their names, the way they spoke English and, often, the way they "looked." The people we interviewed in this group came from diverse class and ethnic origins. They also reflected the various tendencies noted in the literature in terms of occupation and reasons for mobility. Among the people we talked to, one group had teaching jobs in private foreign-language schools. Others, who had moved in and out of teaching in the past, had found positions in corporations or international and nongovernmental organizations, while some had started their own businesses in Turkey. Many had initially moved abroad because of the lack or loss of jobs in the United States, more attractive opportunities elsewhere, or a desire for a cosmopolitan life. A second distinct group had come to Turkey as expatriates because of their positions in multinational corporations. While some had only been in Turkey for a short time, others had ended up staying permanently as they moved between different companies, started their own businesses, and/or became involved with or married people residing in Turkey. For a third group, the primary motivation for coming to Turkey was a relationship with and marriage to a Turkish citizen. However, once in the country, their stories intersected with those of the other groups.

It is thus hard to say that Ethan's story reflects the most typical experience. Nevertheless, his colorful analogy of *Grand Theft Auto* strikes a chord: Many people we have talked to described different experiences of opportunity and privilege. In addition to geographical mobility, these included a life experience many described as freer, protected, and upwardly mobile in terms of status, income, and career trajectories. They also stated that they would not have had comparable lives had they stayed in the United States. Their words were almost reminiscent of an outdated theme in U.S. historiography, where the image of the vast, unknown frontier creates U.S. exceptionalism, the merging of freedom and opportunity, individual hard work and success (Turner 1961). In this chapter we explore their experiences through metaphors associated with the American dream, as the frontier of possibilities that has narrowed for them in the United States moves elsewhere to places of unpredictability, but where their U.S. citizenship translates into a resource to ameliorate risk. Their stories open new pathways of discussing the complicated and tense relationship between citizenship as value and belonging when one is no longer living in one's original nation-state but in places impacted by its global power. We focus on both different possibilities of upward mobility and privilege outside the United States and on the self-fashioning of identities, distinct from home and host societies.

An American at the Border

The number of foreign nationals in Turkey has surged in recent years due to the Syrian crisis, with estimates in 2016 of close to three million (Baban, Ilcan, and Rygiel, 2017). In addition, as of the end of 2016, there were an estimated 650,000 people of non-Turkish citizenship with residence permits in Turkey (T24, 2 February 2016). However, experts express doubt about the accuracy of available data for three reasons, as Icduygu and Aksel (2015a) note. First, because these numbers are based on information on legal residents, they miss the very large number of undocumented migrants. Even state officials responsible for data collection admit that half of the foreign population may be excluded from the collected figures. Finally, there is the issue of those groups whose residence status changes during data collection. Nevertheless, we know that immigrants in Turkey increasingly comprise Iraqi and Syrian citizens, followed by people from Azerbaijan, Afghanistan, and Turkmenistan, who are mostly escaping war zones or dire economic circumstances in countries bordering Turkey (Danış 2011; İçduygu and Aksel 2015b; Kasli and Parla 2009; Üstübici 2018).

In contrast, the number of U.S. citizens in Turkey is much lower. There are different counts based on residence and work permits as well as census data. The most recent statistics from the Turkish Statistical Institute based on residence permits reveal that there are about 10,000 U.S. citizens living in Turkey. According to census data, 12,000 people with residence in Turkey were born in the United States (TURKSTAT 2017a). The low percentage of Americans within the overall migrant population in Turkey suggests the possibility that they are not placed in the same category with others by various bureaucracies governing mobility and migration. We should also note that these statistics are not completely reliable either, in that many American citizens have historically stayed in Turkey on tourist visas that they could renew every ninety days by simply leaving and reentering the country. In fact, the 2013 law change came into effect just as we began conducting our interviews (*Resmi Gazete* 2013) in compliance with ongoing EU negotiations (Icduygu and Aksel 2015a).[1] This meant that people could no longer make "visa-runs" every ninety days and continue to stay in Turkey without going through the hurdle of securing a residence permit. Notwithstanding this recent limitation, many people we talked to initially came to the country and stayed there for a long time on tourist visas until they obtained residence status. These actors had not been part of statistical data on American residents in Turkey.

A final source of information is statistics on foreign nationals who visit (enter and exit) the country (TURKSTAT 2017b). The number of U.S. citizens visiting Turkey increased between 2000 and 2015 to around 1.6 million at its peak in 2015.[2] While this represents only 2 percent of overall visitors, it is 50 percent of visits from all non-European OECD countries, with which the United States shares characteristics of high economic development, high per capita wealth, and large distance from Turkey.[3] The high percentage within this group is evidence of the political and social connections between the two countries during the twentieth century, outstripping those with the rest of the West, a history we have outlined in Chapter 1.

When we asked our interviewees what their entry to Turkey was like, they were puzzled: They had just showed their passports, gotten the visa and entered—no questions asked. This experience is partially due to the more liberal visa policy that Turkey has introduced over the course of the last two decades (Açıkgöz, 2015).[4] However, this ease is also due to the global status of U.S. passports. This group had also traveled extensively so they emphasized that this was not an experience unique to Turkey—wherever they went in the world, with the exception of a few countries, they were able to enter without visas or could obtain them without obstacles at the border. Maya, a journalist based in Turkey, said: "I am aware of the privilege and I don't take it for granted. It makes me even more aware when I get to . . . on the off chance you need to apply for a visa, and there's like a 'Where are you from' box and you choose 'the United States' and the number of questions that follows is like five and then you have your visa." Such remarks confirmed the hopes that Turkish parents have for their U.S. citizen children's geographical mobility.

Once inside the country, one group remained on tourist visas for a while. However, as the rules have become more stringent, everyone eventually filed residence and/or work permit applications. The process appears to have been fairly straightforward, starting with an online application, followed by the collection of documentation on official identification, place of residence, proof of income, bank account, health insurance, etc.,[5] and a visit to the local immigration office. In the case of Istanbul that is Aksaray Yabancılar Şube Müdürlüğü, the police station in Istanbul that accepts applications for residence and work permits. When we brought up Aksaray, however, almost everyone had stories to tell, even those who relied heavily on their places of work to navigate the system. These involved complaints about contradictions in the system; the sheer amount of documentation required; inarticulate interactions with officers in the station; the ever-changing rules; and the rumor mill feeding anxieties about whether they were completely legal or not. Bureaucracy in Turkey, one commented, "was not easy."

Nevertheless, it was easier for U.S. passport holders, not only because of the official hierarchical categorization of nationals that impacted the outcome of the application,[6] but also the experience with the actual process. Everybody went through the hurdles but not as intensely as nationals of countries outside North America and Western Europe. Jack, who had been in the country for six years at the time of the interview and had recently started a managerial job in an international company, used to go through the residence permit application by himself. He told us how he had been overwhelmed and infuriated every time he did it because the process was slow and required documents that he did not even know existed, while clerical errors made everything impossible. We asked him what the actual physical experience of being in Aksaray had been like on these previous visits. He smiled and said:

> You go to Aksaray. It's you and eight hundred people all from different countries, usually people from the Middle East—Iran, Azerbaijan, Syria, people from all over. . . . They all look very sad and

> everything takes a very long time. . . . As for me, every single time I go to Aksaray, I just stand there and soon, somebody says "Come with me!" And you just go to the front of the line. I am not trying to be rude and trying to cut in or anything. It's just how it happens, naturally. . . . It's probably because of the way I look . . . because I'm holding my American passport . . . you know what I mean.

In many interviews, people had similar responses to this question. They could complain and challenge the officers more. They could also get away with much more and could take more risks in terms of their legality. During the interviews, we heard many stories about how people stayed for years on a tourist visa, making the "visa run" every three months and presenting well-rehearsed answers about why they were in Turkey (learning the language, writing a novel, etc.) that were used so often that every party to the conversation probably knew they could not be completely true, but the answers were never really questioned. Even when they still had to suffer through Aksaray, as Natalie put it, despite the desperation in the air and notwithstanding the gendered problems she had dealing with the police officers, "part of me knew that my situation was very different from others, that I wouldn't have major problems, and that I would get [the residence permit]."

Natalie continued that her experience probably had something to do with the U.S. government's global power and also something to do with the bilateral relationship between two countries. Like Natalie, many people reflected on their luck based on what seemed to be a global hierarchy of passports. Michael, an English teacher who by the time we interviewed him had already lived in a number of Southeast Asian countries and traveled around the world, compared his experience with that of the Syrian woman he was seeing:

> I think the random chance that I was born in America has opened every possible door to me. . . . This particular woman, because of her Syrian passport, is absolutely trapped. She can't really go anywhere outside of Turkey, you know. And she doesn't want to go back to Syria obviously, but she can't go anywhere else. She has to apply for asylum, which means that you wait in line for years, basically. . . . Just because of the arbitrary fact that she happened to have been

> born in this place whereas I have this small piece of paper. . . . It's like being born into an upper-class, very privileged family.

With these words, Michael was reflecting on this arbitrary inequality his place of birth created at the international level. An American lawyer, who had lived in Turkey close to two decades at the time of the interview, described this difference in terms of "elite" and "non-elite" passports. She told us that she was actually quite angry every time someone with an "elite passport" (be that a U.S. or an EU passport) violated the rules because they came from countries where they would actually get into serious trouble for doing anything remotely close to what they thought they could do outside their countries of origin, especially in developing countries.

Initially, in the 1990s, mobility studies used to celebrate the coming age of cosmopolitanism, a borderless world, and transnational identities (Appadurai 1996; Hannerz 1996; Urry 2007). Recently, however, more critical work has begun asking questions about the structural conditions under which a minority of actors can cross borders and build lives elsewhere with relative ease in comparison with the majority of the world's population (Rees and Smart 2001; Shamir 2005). Glick Schiller and Salazar emphasize the need to entrench mobility studies within global power dynamics, and propose the term "regimes of mobility" to systematically analyze the impact diverse legal statuses, global racializing categories, and global political economic relations can have on people's ability to cross borders, and on their social status in the places where they move to. Accordingly, mobilities and experiences of movement are multiple, unequal, and impossible to universalize in opposition to another category, that of the immobile (Glick Schiller and Salazar 2013).

In this sense, our interviewees belonged to a lucky minority. They acknowledged that their experiences of seamless mobility and privilege had do with their legal status as U.S. citizens and the ways in which this status lifted them above many others in global racializing categories (Glick Schiller and Salazar, 2013). U.S. citizenship had an aura in Turkey that protected these passport holders against both discrimination at borders and bureaucratic whims once inside. Within the hierarchy of immigrants coming to Turkey, they were never bundled with the majority coming to the country from countries like Syria or Iraq. From the moment of entry, U.S. citizenship placed them in an advantageous position.

"Creating New Spaces" in Turkey

As detailed in the previous chapter, parents who obtained U.S. passports for their children were making intense calculations of future political risk. In general, migrating to the West had become a popular conversation among urban professional classes and people with means.[7] In fact, in 2014 and 2015, when we were conducting interviews with both U.S. and Turkish-American citizens, the political climate had already become more repressive than in 2012–2013.

In 2013, when the Gezi Park protests erupted; they were seen as an uprising of Turkey's urban middle classes against the government (Özel 2014). These protests began on 27 May 2013 to protect the only green area in Taksim Park, next to Taksim Square, the central square in Istanbul, from construction and incorporation into the Taksim Pedestrianization Project. Activists set up tents in the park to prevent it from being destroyed. These protests quickly spread, especially through the participation of groups organized via social media. Police interventions and the insistence of Erdoğan, then the prime minister, on continuing the redevelopment resulted in mass protests that quickly spread throughout Turkey, with parks and streets being occupied in all large cities. However, these were violently repressed within weeks. The second (and third) group of interviewees had lived through these days. Thus, in a climate where Turkey's urban secular classes were feeling more and more the brunt of repression and restriction, we were surprised to encounter in the interviews contradictory uses for words such as freedom and flexibility.

James, who had been in Turkey for five years working in an international publishing house, was the first interviewee who remarked on this feeling.

> There is something about that level, this level of chaos that is attractive. . . . Knowing you can go out of your door and have a strange adventure: That's what Istanbul provides. Something about that chaos creates space for someone who wants to live freely, like someone who doesn't want to really answer to anyone. Even as much as bureaucracy as there is, it is sort of crushing itself. So, you can stay out of the way of the bureaucracy. Or create new spaces . . . You can really do whatever you want. . . . That's why I feel so much freer here.

With these words, James was not necessarily talking about the political situation; rather, he emphasized how he was able to escape social conventions and rules by not continuing to live in the United States. He was reflecting on the flexibility that the relative absence of strict rules meant for him in Turkey. The language he used ironically repeated some of the metaphors of the myth of the frontier, where the American west emerges as a place to expand into and find freedom, a vast territory replete with danger but also opportunities through sheer willpower (Duara 2002). However, James would also continue later to lament the absence of the rule of law and describe how he cherished the freedoms he had had in the United States because of it. Thus, freedom did not mean one thing but connoted different things at different times depending on the conversation and on where the gaze of each interviewee was focused. Once we chanced upon this contradiction, we began paying attention to how others described their lives in these terms.

When James talked about his unconventional life in Turkey, his description was reminiscent of sentiments and motivations surfacing in studies of "lifestyle migration," where people often talk about maintaining high standards of living at more reasonable costs, seeking a "different" pace of life and physical connectedness to the land, and a feeling of being "elsewhere" (Croucher 2007 and 2012; Jackiewicz and Govdyak 2015; Therrien and Pellegrini 2015). Lifestyle migration is necessarily connected to conditions of global political economic relations that determine who can engage in this type of migration (Huete, Mantecon, and Esteves 2013). It is also classed, stemming from individual positions of privilege as well as global macroeconomic inequalities (Benson and O'Reilly 2009; Croucher 2012).

Yet there were several differences in this case. First, when these interviewees experienced an alternative way of being, they were talking about being able to negotiate and escape first from social conventions in the United States *and* in Turkey. These stories were unfolding not necessarily under idyllic conditions, given the political circumstances in Turkey. Second, however, as U.S. citizens, they still recognized their relative ability to maneuver amid decreasing rights and freedoms in Turkey. They relied on the protection of the U.S. government and assumed that their status as U.S. citizens gave them a certain kind of protection and exemption from rules and repression.

Negotiating Social Conventions in Turkey and the U.S.—At the Intimate Level

The kind of observations James made were repeated in several interviews, where people talked about building different kinds of lives that defied what would be expected of them at home. At the time of the interview, Megan had been in Istanbul for a decade working at a multinational company and was about to be married to her Turkish fiancé. They were established in Turkey, with her admitting that it was much easier for her to be in Turkey than for her future husband to start from scratch in the United States. She reflected a similar sentiment to James when we asked her to compare her life in Istanbul to what it would have been like had she decided to stay in the United States.

> I think I would be constantly trying to escape this conditioned pressure of competition. There's this expectation, to be on this conveyor belt . . . You go to college, you graduate, you get a job and that's what you want to do for the rest of your life. . . . I think there's always a state of panic that goes along with that. People are afraid: If you don't set up these things right away, it feels like you're going to fall into a state of chaos later on. . . . I have a lot of responsibilities of course, I have a full-time job, I have bills to pay, I have, you know, the day-to-day life in Istanbul to survive. But I feel . . . it's actually a lot less restricting than maybe a life in the States would be.

Megan said that she did not have to be on a "conveyor belt" of the kind she would in the United States; she could be more flexible in terms of her life-planning because she did not encounter on a daily basis the kind of social pressures that she would have to respond to had she stayed in the U.S., ranging from building a career to settling down, to making a home and establishing financial security. Megan's concerns resonated with the concerns of the Turkish Americans who found the American way of life to be very competitive and restrictive—something we will detail in the next chapter. For Megan, the move also had its costs that had to be negotiated: regarding families back in the United States and "Turkish" familial and gendered expectations.

In the case of Turkish Americans, as we will explain in the next chapter, the topic of families would come up a lot: For them relocating to Turkey had a lot to do with remaining connected with families there and getting support in raising children. However, this was less of a major topic for this group. The younger interviewees, who had, on average, been in Turkey for a shorter period, either talked about being the "black sheep" of their families and not being very attached to them, or emphasized the importance of their regular visits to the United States for keeping in touch. There were a few who felt that there might come a time when they would want to take care of aging parents. The rest, who had been in Turkey longer, did maintain contact with their families, had reciprocal visits, and occasionally expressed doubt over their decision to build a life elsewhere, away from them.

The older interviewees, whose own parents had passed, talked more in detail about how they raised their children in Turkey and/or were taking stock of familial expectations in Turkey. Almost all of those, who had Turkish spouses and children of school age, chose the same private foreign-language schools that also accepted students of only Turkish nationality. This choice was the result of a negotiation: Opting for schools catering only to children of foreign nationals would have meant their children would grow up in a secluded, international environment, isolated from their Turkish surroundings. More "Turkish" schools would have meant their children would only speak Turkish as a mother tongue. Thus, private foreign-language schools were a compromise. The parents hoped that this would enable their children to be truly Turkish and American simultaneously.

Among our interviewees a few had adult children who had grown up in Turkey. In one such case, the American mother predicted her son would never end up living in the United States unless there was a crisis in Turkey. Another, who had two grown-up children, told us that while her daughter, who was more exposed to English and American social circles during her formative years, did end up living in the United States, her younger son had immediately returned to Turkey after his university education in the United States. Overall, those who had children repeated some of the sentiments voiced in the previous chapters: the desire to raise flexible children who would be able to build lives anywhere. Their stories also revealed anxieties about Turkey's political system, the quality of education in Turkey, and worries about what the children were "losing" by not being in the United States. Such feelings resonated with the literature on diaspora communities, who experience anxieties about raising children in contexts where they themselves have not grown up, where the children's home becomes distinct from their own notions of belonging (Tummala-Nara 2004; Tsolidis 2011; Faria 2014). In this case, the fact that the group whose citizenship status is more "prestigious" compared with the host society made the ambivalence around familial choices more acute, with questions frequently raised about how American their children were going to be.

People also talked about the familial support they received and the benefits of tight-knit families in Turkey for the upbringing of their children. Those who were married to Turkish citizens emphasized how they admired and also resented the closeness of families. The latter stories detailed amusing encounters caused by their perceptions of familial expectations of constant communication and the occasional expectations of age- and gender-based deference. There was a lot of talk about women's rights and expectations of gendered propriety that both men and women found hard to understand. Women often told us stories of how they utilized their status as U.S. citizens to protect themselves from some of these expectations.

Suzanne, a newly married young woman, said that her husband's friends often told him that his marriage experiences did not "count" because he was married to an American. She interpreted this "not counting" as her freedom not to be judged by "Turkish standards" when she did not see her in-laws as much as she "should," went out by herself without reprimand, and earned more than her husband did. Rhonda, who had been living in Turkey for the past twenty-five years and married a Turkish man, admitted that she could still play "the American bride" card to escape some of her in-laws' expectations. She added that she still retained a prestige or status that other women in the family did not have: She could get the seat at the head of the table, be the center of attention at a wedding reception, and so on. Unable to explain how this transpired, she said that somehow "this foreign *gelin* [bride] thing is important."

In each of these stories of negotiating social conventions, U.S. citizenship, specifically the status of being an American citizen in Turkey, afforded a flexibility that they thought their Turkish counterparts in Turkey or American citizens from similar class origins remaining in the United States would not have been able to achieve. People could pick and choose to some degree what they wanted to abide by and what they did not—making use of the popular admiration evoked by their decision to leave the United States, a place that was increasingly the object of desire for the Turkish people around them.

Negotiating Unpredictability and Risk in Turkey—The Macro-Level

This perception of flexibility and relative freedom did not apply only to social conventions in the United States and Turkey. People also talked about political risks in Turkey that they had witnessed during and after the Gezi Park protests and mentioned indicators of rising anti-American sentiment and conspiracy theories.

For instance, the journalist Maya talked extensively of her experience of reporting during the protests and their aftermath.

> During the protests, I was far more comfortable being alone than when my partner was with me because if something happens to me, if I get detained for whatever reason, I am an American journalist. I would never want to be detained as a Turkish journalist. As an American journalist, I'm OK. But if he's with me, I get much more scared because if he gets in trouble, that's it. He's in his own country, he's at the mercy of whatever system or non-system is applied here. His rights aren't there whereas mine are . . . you know . . . a quick call to the consulate and I'm OK.

In fact, many assumed that if something went terribly wrong in the country, the U.S. government would send planes or helicopters to airlift them out. While these expectations could be inflated, they contained some truth. The U.S. government could also exercise leverage over the Turkish government during a crisis both because of the power difference between the two and their integral relations, which in many ways meant the latter was more dependent on the former. Furthermore, the U.S. state does officially provide a number of protections to U.S. citizens abroad, beyond those of most other states. This ranges from the FBI's involvement in situations where American citizens are impacted by instances of political violence abroad (FBI 2008) to a Smart Traveler Enrollment Program, which provides regular information to travelers and organizes evacuation from crisis zones.[8] However limited these may be in implementation, they contributed to a feeling that U.S. citizens would be protected. Thus, the freedom they found in the Turkish context had to do simultaneously with escaping restricting rules and expectations in the United States while still relying on the U.S. state's power to protect them under conditions of political risk abroad.

Others talked about their encounters with conspiracy theories, how everyone at both ends of the political spectrum in Turkey seemed to believe that the United States was behind everything. Alan, a Chinese American start-up owner, admitted to no longer saying he was American during one-time encounters in taxis, food courts, and the like, because it occasionally opened up a can of worms. "Let's say sometimes when I tell a cab driver that I'm Chinese, there are only a couple of remarks. But when I tell strangers I'm American, they start questioning me about American policies here. When the topic is American policies in this part of the world, there are always huge conspiracy theories." Eventually he gave up talking with strangers on matters of U.S. foreign policy. He did not experience insecurity in these encounters but described feeling uncomfortable and found a way out by relying on his ethnic identity. He also told us later that he thought hard about this discomfort and how he might be taking advantage of U.S. government's power while also professing to being against its interventionism abroad.

Lisa, a young woman, was more distressed after hearing multiple anti-American speeches made by prominent politicians. She told us that at one point she was so worried that she asked a staff member at the American consulate in Istanbul she met at a gathering what they thought of these speeches and whether there was anything that she should worry about. In 2014–2015, the consulate had not started issuing travel warnings to Turkey and U.S. citizens had not yet been arrested or deported. This officer, she told us, waved a hand dismissively, saying: "That's just politics. The U.S. has an extremely strong relationship with Turkey. We are always working hand in hand with them, so don't listen to anything you see on the news."

Such stories show us the different ways in which anti-Americanism can manifest itself. At this time, in the experience of the groups who were most likely to be "recognized" as American citizens in an increasingly unpredictable setting, anti-Americanism seemed like a populist discourse that political actors used or certain segments of society resorted to, but not something that overwhelmingly determined everyday encounters. Whether in the immigration office or elsewhere, interviewees almost always started their narratives with a sentence like "I've never had bad reactions," describing instances when strangers learned they were American citizens. This phrasing indicated an expectation that being recognized as an American could elicit unpleasant conversations about U.S. foreign policy, as Alan's story attests to, or pose security risks in the worst case scenario. When probed about whether this situation was changing, whether there were moments when they had become more reluctant for security reasons to reveal that they were U.S. citizens, almost everyone still responded in the negative. But they also explained the discomfort they felt when faced with others' experiences with U.S. geopolitical power, almost always opening questions about what it means to be an American outside of the U.S.—questions not easily answered.

Some said their continued sense of personal security might have to do with being in Turkey as opposed to other places, such as Iraq or Afghanistan, where the American presence was more obviously and solely connected to U.S. military power. It should be noted that the political situation in Turkey deteriorated rapidly after we conducted our final interviews in 2015. In fact, many of the interviewees who had been here for shorter time period have moved out of the country since then. Those with whom we remained in touch mainly told us that the unpredictability of the situation had become less tolerable, and that whereas in the past they had never felt a security risk as U.S. citizens, they were beginning to now. Among those who had been in Turkey for a decade or longer, only one person we know of moved to Europe with her family (children and Turkish husband), and another to the United States. We will explore these developments in the conclusion, but at the time of the interviews, our informants felt a sense of protection because of the history of positive cultural relations between the two countries and the global recognition of being an American.

Everyone they encountered in an urban setting knew something about or someone in the United States and wanted to share these connections and anecdotes with our interviewees. A few who had lived in small communities in Turkey or elsewhere in the region used the term "celebrity" to describe how they felt—people were often in awe that they had chosen to leave "the land of freedom and plenty" behind to come live with them. This admiration often shielded them from problematic U.S. foreign policies. They were always in the limelight, which in a sense protected them from prejudice and threats. The majority of their experiences were thus in contrast to the rising anti-Americanism we explored in Chapter 1.

There was something else: When our interviewees said that they were never confused with U.S. government, they were also recognizing a situation in which many migrants have the opposite experience. Critical scholarship tells us how being recognized as "Muslim" has connotations that exceed the actual individual: One becomes lumped into stereotypes, associated with regimes and governments beyond one's control, and is almost always considered a security risk or a victim. The societal gaze places them at the bottom of racial hierarchies in direct relationship with hegemonic security discourses and global political inequalities (Abu-Lughod 2013; Lockman 2004; Mamdani 1996; Said [1979] 1994). In Turkey, however, the global political order worked to the advantage of our interviewees, in that they could both eschew the negative connotations of U.S. foreign policy as individuals and also retain a position of power in criticizing both American and Turkish developments, portraying themselves as free from both. Citizenships, their narratives suggest, are perhaps unequal in spaces outside countries of origin, also in terms of protecting individuals from negative perceptions surrounding their governments' politics—even though they still evoke personal anxieties.

We can continue the analogy of the frontier. When these actors talked about the freedom available to them, a land where they could escape some regulations in comparison both with American citizens back home and Turkish citizens in Turkey, they were almost adopting a narrative already present in the United States' exceptionalist historiography. It was now becoming globalized and reterritorialized in the words of ordinary actors who clearly have nothing to do with the U.S. government. As a result, the word "freedom" could denote both their exceptional lives as Americans in Turkey and become the conveyor of a critical gaze about social conventions and existing (and nonexisting) rules in the United States and Turkey. Their claims of difference became more explicit in identity narratives, something we explore in the final section of this chapter.

Comparing Turkish and U.S. Citizenship

Turkey felt freer for these interviewees because of their American citizenship, but not as free for the Turkish citizens. This hierarchy became more visible in discussions of dual and multiple citizenship. Those who had lived longer in Turkey had the chance to apply for Turkish citizenship. Only a few, all women, married to Turkish men, did apply.

When asked questions specifically about their decision-making, they often said that having Turkish citizenship removed anxiety about renewing residence permits. Talia, who had been married to a wealthy Turkish individual for the past decade, was more explicit about the pragmatic value of getting Turkish citizenship. First, she said that she had started the process because she felt ready to make the commitment. Then she added that it was also her lawyers who prompted her.

> My lawyers have been on my back for the past nine years. They say, "You're an American. You're living on Turkish soil. You have a Turkish husband . . . As a foreigner in Turkey, if one day something happens to your husband, nothing . . . there is a chance you would not inherit anything. . . . If you're living in a home that your husband or his family owns, then you can live there until the day you die. But it is a temporary residence just for you until the day you pass away." So, my lawyer has basically instructed me [to apply for Turkish citizenship].

She told us of friends who had forfeited their inheritance in this manner, so for her Turkish citizenship meant being protected from this fate. However, everyone applying for or who had Turkish citizenship was also ambivalent about the *costs* of Turkish citizenship: Women were worried about whether their children would become subject to military service, were displeased about surname changes, and most questioned what dual citizenship might mean in terms of U.S. government protection and whether it would endanger in any way their U.S. citizenship status. Since the value of U.S. citizenship was higher than Turkish citizenship, they wanted to make sure that acquiring the latter would not hurt their status with the former.

When we asked the hypothetical question of which citizenship they would give up if they could not hold onto both, everyone said they would retain their U.S. citizenship. It was the immigration lawyer, Arianna, who explained the choice in more general terms: Even though there was a sense of loyalty and belonging that defined citizenship for her at a personal level, when it came down to decisions of this kind,

> It's more an issue of having access to an elite passport. So, whether it's a UK passport, Canadian passport, a U.S. passport, if you're living outside of your country of nationality, having an elite passport is very important for global mobility. . . . So there is no question but if I were here and I had a Canadian passport and a Turkish passport or a UK passport and a Turkish passport, that value is not so different. . . . And in fact, having the U.S. passport is a much greater burden, obviously because it's one of the only countries in the world that requires, you know, payment of tax [while residing abroad].

Thus they felt protected by the U.S. passport while U.S. citizenship could be translated into various kinds of privilege outside the United States. That was harder to give up, although U.S. citizenship imposed tax burdens even when outside the United States. At least at the time of the interviews (Donald Trump had not yet been elected), those that had U.S. citizenship in addition to those of various European countries, due to ancestral connections, said that if they had to give up their status as citizens of multiple countries, they would choose to keep U.S. citizenship. For some it was about being an American, for others it was about work histories and retirement plans in the United States. The choice was the same for the group who had a second citizenship in other countries of the Global South, the rationale being the mobility that U.S. citizenship offers around the world.

Moving Up in the World

At the intersection of U.S. government power, its implications for the U.S. passport and the contextually specific cultural prestige associated with U.S. citizenship, it was not only contradictory narratives of freedom and flexibility, suggesting a global hierarchy based on citizenship, that emerged. U.S. citizens in Turkey also experienced multiple kinds of upward mobility, which many acknowledged might not have been possible had they remained in the United States.

Bourdieu has shown that classes and class boundaries emerge as an effect of struggles encompassing not only matters of economic capital accumulation but also what he refers to as social and cultural capital (1984 and 1989). Cultural capital denotes educational achievements, matters of taste, and consumption practices that appear unconnected to economic inequalities—but which are in fact inherently related (1994). Social capital enables us to capture the networks that people can comfortably navigate and/or to which they can connect. The ability to convert these different types of capital into one another endows people with symbolic capital (Bourdieu 1986), a sense of being recognized as belonging to a particular class because of the seemingly natural characteristics they embody. Empirical work emerging from new class studies shows how intense individualized classification struggles based on self-definitions of taste, cultural identity, and consumption habits can be (Katz-Gerro 2002; Le Roux et al. 2008; Savage, Bagnall, and Longhurst 2001). These are intense because they involve multiple, simultaneous, and occasionally contradictory claims of authenticity and difference (Lamont 1992; Mendez 2008; Sayer 2005; Skeggs 1997 and 2005); distinction and disidentification (Lamont and Molnár 2002; Lawler 2005b; Reay 1997; Skeggs 1997), and an alertness to changing value schemes at the macro level beyond one's control (Bourdieu 1987; Lawler 2005a).

What happens when we reconsider discussions of class and classification struggles in transnational spaces? How are nationally situated bundles of capital recognized and/or misrecognized outside countries of origin? Migration studies focus on the likely possibility of downward class and status mobility when people move outside of their country of origin, even for professional classes, because their cultural and social capital repositories become less recognizable (Erel 2010). What if certain citizenships can be translated into a resource of cultural capital that produces upward class mobility?

Translating U.S. Citizenship into Economic Power

As discussed earlier, the U.S. citizens we interviewed had held a spectrum of socioeconomic positions in the United States. Once in Turkey, the least advantaged were those teaching in various private English-language schools or tutoring children and adults. This group had on average been in Turkey the shortest time and had moved here because of the economic crisis in the United States, where they could not find jobs. However, even for this group, although their income was not necessarily high, there was a sense that their money went much further than it would have in the United States. As Paul, a high school teacher, told us:

> I think you have the possibility of living a much better life here financially, economically as a teacher for sure. You know, my friends will see me like on vacation in Italy for example and ask, "How do you just go to Italy?" And the answer is it costs the same or less going from Chicago to Kentucky. . . . There are lots of costs you don't have living abroad: My school pays for my apartment. . . . So, I do feel like, I live much better . . . you're able to save money too, whereas it's harder when you're back home.

This group felt that they earned enough to pay off their debts, live in good neighborhoods, and not think about monetary restrictions when going out or on trips. There was a sense of greater economic power when they compared their current life standards with what life would have been like in the United States, as well as with the general population in Turkey.

Hanging Out with the "One Percenters"

All our interviewees, regardless of their socioeconomic background in the U.S., described how they socialized with a combination of expatriates and university-educated Turks, most of whom had connections to the United States one way or another. This was almost inevitable, one suggested, "because, in order to form friendship and relationships, you have to be able to communicate with each other." There was a second characteristic of the people with whom they associated: having gone to foreign-language schools, or English-language universities in Turkey and abroad, or having lived abroad signifies an upper- and upper-middle-class segment of the Turkish population. This meant that, when the interviewees hung out with them, they were becoming part of a higher-income social circle that they may not have belonged to back in the United States.

Dan, who had been in Turkey for just a few years, already found himself friends with a group of young Turks who were much wealthier than his own socioeconomic roots. When we asked him how this happened, he offered the following description:

> They speak English, that's how. Those who speak English are usually more educated and it takes money to get educated. I don't know if the public school system in Turkey provides as much opportunities to all the different classes. So, if you've been educated outside of Turkey or went to a French or an American or an international school, we tend to have more in common, so we tend to talk more, we tend to dress the same, look the same, act the same, and those things just kind of collide.

These experiences were not only true for teachers and tutors. The group who came from wealthier families in the United States, or had degrees from Ivy League universities, or had corporate jobs in Turkey, expressed a similar sentiment. One corporate lawyer, who moved to Istanbul in search of a different pace of life, explained his status mobility in the following terms:

"I've been very lucky. . . . I went to decent schools and I'm an attorney, and so just by showing up here and being vaguely polite at a couple of parties, you instantly find yourself going from sort of, you know, 5–10 percent to 0.1 percent. You know, you instantly find yourself hanging out with people who seem to be really the upper-class here." Everyone also had access to the expat community at large in the city. These intersecting communities existed because the numbers were small and there were institutionalized networking opportunities organized by the American consulate and the American Business Forum in Turkey, among others. This access was important not only for purely status reasons but because these contacts could translate into job opportunities, and interesting and fast career trajectories. John, who had lived for brief periods in various Middle Eastern and Asian countries before ending up in Istanbul because of college friends from and connections with Robert College, told us that when he first came to Istanbul, he could not find a decent job. When he was complaining about this at a family dinner he attended, a friend's father questioned him about his brief experience as a bartender. He told John that he could send John's résumé to some friends.

> So, I got this email from this restaurant group, "We're opening a bar, can you send us your résumé?" . . . We arrange a get-together in this beautiful hotel, where I meet the owner and the general manager, who is doing the hiring. . . . I was going to be a bar manager even though I had no experience. . . . In America no one would take that risk. You need to be a seasoned veteran in the industry if they are going to let you open up a restaurant with them.

At the time this happened, John was only twenty-six years old, and he had been operating this new bar for close to two years when we conducted the interview. In the long run, he hoped to open his own business in Istanbul. John's experience was unique in many ways but we also met various individuals who were establishing business development units at international firms at a very young age, had been asked to start new departments in firms soon after moving to Turkey, could comfortably meet with high-level officials in Ankara for their start-up companies, or have their art work included in well-publicized exhibitions, even though they were initially very much on the outside of the Istanbul art scene.

"The Prestige of American Citizenship"

Such stories prompted the question of why. In response, many people repeated Dan's assertion that hanging out with upper-income groups enabled access. A second common interpretation was the narrative with which we began this chapter. As American citizens, they were "rare" in Turkey, which opened opportunities that would not have been available in the United States. In general, when they ventured outside of the United States, especially to developing countries, U.S. citizenship and Americanness became an exceptional asset.

We met numerous interviewees who had initially left the United States during the 2008 economic crisis after failing to find jobs in their chosen sectors. The same was true for the group of Turkish Americans who decided to relocate to Turkey after years or decades of living in the United States. A young NGO director said that he was able to get the positions he did in the Middle East—prior to coming to Turkey—because the NGO was looking for a U.S. citizen to run the local operations and he had few competitors, which would not have been the case for a comparable position in the United States. An Asian American remarked that on the U.S. East Coast he was just one of many Chinese Americans who went to an Ivy League school, got an economics degree, and worked on Wall Street; but here these credentials were seen as unusual and therefore attractive. A lawyer said that due to her U.S. citizenship, she was offered a job in the newly established immigration department of an Istanbul law firm. Her work experience would not have been anything special among immigration lawyers in the United States but in Turkey her U.S. citizenship, American legal expertise, and language skills could translate into progress in her career.

Other interpretations of the advantages of the rarity of American citizenship also tiptoed into the conversations. Becky, for example, had moved to Turkey because she did not have any immediate job prospects in the United States after graduate school. Having worked during her university years in a summer camp for young students organized by Robert College, she decided to use her connections to find a temporary teaching job in Istanbul. What was supposed to be a brief stint was about to become five years when we met her because, after she began tutoring two students from a very wealthy family, the word had spread: She was now a full-time tutor for children between ages two and sixteen for some of the wealthiest families in the country. The job also involved organizing immersion experiences, traveling with the families on vacation because her U.S. passport and language skills made it easier to go abroad than it would have been for a Turkish nanny, and even joining the families when they had international guests. When we asked her why she thought these families wanted her around for more than just the tutoring, she pondered for a while before saying:

> I think part of the reason why they want me around is that the[se families] have fun memories of the United States. I feel like sometimes it's a bit nostalgic for them to have Americans around. So, they also want their kids to be exposed to Americans; they like the mentality. [A famous businessman] is very curious, he loves to learn new things and he wants this for the children. . . . He does not like to bring the Turkish nanny [on trips abroad] because she won't eat the food . . . you know; she will bring her Turkish coffee with her. So that's a difference, the kids pick up on that because they're with their nannies all the time.

Thus, according to these narratives, the small wealthy segment of Turkish society with previous exposure to the United States and a cosmopolitan socialization prefer to be with or to hire Americans because it creates a comfort zone around them. This keeps alive their own experience in the United States while making it possible for their children to be exposed to "non-Turkish" practices. We also encountered stories about less wealthy and less cosmopolitan individuals who also saw value in hiring Americans. We heard many remarks about the "prestige" of having an American employee, similarly to the narratives of Turkish Americans in the following chapter. In one interview, when we asked Natalie why she was hired on the spot as a speech therapist in her school, even though she had not yet completed her training, she responded with a story about someone else's experience:

> I had a friend who had the craziest job: She was paid a teacher's salary to be a consultant for this guy's business and she did not have any experience in his line of work whatsoever. He would just take her to meetings as "the American" (laughter) . . . I am serious . . . and he was like, "Drop some business lingo; just say this is how we do it in New York." And that's what she did basically, and everyone

> would be like "Oooh, OK" . . . but I guess it is not true for all foreigners. . . . I mean I think it's like in the U.S., too, when I think about it. You know being French there . . . it's like people love anything French. . . . A lot of people study French, love the culture and know about it through movies, whereas if you're coming from a poor Latin American country, there's a different perception.

When she recited this story, we broke off into laughter because it was so absurd. Even though this employer did not really require a consultant, he liked the idea of taking "an American consultant" to meetings. John, the twenty-eight-year-old bar manager, said that the owners "knew that it'd be really cool to have an American behind the bar. It was a marketing thing, you know, we have an American bar manager, blah blah. . . ." Michael, one of the lawyers, said that he was overpaid for the job he was doing at his first company—there was not much to do, but the partners insisted that he hang his Ivy League diploma in his office and that he attend all meetings with outsiders. Abigail, who married into a wealthy family, was asked to become the visible face of their company, even though she had no business expertise, because the older members of the family saw the involvement of "the American bride" as prestigious. Another remarked on this cachet in more general terms: "Here you're instantly given status that you would never be given in the States. Here, you're just instantly given it because you're American."

In other words, the notion and the status of U.S. citizenship translated into specific opportunities outside of the United States, which ranged from easier geographical mobility through fast-track career paths to interesting job opportunities. Even when people experienced a career downturn, they still could claim improved purchasing power and social status as Americans outside their country of origin. The sheer difference between U.S. government power and the power of the Turkish government also increased the value of being a recognized member of the United States abroad. Because being part of the elite in Turkey is associated with having robust U.S. connections, U.S. citizens benefited from this association. Our interviewees experienced upward mobility outside the United States because their U.S. citizenship provided a status that the majority in Turkey did not share. The connections between their experiences and their standing as U.S. citizens indicate that there is a hierarchy of citizenships that influences people's status outside their country of origin.

However, Becky, the tutor, also admitted that she lived in a bizarre bubble: While she was being picked up from the dock by boat three times a week to go to her job, networked with people whose names adorned newspaper society pages, and traveled abroad for free, she was still just a tutor, she commented. This was a conflicted experience: She did feel upward mobility in her everyday life, but she also questioned whether this was the career she had envisaged for herself. Some others also repeated similar sentiments, juxtaposing narratives about high social status with questions about what might have happened had they stayed in the U.S. The younger crowd expressed the hope that their experience abroad might open up new paths if they decide to go back. Others, who did not foresee returning, emphasized the choice in terms how they had come to feel more "at home" outside of the United States, among other like-minded Americans and Turks. This was a home where they still identified as Americans and American citizens, but they had ambivalent relations with both the United States and Turkey.

Being a "Special" American: Ambivalences and Negotiations of Identity

Our conversations were not only about the hierarchical utility of U.S. citizenship in Turkey. People also reflected on why they had their privileges in terms of self-attributed definitions of *who they are* as American citizens living outside the United States. On the one hand, people used notions such as diversity or cosmopolitanism in stories in which they established personal distance from racism, isolationist perspectives, and inequalities in the United States. On the other hand, they referred to "American" sensibilities of diversity, freedom, and the value of hard work for individual achievement to depict what was problematic in Turkey. The narratives became the basis of self-identifications as "special" kinds of American citizens, who are different from the majority who remain inside the United States, as well as the majority of Turkish society.

An American Outside America: Claiming Difference Through Cosmopolitanism

Some of the interviews we conducted coincided with the Ferguson riots in the summer of 2014.[9] Several people we spoke with asserted that they did not idealize the United States. Suzanne, who had previously explained her fast career trajectory at an international company by referring to her analytical skills and sense of responsibility, said that she did not see the United States as a utopia.

> In America you're told that . . . at least where I grew up in Texas, in rural Texas, people say: "Why would you ever want to live anywhere else? We Americans have true liberty of speech, we have a good education system, you can get rich in America if you want to, you can better yourself, like pull yourself up." You know the bootstraps rhetoric. But I don't think it's true. Look at the crackdown in Ferguson right now, which is no better than what Erdoğan did in Gezi, maybe a little better. But not much! Look at all the restrictions they are trying to put against abortion. No different from Turkey. . . . I look at the education system and the student loans; it's insane! So I don't see it as a utopia.

She then went on to explain that she did not necessarily feel patriotic and that she felt "more like a global citizen than just an American one. Of course, if you will ask me, I'll say I'm American." Our interviewees also often found it hard to connect with their friends and family once they went back home. Sarah, who had tried going back to the United States twice and ultimately decided to settle in Turkey for the indefinite future, described these return attempts as "reverse culture shock." "I had a hard time to adapting back to American life. I think I actually felt a reverse culture shock. . . . I just felt like I wasn't connecting with people. I was back in my hometown where I grew up, and the people that I've gone to high school with weren't the type of people that I would . . . we didn't have anything in common, I couldn't connect with them and I just basically stopped trying to reach out to them." Like Sarah, many had a feeling of not being able to share their experiences with the people in their former lives because they were not interested. Others described being put off by the sheer size of everything in the United States, the everyday life built on constant consumption, and the obliviousness about everything outside one's own town. It was also a feeling that their political views had changed so much that they felt completely disconnected. Questions of who they were and what it meant to be an American citizen who no longer felt as at home in United States frequently came up in conversations. Summing up these feelings was

Jessica, who asserted that she was different from most Americans because she had an outside view of U.S. politics and society. She had lived for extensive periods in Latin America, Southeast Asia, and now Turkey. She could compare:

> Many Americans don't have that window looking in on themselves. They think America is wonderful, and they don't realize the wonderful education systems that some countries have and the wonderful inclusiveness that some countries have. . . . I mean the fact that a South American country can legalize gay marriage before the U.S.; many Americans don't even know that. . . . I mean things like "the right to bear arms." . . . In Korea, it's illegal to own a firearm; you cannot have guns. . . . And Americans think they have the right to own and carry around automatic weapons, and I don't think they realize how strange that this is in the rest of the world.

In other words, they wanted to convey to us that they could turn their critical lenses on American society, politics, and disproportionate global power better than the majority of U.S. citizens at home because they had a different vantage point. These assertions of critical distance were often combined with self-identifications as a "different kind of American": they were transnationalized Americans who combined "the best" of two worlds. They were the Americans who could escape the negative connotations of the United States because most people in the countries where they lived did not confuse them with the U.S. government and/or because they themselves were sufficiently distant from and critical of U.S. foreign policy while benefiting from the geographical and upward mobility opportunities that U.S. citizenship enabled.

An American in Turkey: Stories of What Is Missing

Janet, who had lived for quite a long time in Saudi Arabia and now in Turkey, explained how she felt about her status as an American inside and outside the United States. "I have always felt like a little bit different. Yes, I know that I am an American; I know that that's where my parents are from and whatnot. I am like a very international, not just like a normal American. . . . In the U.S., I'm like 'the special' or 'the weird American.' In Turkey, I'm just an American, weird again, but like, you know, I am an American."

In other words, back home, she was "weird" but elsewhere her "weirdness" was what made her a "regular" American. And as "regular" Americans in Turkey, our interviewees were still "different." It was in these moments that people often turned their critical gaze on Turkish society. When, for instance, asked about their upward mobility—in addition to reflections about the power of the U.S. passport and "the prestige" of employing an American citizen, which had to do with the contextually specific connotations of the United States in Turkey—they also suggested they had certain characteristics that most Turkish people did not. According to these narratives, they could bring honest hard work to the table because that was ingrained in American culture; they had analytical thinking skills because the American education system, whatever its failures, taught this to a greater extent than the Turkish one (or others in the region); they were culturally open because they came from such a diverse society. Given the existing connotations of America in Turkey, its hegemonic associations with freedom and opportunity backed by U.S. global power (Bright and Geyer 2002), this critical gaze assumed authority.

Suzanne, for instance, suggested that when people were brought up in settings where they were likely to be afraid to think independently or voice dissenting opinions, employers might turn to outsiders to fill critical positions. Several also noted a general tendency to refrain from voicing one's opinion publicly if that happened to be in opposition to the government or hegemonic norms. Some connected it to the public education system, which encouraged rote memorization, or to people's survival strategies in the existing political climate. Megan contrasted this state of affairs to the right to freedom of speech she had through U.S. citizenship, and described how she came to appreciate what many others take for granted.

> In the U.S., you're not going to be put in a jail for saying that you hate the president, or you wish there would be some major change in that society. And that is something that's very threatening in many countries. . . . Journalistic freedom, things like that. . . . I think that was one of the major realizations that I had: the simple ability that you have to express your opinion as an American. Again, it's not perfect, it's never a perfect system but you can feel much more comfortable being public about any opinion that you have than you can in other places.

With these words, Megan, who had spent the much of her adulthood in Turkey and a post-Soviet republic, reflected on the tradition of free speech in the United States and how she came to appreciate it once she was outside. Many others had similar sentiments, and ended up moving from a position of criticizing the United States and American society to voicing pride in being able to take freedom of speech for granted as an American.

Others were proud of coming from a country where it was not your ideological conviction, how you looked, or proximity to the people at the top but your individual ability and will to improve yourself that supposedly determined your life chances. Interestingly, as discussed earlier in this chapter, some of these interviewees had experienced difficulties in the U.S. job market, lost jobs in the 2008 crash, and/or said that the opportunities they had in Turkey were far better than the ones available in the United States. One Syrian American even remarked that not being able to find a job had made him feel as if the U.S. rejected him. Many also talked about racism in the United States. Nevertheless, being away somehow cemented their belief in the so-called American system and, as one put it who had lived in Turkey for the past decade, "Whatever your gender, religion, ethnic background, what you look like, picking yourself by your bootstraps, I miss that."

For Megan, it was not only about freedom of speech, but her freedoms and rights in more general terms as a woman compared to the norms she was exposed to outside of the United States: "The clash of cultures when you experience growing up as a young woman in the States versus a rural . . . community with very strict expectations of what women do and if you're a foreigner what that might imply. . . . So, I was detained quite a few times by the police because they did not want to believe I was in [a post-Soviet republic] for what I said I was there for: For them, I was either a spy or a sex worker. . . . So, it wasn't just an identity on my passport, but it was also my physical identity and what that implies." Other women, too, often talked about gender norms in Turkey. In addition to previous stories of how they used their status as U.S. citizens to cope with the difficulties of being a woman in Turkey, they still expressed how troubled they were when men harassed them on the street, especially because they looked "Western" and were therefore expected to be "loose," or were expected to have no one to stand up for them in everyday interactions. They could see that being recognized as an American (or Western) woman signified something different from the way they perceived themselves. What emerged out of this disjuncture was not only negotiation strategies, but also an identity assertion, an appreciation of their upbringing in the United States.

A similar observation was also true for those interviewees who were often asked intrusive questions because of their ethnic background: "Where are you really from?" Khalid, whose father had immigrated to the United States from Bangladesh and who himself had lived in Turkey for the last two decades, said that U.S. citizenship certainly helped his job opportunities during his time in Turkey. Yet he added a qualifier that he probably benefited less than he imagined a white American would: "I think you're not going to say 'Oh, he's an American' just by looking at me. You can't tell till I open my mouth. As soon as I open my mouth, then I can see everybody has questions in their mind: 'Who's this person?' " A Palestinian American was so bothered by the question "Where are you really from?" that he had stopped saying he was an American in everyday encounters with strangers. Several also acknowledged that the United States had its own problematic immigration policies before asserting that it still was inclusive. Besides, this sort of questioning would never occur there, out of sheer propriety, because "being an American is not about ethnicity," as one contended, even though the same interviewees would also talk about racism in the United States.

These descriptions of difference in Turkey were voiced in tandem with critical distance from hegemonic Orientalist discourses in the United States. Those who had also lived in the Middle East told us stories of how they reacted when they were asked racist questions about Arabs. The younger group talked about their discomfort when people in the United States saw their life in Turkey as "a curious adventure" or were oblivious to the world outside their small towns. And yet precisely because they could assert a position of geographical and emotional distance from the United States, they often became embroiled in incongruous descriptions. Just as Young reminds us, in Poirier's words, how the writers most critical of the United States are often the most ardent defenders of "American" values (and are disappointed because America does not live up to them) (Young 2002), these individuals who combined criticisms of both American and Turkish societies ended up contributing to a very specific imagination of the United States outside of its borders.

The autobiographical stories of our interviewees suggest that American citizenship outside the United States allows for very specific subjectivities. These narratives, which are very individual, are nevertheless connected to global power hierarchies. U.S. global hegemony, both political and cultural, contributes to their comparisons between the two countries, selective deployment of "American" tropes, and an ability to find a space in between for themselves. This doesn't mean that this space does not come with its own anxieties of identity, both for the individuals and their families. Being an American citizen outside of the United States raises tense questions of identity and belonging, but also provides a way to resolve them in tandem with hegemonic narratives of their host society, in this case Turkey. Andrew, who had lived most of his adult life in Britain and India but had recently moved to Istanbul with no plans to go back to the United States any time soon, explained this aptly:

> To be fair, I mean I know a lot of people find Americans obnoxious. . . . You know our foreign policy is unpleasant. We cause a lot of problems throughout the world. But I've never really had a very, very bad situation because I was an American, officially or unofficially. So I would say in some sense it's always a good thing, which of course is ironic: It makes me an ingrate because I don't have much interest in my country in terms of actually living there. But I do benefit from the fact that I don't have a Syrian passport or a Bulgarian passport, or a Nigerian passport, or you know, a Cambodian passport. I know life would be far more difficult [if I did].

The American Dream in Transnational Spaces and the American Empire

One major finding that emerges from the literature on migration is that whatever the cause of migration, immigrants tend to experience downward mobility in terms of status, recognition, and economic prospects (Erel, 2010) in relation to their host society. Those who don't are separated by name: expats, lifestyle migrants, etc., emphasizing positions of a priori privilege. These studies emphasize the structural conditions and inequalities under which only a minority of mobile people can be described using these terms. These inequalities include the class positions of these groups in their home countries, their higher earning power and wealth relative to their host countries, and the wider political and economic relations that order states internationally (Croucher 2012; Glick Schiller and Salazar 2013; Huete, Mantecon and Esteves 2013).

The narratives of the U.S. citizens we have traced in this chapter suggest such a source of a priori privilege: In these narratives the official status of U.S. citizenship and being recognized as American matter. This is more obvious in transnational spaces, where status and recognition can be translated into opportunities that cannot be found even within the United States itself. The age of transnationalism, therefore, does not mean that national membership is no longer important. Nation-state-based citizenship is alive and well, more than ever, because people's citizenship plays a fundamental role in the types of recognition they can elicit beyond their state's borders, opportunities they can take abroad, the protections they can rely on even when outside their countries of origin, and the voice of authority they can adopt concerning both home and host societies because they are elsewhere.

In this particular case, it is the institution of citizenship through which class positions move across borders and refract in correspondence to existing interstate inequalities. The social group whose stories we explored in this chapter came from diverse class origins; not all had internationally recognized schooling; neither could they all be said to have unique skills or professional experiences. Nevertheless, many related stories of upward social mobility outside of their country of origin. They were able to befriend, connect with, and become part of social circles to which they did not belong in the United States. They were able to achieve professional progress, finding themselves in positions of influence at a younger age or in interesting jobs, paths that might have been closed off to them in the United States. Even when their jobs did not appear to be prestigious or unexpected, they still spoke of improved living standards in comparison with the United States—especially because they had moved abroad because of the lack of jobs back home.

For most, the American dream is no longer possible in the United States. Surveys indicate that the present generation is not looking at a realistic possibility of surpassing their parents' class position because of economic crises and businesses moving abroad or closing (Saez and Zucman 2016). The American dream has become just that: a dream, a myth that is upheld rhetorically but not so much in reality—in the United States at least. Yet this case shows its enduring power outside the United States. U.S. citizenship translates into a resource that its possessors can utilize in a number of different ways to achieve upward social, cultural, and economic mobility so long as they are in the developing world. The dream has thus been extended temporally and geographically to the world beyond the

United States. The idea of America, where anyone can make it, survives in the lives of these American subjects who live elsewhere.

Another recognizable discourse emerging from these narratives is one of inclusiveness and multiculturalism (Grewal 2005)—except that growing evidence of racial inequalities, tensions, and police violence, as well as a growing systematic attack on women's reproductive rights in the United States may tell a different story. The people we have interviewed offer an alternative interpretation from afar. When people are asked where they are really from, when white men become aware of their disproportionate privileges as opposed to women and minorities, when women reflect they will never be "Turkish" even if they have Turkish citizenship, these uncomfortable experiences in Turkey can be contrasted with the dream of an accepting, multicultural, immigrant society in the U.S. Things lose focus; become blurry at the edges from afar. On the other hand, these Americans abroad also assert that they are critical of the problems of American society and U.S. politics. As one of them said, no one sees the country as a utopia.

In her autobiographical work on her years in Turkey, Suzy Hansen says that Americans are very unlikely to think about how their personal identities relate to their national identities. She suggests that this is a position of privilege, that people do not have to reflect on the connection because its impact is felt elsewhere in the world, not in the U.S. She then documents how her life outside the United States revealed the impact of American foreign policy and how, until that point, her obliviousness was part of her many privileges and her sense of what being an American meant. In the end, she feels disjuncture, shame, and loss. In a sense, hers is a story of American innocence and its questioning, precisely because it has been made possible by the not-so-innocent presence of U.S. government in the world (Hansen 2018). Hansen's book is a story of finding onself in foreign lands and building complex narratives of identity, which are simultaneously "American" and distanced from U.S. politics. Possibly this is another privilege enabled by the same geopolitical relations she sheds light on, questions, and criticizes. In a similar vein, the contradictory perceptions of our interviewees reveal the persistent power of citizenship in evoking complicated feelings of national belonging and identity. Theirs are stories of becoming American, albeit a different kind, as they put it, elsewhere in the world. There is also a larger process here than the individuals' own life trajectories: Through their critical evaluations of the U.S. government, they become American subjects who are capable of extending what is "good" about the

United States to foreign lands while acknowledging its failures. It is the frame of critique that makes the dream of a multicultural America, where anyone can make it, credible. America becomes transnationalized in the experiences and narratives of its subjects beyond its borders. Their experiences of transnational mobility and privilege create a global desire for membership in the U.S. across the world. This is how the power of the American empire unfolds, in the seemingly apolitical, everyday lives of its subjects beyond its demarcated territory.

In the next chapter, we continue with these stories of mobility—geographical and status-based—but we also introduce the intensifying experiences of unpredictability in this same period through the voices of Turkish Americans who have made the choice to *return* to Turkey. We explore the strategies they develop around their dual citizenship status along with the complex emotional bonds their status entails. We explore in their narratives conditions of hybridity and ask what these mean in terms of the transformation of national citizenship in an age of transnational identifications and mobility.

Chapter 4

Returning from an American Dream

Turkish Americans in Turkey

Esen was a middle-aged artist who completed her university degree in Turkey before moving to the United States after winning the diversity lottery in her mid-twenties. She then lived in the United States for about fifteen years, bought a home there, and established a career. In her early forties, however, she began considering returning to Turkey, an idea she would have never imagined when she first moved to the United States. Eventually, she did move back because, she told us, she missed her friends and her family in Turkey, more intensely than she had imagined. This was a risky move as she had neither property nor a job waiting for her, but she was willing to take the chance to rebuild her life from scratch. When we spoke to her, however, she was growing increasingly anxious about political developments in Turkey and was considering moving back to the United States, this time with her son, who was born in Turkey. As we were completing this book, she was in Los Angeles with her family, leaving behind a career that she had restarted in Istanbul to begin yet another cycle of uncertainty. Her story shows how decisions about living in Turkey or the United States are never final and can change due to life opportunities and political developments.

Migration studies tend to consider the developed countries of the West as magnets, especially for skilled migrants. As a result, we often have a skewed view of such places, including the United States, as receivers but not senders of migrants, which the previous chapter has begun refuting (Boller and Halpert 2015, 300). The more dominant popular perception is that migrants who leave after coming to Western countries are the vulnerable ones who could not establish the necessary social, cultural, and economic ties in the receiving developed country. In many cases, according to this view, they leave not because they want to go back to their homelands, but because they have to—due to precarious living and working conditions and/or exclusionary migration laws.

There is some truth in this perspective, given that the number of international migrants increased from one hundred seventy-three million in 2000 to two hundred forty-four million in 2015. As of 2015, Europe hosts the largest number of international migrants (seventy-six million) while North America hosts the third largest (fifty-four million). Overall, high-income countries host more than two-thirds of all international migrants (United Nations 2016, 9). Since the 1980s, the same high-income countries have also been designing selective immigration policies (such as quality-based point systems and quotas) to attract a larger proportion of highly educated and skilled migrants (Docquier and Rapoport 2007). As Shachar and Hirschl (2013, 72) argue, governments in high-income countries "have come to subscribe to the view that something else is required in order to secure a position in the pantheon of excellence: It is the ability to draw human capital, to become an 'IQ magnet' that counts." Shachar and Hirschl call this "Olympic citizenship," a form of citizenship designed to attract the wealthy and highly educated scientists, athletes, artists, and successful entrepreneurs and innovators, for which governments compete with one another (2013, 73). U.S. policymakers have joined this trend with the Immigration Act of 1990 and the decision to relax quotas for H-1B visas, a category assigned to highly skilled professionals.

The diversification in migration trends, a result of changes in global economic patterns, however, complicates assumptions about return migration. The classic story in which the migrant moves permanently from a poor to a rich country is increasingly no longer true. Migrants now appear to be lifelong mobile subjects between their country of residence and country of origin (Nguyen-Akbar 2014). As the job markets for skilled and middle-management jobs in North America and Western Europe shrink, we are witnessing a trend where highly skilled migrants may expand their job searches to opportunities in their countries of origin as well (Nguyen-Akbar 2014).

The group investigated in this chapter consists of highly skilled migrants who had at some point moved to the United States for education or work.

Their life stories reveal complete integration with and the establishment of institutional ties to the United States, either through residence permits or U.S. citizenship. Apart from a few cases of people winning the diversity lottery (also known as the green card lottery), these people had acquired their official status through long-term stays in the United States. In many cases, they had also been educated in the United States, and none had been jobless there; in fact, they all had well-paying jobs. Several were married to U.S. citizens, having met their spouses during their university years or through their professional circles. In short, this is a group of migrants who were culturally, socially, and economically integrated into the United States. Nevertheless, they had all decided to return to Turkey.

As U.S. citizens, this group was experiencing what the parents in Chapter 2 anticipated for their U.S.-born children who were not growing up in the United States. Their stories revealed the meanings and strategic values of citizenship experienced by *naturalized* American citizens. Not only that; their decisions to return from the United States to live in Turkey allowed them to compare life in the two contexts, uncovering yet another layer of meanings of belonging and identity around citizenship regimes (Yuval-Davis 2009). Their circulation between the United States and Turkey suggests the enduring ties migrants retain with multiple societies as they expand transnational social spaces (Faist 2000). In this chapter we inquire into the meanings and values attached to multiple national citizenships within these spaces.

Migrating to the United States

The composition of our interviewees reflected a shift in the 1980s that happened in migrations trends from Turkey to the United States. As we have indicated before, emigration from Turkey to the United States remained low between World War I and the early 1960s due to restrictive immigration laws. Only about a hundred Turkish immigrants entered the United States per year between 1930 and 1950. Although the numbers increased to 2,000–3,000 annually after U.S. immigration laws were liberalized in 1965 (Kaya 2005, 427), it was not until the post-1980 period that significant numbers of Turkish citizens began emigrating to the United States.[1]

From the 1980s onward, the rise and consolidation of neoliberalism in Turkey enabled a new generation of transnationalized professionals (Emrence 2008). These actors were now even more intensely connected with Western lifestyles and consumption patterns because of their disproportionate economic power and the increased availability of such goods and services. Their everyday consumption practices became corollaries to their claimed distinctions from other social groups and identification with certain factions of the newly urbanized middle classes around the world (Ayata 2002; Öncü 1999). For these classes, the West became synonymous with the United States, so they began to go there for education, work, and investment in increasing numbers (Bali 2002). As a result of increased macropolitical connections between the two countries and the opportunities made available to the cosmopolitan, educated middle classes during Turkey's transition to a market economy, the number of Turkish citizens moving to the United States began to escalate.

During the 1980s, these people also made more use of the transformation of citizenship regimes in both countries that relaxed the "one nation, one person" rule in tandem with a significant number of states worldwide, as outlined in Chapter 2.[2] Now that they do not have to worry about losing rights in their home countries (property ownership, inheritance, etc.), the number of people of Turkish origin being naturalized in the United States, while still a very small proportion of total U.S. immigrants, has grown in the past decade. According to current estimates, approximately 500,000 Turkish American citizens live in the United States,[3] mainly in metropolitan areas, with New York City and its vicinity as their first choice (Kaya 2003, 211). The vast majority are first-generation immigrants, belonging to the wave of immigration that began in the 1980s and has accelerated since the 1990s (Kaya 2009, 620). In this wave, a significant number are college-educated, speak excellent English, and pursue careers in medicine, engineering, or business. This pattern of skilled migration to the United States is generally described as a "brain drain," since they are assumed to be lost from the home country's labor market (Kurtuluş 1999; Akçapar 2009b). Bayraktar-Aksel (2019) argues that this population is politically attuned around "Turkishness" rather than a Muslim identity due to their education in the Turkish national curriculum. They have easily adapted to American professional life and society, and usually identify themselves as "Turkish Americans" in their country of residence.[4]

Our interviewees who were return migrants display these general characteristics. Most had initially migrated to the United States for college education, vocational training, or to find work. In general, they felt familiar with the social fabric and experienced a welcoming attitude in the United

States. Those who had initially gone for a short term found themselves staying as new opportunities presented themselves. Rana, for instance, who had moved to pursue an MBA, had planned to stay for two years, finish her degree, and return to Turkey to find a job. However, as she was finishing her MBA, she was offered a great position in a major international finance company that she could not refuse. Her employer also supported her green card application. So, she stayed. As she told us: "My intention was to move back to Turkey once I finished the MBA. I never planned to stay longer in the U.S. But your plans change. You change."

Those who had moved there abruptly after winning the diversity lottery shared stories of excitement. Deniz, who was working as a journalist in Turkey at the time we interviewed her, had won the lottery in the early years of the twenty-first century. At that time, she possessed no transferable skills. However, her sister was working at a major software company in the United States and offered to cover Deniz's educational costs so that she could acquire skills that would make her acceptable in the U.S. job market. Deniz sold all her belongings, completed an intensive English course, and moved. She was initially accepted in a graduate program in business administration before finding a job in the human resources department of a large company. She recalled the excitement she felt when she first received the letter from the U.S. government in the following words:

> It was my fourth time [applying for the lottery]. One day I received a letter. I read the letter; but my English was so bad those days that I don't think I understood it correctly the first time. I mean I always knew it as the green card lottery, so I was expecting something like "You won the lottery." But it was something like DV200x, a one-page letter, which I could not quite figure out. It stayed on the shelf for a week. Then I read it again with the help of a dictionary. It was *the* green card! And they were expecting me to send so many documents! I was then assigned for an interview with a consulate official in Ankara and I was interviewed. It was very easy. They told me my permit would be mailed to me in a week. I was surprised and shocked. "Is that it?" I remember asking myself, "Am I becoming an American?"

In a sense, Deniz's expectation of "becoming American" was realized in many cases because most of our interviewees came from relatively privileged backgrounds and had the kind of cultural and social capital that could reduce the likelihood of the downward mobility that migrants often experience. Their stories of integration and their praise for the meritocracy of the American system reflected this. Mehmet, a professional working for an international organization who moved to the United States after winning the diversity lottery, echoed this sentiment. He recalls how he was amazed at the respect for different cultures even in his oath-taking ceremony.

> At my ceremony, there were around a hundred people from seventy different countries. Some were refugees from Africa. Some had been in the States for more than thirty years. A judge was leading the ceremony. He said we were Americans, but we should not forget where we come from. He said people like us founded this country and their memories of their homeland keep the nation alive. I thought about our political system. We want to Turkify everyone, even the refugees . . . We are so intolerant of difference. But the U.S. is not like that. It is not who you are, it is what you do. That is why America is so attractive.

For many of our interviewees, being able to hold the U.S. passport in their hands meant a major change and a huge opportunity for their lives. They all emphasized their newfound freedom of travel, confirming the expectations of the parents in the earlier chapter. Having a citizenship that was valid not only for the country issuing it but also throughout the world translated directly into a kind of freedom of movement that they had not experienced before with their Turkish passports. For example, according to Selma, "An American passport has one great advantage: travel freedom. I can get to anywhere. Europe, Egypt, Italy, Spain. Wherever you want to go, you can go. You don't have to plan anything in advance. You also feel secure with it. You are a citizen of the world. A global citizen." Defne, a middle-aged female academic who moved to the United States for her PhD before becoming a U.S. citizen, underscored how important this mobility was by describing U.S. passport holders as a different class of people, one that possesses many rights:

> Before I was an American citizen, I had many problems with getting visas. For instance, Germany can be really ridiculous in issuing visas. Because of their unpredictable requirements, I could not be with my sister when she gave birth to her first child. People say that there are

> no rules in Turkey but there is no predictability in the visa policies of European states, either. But if you are an American, then there are rules. Travel freedom then becomes a primary right for you. When you show your U.S. passport to an officer, you show that you possess full rights. But when you show a Turkish passport, it means that you deserve less; you have fewer rights. With the U.S. passport, you belong to a different class.

Echoing the anticipations of the Turkish parents in Chapter 2, for the middle and upper classes in Turkey this opportunity to travel seamlessly was extremely important. This group of interviewees also agreed that U.S. citizenship had significant instrumental value because of this. They frequently talked of how the passport affected their treatment in the countries they traveled to. Furthermore, once they had residence permits and/or U.S. citizenship, this group had all the institutional means in their hands to fully integrate into American society, in addition to their prior cultural predispositions, higher education, and job skills. And for years, they did so, fully aware of the international advantages they now had.

Our interviewees often stated that they were generally happy about the living standards that they had achieved in the United States. Depending on the region where they resided, some admired the close-knit communities they found in their neighborhoods. Those who had children could not speak more highly of the quality of the schools they attended. Above all, all were impressed with the predictability of the political system. Overall, they had established a life in the United States beginning usually in their late twenties and had every reason to stay. Most had undergraduate or graduate degrees from U.S. institutions of education, they had high-end jobs, and they had established a social life that seemed valuable to them. After all, they were American citizens now and they were not going to be expelled from the country even if the political climate suddenly changed for the worse.

Yet it was not all smooth sailing. Deniz, who took up the position at a large financial institution, told us that her change of plans did not mean she did not miss her family and friends in Turkey. "In Turkey, I had my family; my boyfriend was there. Moving to the U.S. meant that I left all my friends, family, and loved ones behind. At the time, this was the best choice for me. But when I moved to the States, I felt an intense loneliness and emptiness inside. It was very difficult." Others too experienced similar sentiments. Sezin, for example, a computer engineer in her mid-forties, told her story of moving the United States in the following words:

> I graduated from the computer engineering department of one of Turkey's most prestigious universities. I was the top of my class. I started my MS in the same department. One day, a friend of mine emailed me a job announcement at a major software company. I thought it was only for American citizens but there were no restrictions in terms of citizenship. I applied . . . along with a lot of friends in my department. I mean, what could be more appealing than the idea of working for [name of company] in the U.S.? It was a dream job. There were so many applications from Turkey that year that officials from the company actually came to do interviews in Turkey! I think they may have hired almost the entire MS class that year!

However, working for this huge software company was nowhere near the dream job she had imagined. There was always stress in an extremely competitive work setting, and she had to work incredibly long hours, which left little room for a social life outside the company. As she noted: "I had moved to the U.S. with friends. But we could never see each other once we moved there."

Subtle patterns of exclusion also emerged in these narratives. Whereas their cultural capital, defined around an affinity with the West, gave them symbolic distinction at home, it did not always pass as "Western" enough outside Turkey. According to one informant, this was especially the case following 9/11 and changing perceptions of people from Muslim-majority countries. Others attributed it to the fact that they never looked or sounded "American" enough. These conflicted descriptions of life in Turkey and the United States were revealing of the dissonances in their cultural register (Lahire 2008). In Turkey, their historical distinctions relied on affinities with the West. They were the actors more likely to study, live, and adjust to the expected behavioral repertoires of the United States. However, the United States, despite all its imaginaries of inclusiveness and multiculturalism, still invoked in these people a feeling of homelessness in that they felt excluded from the imaginary with which they asserted affinity.

It was in these moments when they began considering returning to Turkey, that a second expected value of the U.S. passport emerged. While they were ordinary in the United States, they could already see from their travels abroad the high status attributed to being an American outside the United States. Could the same be true for their return to Turkey as Turkish Americans? Their return decision was partly encouraged by their ownership of the U.S. passport: they could easily relocate if anything went wrong in Turkey. This enabled them to consider the strategic and emotional advantages of returning to Turkey.

Difficult Decisions: Returning from the United States

Thus, our interviewees returned to Turkey from established lives in the United States. "Don't you regret returning to Turkey?" was a question they were often asked. Why had they given up the chance to live and establish a future for themselves in a safe, powerful, and stable country with a sound economy? Many interviewees told us that when people asked them such questions, they were not interested in what it was about Turkey that drew these people back home: Rather, the rhetorical question was born out of the assumption that their decision to return to Turkey after living in the United States was irrational and wrong.

As the authors of this book, we too decided to return to Turkey in the mid-2000s after completing our educations in the United States when the political and economic climate in Turkey appeared more hopeful. Not only did we return to Turkey, we chose not to give birth to our children in the United States; we refrained from giving them the "gift" of U.S. citizenship. We also heard the same question from everyone we recounted our life stories to, especially as the political situation in Turkey has become increasingly unpredictable: Do you regret returning to Turkey? Why did you make such an irrational decision? However, ours were different cases in that when we returned to Turkey, we had no institutional connection to the United States. Although we had each lived there for close to a decade, we had acquired neither U.S. citizenship nor a green card. Therefore, the decision to return meant that our relationship with the United States from that point on would be as a tourist. Returning to Turkey without securing a residence permit or U.S. citizenship meant nearly completely forgoing the possibility of resettling there.

In contrast, the group we interviewed had an institutional connection with the United States through either citizenship or a green card, which they had obtained by various means (e.g. marriage, work visas, and, albeit rarely, the lottery). The majority of the interviewees who had U.S. citizenship felt secure in their status. As for the permanent residents, they also saw their green card as a right that could not be taken away from them. At the time of our research, President Trump had not yet imposed his executive order restricting travel to the United States, including individuals who came from a list of countries including Iran, Libya, Somalia, Syria, Yemen, and North Korea. In the absence of such erratic changes governing travel to the United States, they believed they had a clear right to return to and live in the United States. The literature on return migration suggests that when migrants gain citizenship of their host societies, this can actually induce return migration because ownership of a second passport enables not only transnational mobility but also represents a way out if migrants' expectations from their return are not fulfilled (Mortensen 2014). This means that there is a positive correlation between transnationalism and return intentions because, so long as immigrants maintain connections to and some kind of presence in their countries of origin, the decision to return becomes more feasible (Carling and Pettersen 2014, 15).

This was the case for our group. Their institutional attachment to the United States in the form of citizenship made them feel safe. It made them feel that they might have other opportunities to resettle in the United States if everything did not go as planned in Turkey. Thus, their answer to the question "Do you regret that you returned to Turkey?" was generally, "I can go back any time if need be; I'm living here now because it's better for me to be here right now." In other words, the U.S. citizenship connection contributed to their decision to return. Having ties to the United States through citizenship provided the security of knowing that they could change their decision at any time in the future. More broadly, the official recognition as American citizens provided the opportunity to live and travel anywhere in the world. It should be pointed out here, however, that those who felt that they might have another chance in the United States also wondered how realistic it was to think like this. Even if they had U.S. citizenship, without a job or an established life to look forward to, returning to the United States was likely to be a distant possibility. Nevertheless, they believed that if Turkey's political climate and economic opportunities radically deteriorated, then having U.S. citizenship would give them, at the very least, a way out.

So did they regret returning to Turkey? All the people we interviewed said that their decision to return had not been an easy one, involving serious thinking and consultation with families and friends. Family and friends were crucial: They missed their friends, wanted to take care of ailing parents or wished their own children to be close to grandparents. Besides emotional bonds they could not shake, they also saw the possibility of finding better jobs in Turkey than in the United States and the likelihood of faster-track careers, given their experience in the United States. For nearly all of the interviewees, returning to Turkey meant a rise in social status compared with the United States. Thus, it was in Turkey, not in the United States that U.S. citizenship translated into upward mobility, similarly to the experiences we recounted in the previous chapter. Nearly all our interviewees had put down roots in the United States, made good money, and had decent lives there. What was their decision-making process like?

Family Ties

Research on return migration suggests that the decision to return is not only influenced by networks in countries of origin and residence, but also by a variety of emotions that shape people's everyday experiences, remembrances, and interpretations of their commitments to their broader web of relations (Carling and Erdal 2014, Carling and Petersen 2014). Thus, thoughts of family members left behind, especially a desire to establish intergenerational ties between emigrant children and their grandparents, can become crucial factors in the decision to return or retain mobility between the two countries (Yahirun 2014).

For our informants too, the desire to reunite with family left behind in Turkey was one of the most important reasons to return, particularly for women. This was especially the case when they had aging parents with no one else to look after them. Many of our interviewees told us that they returned to Turkey because they wanted to keep their families together, take care of their parents, and spend time with them. Zehra, an urban planner in her mid-forties, stated that this was the most important factor behind her decision:

> My mother and my father are with us today and won't be with us in the years to come. I do not know what it means to lose a parent. I have always heard stories from my friends, though. They always say that not having had more time to spend with your parents before they pass is such a big regret. I guess for me it was important not to

> feel that when the day comes. That's why we decided to return: to reunite with our parents; to give our children a chance to know them more.

Many also talked about the difficulties of raising children in a place they knew but had not grown up in. Such sentiments reflect how parenting across cultural contexts and practices poses difficulties for both parents and children. Parents struggle with coexisting emotions of sadness, guilt, and anxiety in coping with divergent cultural contexts, which for children often mean different identifications than those of the parents (Tummala-Narra 2004). More important, everyone with children also highlighted the difficulties of raising children without social support systems: Indeed, the strength and inclusiveness of social networks in Turkey were a major factor in making the decision to return. As they often repeated, it takes a village to raise a child, but because most of these families were first-generation immigrants in the United States, they were alone. Many looked forward to the social support they would have for their children if they were in Turkey. In Zehra's words, "we have a social network here [in Turkey]. Our families support us, physically and emotionally. They look after our kids. We don't have to take care of everything alone. We don't have to hire babysitters, either. We have property here or the rents are cheap; so that means we get to spend each dime on our kids and for ourselves. [When we were trying to decide], we made a list of the advantages and disadvantages of return. And here we are." Nevertheless, many families were also aware of the advantages of raising children in the United States. They frequently talked with anxiety about the low quality of public schools in Turkey and the higher quality of public education in the United States. Many told us that they had to send their children to expensive private schools in Turkey. Mehmet, an engineer in his mid-forties, struggling with their decision at the time we spoke to him, told us that they wanted to resettle in Turkey and raise their only child with the help of grandparents, but now he had serious doubts:

> You pay around twenty thousand dollars for a farcical, foolish education. You question this absurdity. Why should I pay this much? What will I get in return? What is the value of the education that my child gets in Turkey? . . . There is no real sense in it. The curriculum changes every single year. There is no foundation to it. There is

> also a lot of stuff which go against your personal values. You don't know what you are paying for. You don't know what the ideology behind it is. You don't know who will profit. And you go on paying ridiculous amounts of money, especially people with our social status. The education my child gets here has no international validity either. It does not guarantee my child's future.

Many interviewees shared Mehmet's feelings, as did the parents who traveled to the United States to give birth to their children. Aside from the recent desecularization of Turkey's national education, the Turkish American interviewees were also concerned about privatization of education, something that was not mentioned by our first group. This was mainly because when this group had lived in the United States and they had sent their children (or knew people who sent their children) to good public schools. While they recognized that the quality of public schools depended on where they lived, they were also very much aware that there were still the contextually specific possibilities for good quality public education, which was not the case anywhere in Turkey.

Since the 1980s, Turkey's educational system has been radically monetized through neoliberal reforms, which has led to an exorbitant increase in parental contributions to the public education system, a sharp decrease in the overall quality. and a rapid increase in the number of private schools (Koşar-Altınyelken, Çayır, and Ağırdag 2015). While state schools suffer from serious financial difficulties, the government has channeled public funds to establish private schools, supporting them through tax exemptions and land grants. Given the deteriorating resources and quality of public schools, the number of private schools has exploded because more and more parents are scrambling to get their children out of the state system. However, their options are limited within the private school system, where many offer an education no better than that had previously been offered by state schools, and the rest are exorbitantly expensive. The Turkish educational system is also highly centralized, which limits schools' ability to diverge from the nationally designed curriculum.

Thus, desecularization and privatization of education concerned many families since returning to Turkey. They constantly struggled to find good schools for their children that provided quality education alongside secular values. In some instances, they turned to international schools that do not operate under the auspices of the Ministry of National Education. However, their diplomas are not accredited in Turkey. Many families were sending their children to a group of private schools that could provide a certain degree of autonomy in their education. Such schools are proud of their secular identity and market their relative autonomy from the Islamization of education as an asset that cannot be found in state schools. These schools, however, are expensive and usually offer little to no financial aid. Many of our interviewees stated that they needed high-paying jobs just to provide a good education for their children. In short, the children were a major concern in the decision to return, with extended family dynamics being a positive factor and education being a negative one.

Precariousness

In the classic migration story, as mentioned above, the migrant moves from a poor to a rich country before settling there permanently. This was not the case for our group. In fact, another critical factor contributing to their decision to return to Turkey was the precarious working conditions in the United States. For several decades, the workplace has become more uncertain, unpredictable, and risky worldwide, with layoffs a regular component of employers' restructuring strategies. Conditions of precarity has spread to all sectors of the economy, including professional and managerial jobs. These are usually seen as much more pervasive in the United States than in economies with tighter controls over employment practices and state-funded social safety nets (Kalleberg 2009).

Although skilled migrants make good money and may have high-status jobs, the U.S. labor market is seen as merciless, especially for older people and immigrants. These people had well-paying, prestigious jobs but were anxious about how long they could keep them. Many of our interviewees noted that young workers are valued more in the United States and that there is no job guarantee after the age of forty. Since they already felt insecure as first-generation immigrants, the fear of losing their jobs increased their motivation to leave the United States. In addition to an insecure job market, working conditions were a serious burden, with long hours, demanding bosses, and excessive workplace competition driving them to find jobs in Turkey. Aylin explained how extended she felt in her work in the United States:

> My company was a small one. It was small by American standards of course: forty people. After I had my child, I was not even allowed to take a break. My maternity leave was just six weeks. It was insane: Can you imagine, six weeks?! [After giving birth], I decided to reduce my working hours and shifted to an 80 percent workload and salary. I was getting 80 percent of my salary, but my job requirements were the same! No one really was willing to reduce my workload. I had to start working at 8:30 after dropping my daughter at school; I had no lunch break whatsoever and left the office around 14:30. I ran to Defne's daycare, picked her up from there, went home, prepared dinner and took care of her. Then I had to finish the things that I could not finish in the office after she went to sleep. And we were done with the day. I was in America, supposedly living the American dream but it did not feel like a dream at all.

Moreover, many interviewees considered Turkey as a better place for retirement because they expected to be surrounded by their families and friends, with a dense network of professionals, and lower health care and living expenses. In particular, the quality of the health-care system was regularly mentioned in our interviews. While they were very concerned about education in Turkey, they were even more concerned about the unaffordability of the U.S. health-care system. Therefore, they considered it the best of both worlds to have worked in the United States at a younger age before moving back to Turkey after reaching middle age. That is, they thought they could escape the ageism in the United States and receive better social services in Turkey. Mehmet, whose job requires constant travel between Turkey and the United States, was keenly aware of this:

> Turkish citizenship is not something that I had actively sought. I was born into it. It was an accident. But still it is good to belong somewhere. It is also good to belong to two places, two cultures. Having multiple places where I belong truly reflects my personality. That said, the best part of Turkey is that it is a safe place for your old age. It is good to retire here. I feel it was good to have spent my youth in the U.S. and then to retire here [Turkey]. My family is here, I have a network here, it is cheaper to live here, you have a lot of social security here, and health benefits are better than the U.S.

The U.S. Economy in Crisis

Most of our interviewees had returned to Turkey in the first decade of the 2000s, when many countries of the Global South, including Turkey, were experiencing significant economic growth. Turkey's economy had also become an attractive center for multinational businesses and investment. Thus, the expanding job market, the new and enticing investment opportunities on offer, and economic stability attracted Turkish citizens with U.S. work experience. As the middle and upper classes shrank in Western economies due to recession during the early 2000s, countries like Turkey were becoming the locomotives of the global economy.

For the business owners among our interviewees, Turkey was not only their home country but also a market in which they could invest. The competition in the market was not as great as in the United States, and there was room for new companies. With the experience they had acquired in the United States, they stood to gain significantly from investing in Turkey. In this new market, people with experience and networks in both countries and dual citizenship were in an advantageous position. Therefore, having settled in the United States, many decided to come back to Turkey because of these opportunities. One high-profile middle-aged investor in the IT sector decided to return to Turkey after the 2008 crisis hit the U.S. economy:

> I had an American business partner. At the end of the 2011, we had this business idea and we were looking for places to invest. Then I thought of Turkey. I mean the market in the U.S. was very competitive, but Turkey was new and emerging. The competition was less; investment opportunities were open. Besides, I had a lot of connections we could utilize. We said why not, and I began to develop business models with my American partner. I began to travel here and then we founded this company. I moved to Turkey to oversee our operations here.

Similar stories reflected the way that a U.S. passport is basically insurance against political risks around the world, while resettling in Turkey as dual citizens was instrumental in escaping economic risks in the United States. The key difference between the two moves is that whereas an institutional affiliation is necessary to resettle in the United States in case of political crisis in Turkey, many investors did not face any restriction in investing in Turkey after economic recession hit the United States. In fact, like many countries, Turkey has established institutional mechanisms to attract direct foreign investment regardless of individuals' citizenship status.

Some of our interviewees returned to Turkey to launch start-up companies in this relaxed investment climate. More made the decision to move in response to the shrinking U.S. job market after the 2008 crisis. Surrounded by stories of people losing their jobs and homes, our interviewees felt even more worried about their long-term economic prospects in the United States. Engin told us how this affected their thinking as a family: "I had a job offer from Turkey. My husband wanted me to accept it. This was around the time when the U.S. economy was hit by the crisis in 2008 and I was having difficulty finding any kind of job there. Everything was as if frozen. We could not see our future in the States whereas the economy in Turkey was booming, so we decided to move back."

Status Mobility

It was not just investment and employment opportunities that made returning attractive. Holding a U.S. passport and having real experience of the United States also increased chances of upward mobility in Turkey, for reasons similar to the cases described in the previous chapter. While these people were one in a million in the U.S., where they could easily be bundled with the category of first-generation immigrants, their U.S. experience and citizenship conferred a status and level of comfort once they began working in Turkey that was unlikely to be available to them in the United States.

Several people told us that they gained higher social status in Turkey because their experiences with the United States were more than short-term visits: They intimately knew its culture, working conditions, and the principles of how to do business there. Consequently, they returned as "prestigious employees" and people who hired them saw them as a link to the world. Their U.S. work experience enabled them to claim the ability to introduce an organizational culture not usually found in Turkish companies. Their English language skills made them more desirable to international companies. Thus, their U.S. citizenship was translated into upward mobility only after they returned to Turkey.

There was more: These people ended up in positions where they conducted high-level business interviews and negotiations and went on business trips for international companies. Their passports enabled worldwide travel. Some interviewees talked about how their American experience became all the more valuable for companies located in Turkey because of their U.S. passport. Others talked about familiarity with "the American way of doing business" as a plus for these multinational companies. "If I want to move to another company, having an American citizenship of course will matter, especially when negotiating with large global firms. They look for people with transnational connections. Having lived in the U.S. matters a lot to many of them, both in terms of the language skills and also the business culture you acquire working in the U.S." For Selma, people like herself become "special" employees in Turkey not so much because of the U.S. passport per se but due to the work ethic and culture that one develops working in the United States, and the knowledge of both worlds.

> It was my fluency in English that helped me find a job. No one gives you a job just because you are an American. This might be different from sector to sector. American citizenship might be more helpful in a different sector, but it was not the case in mine. Besides the language, it was the work culture that made a difference. I can switch between the two cultures. I belong to both worlds. I can understand both worlds. I can connect with the business networks of both countries. This is very important, I guess. I am flexible.

Others often remarked how American citizenship meant they had credible options outside Turkey, thereby increasing their ability to negotiate salaries, responsibilities, and positions. Moreover, while they were first-generation immigrants in the United States, they could make claims of being "cosmopolitan" when they returned to Turkey. Despite doing jobs similar to those they did in the United States, colleagues saw them as having a different experience and as "special." Being a "different Turk" was an important status symbol, which they took advantage of to achieve upward mobility in both personal and business life.

Savage, arguing against proclamations of "the death of class" and the emergence of "classless societies," has written that class today is to be discovered in the ways individuals differentiate themselves through classification and boundary-drawing strategies (Savage 2000). These people's stories reveal that struggles for distinction have created a new capital accumulation strategy, especially in non-Western contexts: acquiring status through acquiring citizenship. This takes place beyond national borders and is intended to further enhance class positions within and outside the country of residence (Altan-Olcay and Balta 2016). U.S. citizenship and the assumed set of experiences that Turkish-American citizens bring with them has this value that the interviewees could experience only outside the United States.

However, all these motivations for return must be put into a macropolitical context. Indeed, the vast majority of the people deciding to return to Turkey did so because they were hopeful about Turkey's stability and prosperity. Although Turkey had not reached the same level of political stability as more developed countries, it did provide many economic opportunities. These returnees desired to play a role in the country's political and economic future at a time in the 1990s and the early 2000s when this motivation seemed feasible in a growing economy. Moreover, they saw in the open economy abundant possibilities for utilizing their transnational connections and building new ones. They believed there was a place in the country for them, that they would be able to determine both their own futures and also impact the political and economic future of the country. Despite all the problems they foresaw, this hope was a critical factor in their decision to return.

The Country Is Not Doing Well!

Personal lives and a country's political and economic stability (or how these groups perceive this stability) are tightly intertwined. Whereas a significant number of our interviewees decided to return to Turkey at the beginning of the 2000s, as we mentioned earlier, we conducted our interviews between 2014 and 2015, when the political situation in Turkey had begun to be perceived as unstable. The Gezi Park protests, along with the escalating political repression that followed, gave us the chance to examine how this change in macropolitical perceptions affected personal decisions. When explaining why they returned, our interviewees said that they had been tremendously hopeful. Now they were anxious.

Almost everyone brought up the protests: Unlike the American citizens, who witnessed these protests and sympathized with the protestors but did not ascribe life-and-death importance to them, this group talked fervently about them. Some had participated in the protests for days after their work hours ended; others who were not in the squares physically expressed sympathy for the protestors. They then lamented the euphoria they felt in those days about the possibility of taking control of their lives in Istanbul and the speed with which their hopes were crushed. Ahmet, for example, was a very successful middle-aged professional who developed his own business, overseeing the investment portfolios of companies, after receiving an MBA degree in the United States. When he began thinking about returning to Turkey, he decided to go into the restaurant business and bought the franchising rights of a major U.S. restaurant chain. As a well-educated son of a middle-class family, he had transformed himself into a rich businessman through his education in the United States. His decision to resettle in Turkey was economically motivated, although now he was very anxious about the political atmosphere in Turkey.

> I know what Turkey is all about. Politically, I have never had high expectations. This is my country; I know its limits. But economically, I want a stable system. It is not even economically stable now. In the U.S., I was not even interested whether the president is a Democrat or a Republican. They have a system there. Politics does not affect my everyday life there. Here, politics is life and life is politics. It is not stable because everyone [who comes to power] wants to redesign the whole country from scratch. . . . Living in this city is a problem because of this culture of governance. Gezi Park is a good example of this. What is your plan? Are Americans stupid people to build a park in the center of New York? Why have they given up land profits? You need to have a long-term strategy, a development strategy, and an urban planning strategy. These people live for the day and don't plan for the next. It doesn't seem like a big deal now, but if they go in this direction, Turkey will be dead in the next five to ten years. They are killing the country. And the American passport is my Plan B. There may come a time that I need to resettle in the U.S.

Berk was another interviewee who wholeheartedly supported the Gezi Park protests. For him, it was not just about a few trees; it was about demanding that the government respond to public interest instead of private profits. Working for a large conglomerate and with a business administration degree, he emphasized that understood profit-making, and that it is a good thing. Yet, he continued, it must be companies that concentrate on profit-making; governments should consider the public good even when the choice may not be profitable. He said that he found the profit-oriented logic of Turkey's current government unacceptable.

> I participated in the Gezi protests. Isn't Turkey a democracy? If it is democracy, I can protest anything I want, can't I? We were foolishly thinking that we have been progressing in the last ten years. I suppose we are not. Look at Istanbul: How many parks do we have? Very few. This is the way they govern us. Parks show that you value the public; if you build shopping malls, it shows you value profits. . . . We want a government that values the public not profits. This is a giant concrete city. They are building even more concrete . . . no room to breathe.

The Gezi Park protests were driven also by government practices since 2012, which fueled urban middle-class fears that it was intervening in their lives and lifestyles (Tuğal 2013). In addition to our previous discussion about the increasingly religious tone of the state schooling system, people were alarmed by the desecularization of public spaces, restrictions on alcohol consumption, public policy attempts targeting women's rights, and public discourses regarding rules of propriety for women. The Gezi Park protests were against all of these developments and represented hope for Turkey's future for the urban middle classes (Arat 2013; Yörük and Yüksel 2014). However, they were quickly and violently repressed by the government (Arat 2013; Yörük and Yüksel 2014).

Since the protests, Turkey has undergone a major transformation in terms of both domestic and international policy. The AKP government has taken an authoritarian direction while its cadres have increasingly been turning to more radical interpretations of Islam in response to the global economic and political crises that have begun to affect Turkey. Meanwhile, growing international and regional conflict, especially the Syrian crisis, has destabilized Turkey's foreign policy (Balta 2015; Öniş and Yılmaz 2016). As the economic and political situation deteriorates, the urban middle classes have been withdrawing their support from AKP.

After 2013, the political climate became characterized by conflict, within both the government and society. Following general elections on 7 June 2015, the AKP government lost its overall parliamentary majority but refused to form a coalition. In a political climate marked by increased violence and bombings, Turkey held new elections on 1 November 2015. This time, AKP was able to form a government without a coalition (Balta 2016). However, these elections were soon followed by a failed military coup on 15 July 2016, organized by a religious sect that was previously an ally of AKP, now trying to usurp power. After the failed coup attempt, a national emergency was declared and expansive political restrictions were put in place. In less than a year, the long-running political debate over increasing the powers of the current president of Turkey, Erdoğan, concluded in a constitutional referendum on 16 April 2017, which narrowly approved a new presidential system by 51.4 to 48.6 percent of the vote. Erdoğan was elected president on 14 June 2018. Over the course of these few years, Erdoğan has faced unprecedented challenges to his rule and the country has become polarized around almost every issue, ranging from education to international alliances (Aydın-Düzgit and Balta 2017). At the time of this writing, this conflictual climate in Turkey was uncertain and the storm had still not subsided; in addition, there was a deepening economic crisis.

We continue tracing this macropolitical situation in the conclusion. Although at the time of the interviews Turkey was not yet engulfed in the political and economic whirlpool that it found itself in after 2015, fear and anxiety were common among this group as well. People who had decided to resettle in Turkey in the early 2000s were no longer so sure about their long-thought-out decision. Ayda underlined this feeling of anxiety and explained how having an American passport helped her to ease her anxiety for herself—albeit not for her parents.

> We live in a very conflictual region. I am very anxious about the future of my country. I don't think things are going well. When I feel really overwhelmed, I try to put a distance between what is going on politically and myself. I try to convince myself that I can always move to the States because I have a second passport. But I know that there are many people who do not have this opportunity. These are my friends, my mother, my father. . . . They have gone through this farce over and over again. I don't know how they feel when they read a newspaper.

Gender inequality and the public declarations supporting it also came up frequently in this group. Özlem echoed this feeling:

> As a woman, I was harassed only once in the U.S. Whatever you wear, you feel safe in the streets. In Ankara—and mind you, we are

> talking about the the capital of Turkey—there are districts where I cannot even wear short sleeves. Sometimes when I do have something with short sleeves on [in the "wrong district"] it is not unlikely that a car will stop and [the occupants] will say something about the way I dress. If I want to be an astronaut, no one would dare to say "no" to me in the U.S. A woman can be anything there. When we returned to Turkey in 2007, this was not the climate here. I thought my country was progressing. It was getting better in terms of gender equality. I cannot believe how fast we lost that track. Now the atmosphere we breathe is so different. The conservative culture and how widespread it has become is so unbelievable. I cannot understand how we came to this point. I am so concerned about my daughter's future.

Like Özlem, many of our interviewees expressed awareness of the enormous difference between the country that they had decided to return to and the country that they currently lived in. This dramatic change worried them. Nearly all thought that a serious crisis was imminent. What is more, they had made the decision to bring their businesses to and invest in Turkey so returning to the United States would not be at all easy. Their families, homes, and their children's schools were all major issues. Yet perhaps even more important was that they had been younger when they returned to Turkey. At the time of the interviews, several worried that they might be too old to make such important life-changing decisions yet again.

Nonetheless, they said that if they lost faith in the promise Turkey once held for them and they could no longer provide a future for their children, they would leave. In other words, in addition to the global mobility the U.S. passport made possible, our interviewees saw the United States as a safe zone. Because they were officially included in this safe zone, they saw themselves as relatively shielded from any political crises that might erupt in Turkey. If everything in the country were to take a turn for the worse, they knew they could withdraw to their secure sites, all the while retaining their Turkish identities.

Ulrich Beck uses the concept of the "risk society" in discussing how citizens in modern societies tend to expend great efforts to control future uncertainty (Beck 1992). We have already discussed in previous chapters the way U.S. citizenship is imagined and experienced as a factor with a tremendous impact on people's individual abilities to take precautions against diverse risks at home and abroad. These narratives here reveal cases where homes multiply along with the risks and opportunities associated with them. This is a case where the U.S. passport builds a transnational social space (Faist 2000) where people can reasonably imagine the possibility of traveling with ease between countries of origin and adopted countries, juggling anxieties of belonging, and strategizing to fend off risk, all at the same time. This imagination is possible for this group precisely because of their legal right to go back to the United States. From this perspective, in the case of dual citizenship, certain citizenships are clearly seen as more valuable than others in creating geographical safety zones and protecting their owners from the risks associated with their other citizenships. This membership in a safety zone through citizenship provides material opportunities, such as flexibility, risk management, and increased status. These "use areas" are geographically differentiated. For example, while being born a U.S. citizen may not bring privilege within the country, it can provide opportunities abroad. People can stumble upon the privileges of a citizenship like that of the U.S. outside the United States, as in the previous chapter, and/or can actively strategize around it to neutralize future risks as the narratives here show.

In this sense, having a passport from a developed Western country adds a new dimension to inequality within developing countries while also highlighting the limits of certain citizenships. Similarly, our interviewees were clearly aware of the limits of their Turkish citizenship and the inequality between different citizenship systems. Meltem, a forty-five-year-old female artist, had followed her boyfriend to the United States before becoming a U.S. citizen by marriage. Eventually they divorced and she married a second time in the United States, this time to someone with Turkish origins. When their child was born, they decided to raise her in Turkey. For Meltem, her U.S. citizenship signified freedom: "U.S. citizenship is freedom. It gives you the opportunity to live anywhere. It is the freedom to raise your kid wherever you want. Turkish citizenship does not provide that. It is not a prestigious citizenship ultimately. It is not globally accepted." According to our informants, although living in Turkey may have offered advantages as they perceived them at the time of the research, having institutional ties with Turkey offered little. On the contrary, some perceived being Turkish citizens as being held hostage. One young woman who moved to the United States with her mother as a teenager resettled in Turkey after the 2008 crisis. The only advantage she could identify of being in Turkey was being an

American there. She had trained as an economist but could not find a job in the United States for a couple of years, so she decided to use her dual citizenship as an asset in Turkey. "Turkish citizenship has no utility. Although my mother is a true patriot, even she sometimes says she would renounce her Turkish citizenship if need be. We are really unlucky to have been born here. There are major differences between citizenships. Differences that shape your life chances. And it is all a matter of luck."

While we were writing this book, some of our interviewees like Esen, whose story opened this chapter, had actually left the country or were preparing to do so. The upshot was that the institutional ties they had previously established with the United States would enable them to leave Turkey if circumstances began to change for the worse for them. As we have noted, they saw U.S. citizenship as a kind of insurance, and a state of affairs where this insurance would be valuable had indeed emerged.

"I Have More Homes Than One"

We have said that our interviewees thought long and hard about whether to live in the United States or Turkey, and considerations like family ties, work opportunities, and macropolitical issues such as security and stability were factored into their decision-making. This raises the question of how accurate it is to see them as purely rational decision-makers. Where did they feel they belonged? Where was home? What were the meanings for them of their Turkish and U.S. citizenships, beyond their use values? We should note here that, when we asked what they thought their principal identity was, people said they were Turkish, but they qualified this identification with other descriptions, drawing from their depictions of their lives in the United States. While some emphasized that they were Americans as well, a significant number stressed a local identity. They said that they were, for instance, from Istanbul, Izmir, or New York, demonstrating an affinity with a city rather than a country.

In the previous chapter, borrowing from Yuval-Davis (2009), we argued that citizenship is multilayered and involves complicated negotiations of belonging. In line with the literature, our interviewees showed two contrasting tendencies about establishing an affinity to more than one nation-state. For some, this dual identity meant being a cosmopolitan citizen of the world. They described a worldliness that made them feel that they belonged neither here nor there. They also felt as though they could live anywhere and asserted an affinity with more than one place. These people, commensurate with the literature's definition of cosmopolitan citizenship (Appiah 1997; Hannerz 1996), described their ability to exist and conduct themselves transnationally and their desire to do so. In this sense, the ways these groups live transcend nation-state boundaries.

An example of these transnational claims came from Zehra, a PhD student in computer engineering who had lived and worked in the United States for years. She liked her life there, but she told us that she imagined she would have a more relaxed pace if she returned to Turkey. Therefore, she decided to quit her well-paid job, return to Turkey, and resume her graduate studies. She did not regret having done so, because she believed her U.S. passport gave her flexibility in terms of where to live and work. She considered herself a global citizen because of her U.S. passport.

> The mobility and travel utility of the American passport is so enormous. It gives you such a sense of security. If everything goes bad here, I can move to the States. If I have cancer, I can go to the States for treatment. If I want my kids to get educated in the U.S., I can move there. I can even move to Europe with an American passport. This passport has transformed me into a global citizen, not just into an American citizen. I can even go to China. I can travel and live anywhere, thanks to this powerful passport.

In many cases, this feeling of transnational belonging was accompanied by emphasis on local roots. While many of our interviewees characterized themselves as global citizens, they also emphasized their local urban identities. For some of them being a local of a cosmopolitan city was very much part of the definition of leading transnational lives. Thus they were neither Turkish nor American, but rather identified themselves as cosmopolitan Istanbulites, while also referencing the major urban centers where they used to live in the United States in describing their identities. These self-descriptions resonate with the literature that argues that the production of globalization entails the production of localization. De Sousa Santos, for instance, suggests that what we offhandedly call globalization is nothing but the globalization of particular localizations (2006). In this case, there are two localizations in question. One local geography is the United States itself because a U.S. passport (a particular locale) transforms these people into global citizens. This local geography comes also with its recognizable landscapes: U.S. citizenship signifies people's intimate knowledge of New York City, Chicago, Boston, and so forth, and that knowledge is almost always part of identity narratives. There is also a second localization involved, which goes beyond the U.S. passport to the urban identities in Turkey. It is at the intersection of these multiple locales and familiarity with them that they can assert a transnational identity. For example, Semra is a US-educated psychologist who won the green card through the lottery when she was a student there. She considered herself a global citizen yet also a person who belongs to Istanbul more than anywhere else. She said she did not identify herself in terms of nationality categories; rather global and local belongings defined her: "I feel I belong to Istanbul more than anywhere. I have always felt this way. I am actually happy that I have the opportunity to resettle here. I feel in love with this city. I feel that I belong here. I don't like Turkey that much, but this city is different. You won't find me complaining even about the traffic. I just do not register the bad things. This is my home. . . . I belong to Istanbul more than anywhere. Being at home in Istanbul makes me a global citizen." The local belongingness that Semra asserted also enabled her to identify herself with the other cities where she had lived. When she was in the U.S., she said she also felt at home in New York, which reminded her of the cultural cosmopolitanism of Istanbul.

Others shared similar sentiments. For example, Edgar, a thirty-five-year-old engineer, felt at home when he first set foot in New York: "We were not like Turkish people in Germany, who went to a big city directly from their small villages. I was not like that. I went there for education. I passed all the tests. I was fluent in English. I remember vividly the moment I arrived in New York. I took a cab from the airport to Manhattan and when I saw the lights in Times Square for the first time, I had this familiar feeling, a feeling that I was at home—as if I was born and raised in NYC." Edgar's words echoed the literature that traces patterns of globalization in the fast-paced flows of cultural products and media across borders (Appadurai 1996; Castells 2000; Hannerz 1996; Urry 2007). Imagination as a social practice creates the cognitive maps through which people travel to places that they have never been (Grewal 2005). In these excerpts, people were asserting their ability to align preexisting cognitive maps with actual experiences and official status of American citizenship. The same narratives also rested on a tacit privilege, the assumption that they were distinct from the majority of the world's population, who could access these cityscapes only through their screens.

Other interviewees described a regional belonging beyond the urban landscape. Can, a young freelance photographer, told us how he was raised in a strictly patriarchal Turkish family even though his mother was an American citizen. The mother had learned Turkish and had completely integrated into everyday life in Turkey, always telling him that she never felt like an outsider. Can and his mother used to visit the United States frequently when he was a child to spend time with Can's American grandparents. However, he told us, he never felt his mother's sense of belonging in Turkey or the United States; instead, he was in-between, a person who belonged to both worlds. In time, he had come to identify himself as a Mediterranean.

> I don't think I can say I am from here or there. I cannot say that I am either American or Turkish. I have both in me and I cannot choose. But I can confidently say I am Mediterranean. I feel like that because I carry this down-to-earth disposition that Mediterranean people have. Portugal, Greece, Spain, Morocco. . . . Whenever I go to one those places, I feel at home. I am drawn to the food, the culture, the personal relations. . . . Someone who is raised in Izmir, for example, would never feel like a foreigner in these countries. I find this enormously important.

However, this "local cosmopolitanism" suddenly shifted to being Turkish when a connection was made with citizenship. Regardless of the degree to which interviewees saw themselves as citizens of the world or a local of a city, the most important cultural component of their identity was being from Turkey. All our interviewees emphasized how the language they spoke, the food they ate, and their cultural practices had all been shaped by their upbringing in Turkey. This tie could not be easily severed. In this sense, even though they had an emotional connection to the United States and saw their life there as also formative of who they were, this connection always lagged behind their emotional ties to Turkey.

Many interviewees did aver that becoming a U.S. citizen represented a genuine cultural transformation and that living in the United States had made a major contribution to them as individuals. Some of the culturally ingrained aspects of living in the United States included in the narratives were a sense of predictable order, strict adherence to rules, and respect for privacy and other people's personal spaces. Moreover, nearly all emphasized how much they appreciated tolerance of difference as one of the most important aspects of what they saw as the American culture. This tolerance was especially felt with regard to their religious identity. Interestingly, only a few identified themselves as practicing Muslims, but even for them the religious tolerance in the United States was remarkable. Arda, a middle-aged professional working for a private religious foundation, remembered his first trip to the United States in 1999. At that time, Turkey was experiencing an ultra-secularist turn so that people with religious backgrounds (who attended religious schools and/or wore headscarves) faced discrimination.[5] Thus, the tolerance towards his religious identity in the United States was something he never forgot.

> We decided to go on a road trip together. We were five young men, all practicing Muslims. At some point we needed to find a place to pray so we stopped at a gas station. We were using the restroom one by one to wash and pray. I was the last one. While I was praying, a policeman came and pointed a flashlight toward me. He asked me what I was doing. I was really scared. I said that I was praying. He was so polite in his response. He apologized and said that people had complained because they could not understand what we were doing. I never thought a policeman could be this polite. I never felt discrimination against my religion in the U.S. I was born and raised in a Muslim country, but I had always felt excluded [in Turkey]. Not in the U.S.

Nevertheless, all the interviewees also maintained a certain distance from "American culture," continually using the expression "our culture." The closeness of kinship ties, being able to visit your neighbor, and being able to form strong intimate relationships were aspects of "Turkish culture" emphasized by nearly all of our interviewees. Of course, this can be explained by their having been born and raised in Turkey. However, it was interesting that those born in the United States but settled in Turkey also made similar observations.

However, they also distanced themselves from what was wrong with the "Turkish culture." According to many, the most distinctive aspect of Turkish culture was that people would always break the rules in the absence of an authority to uphold them. Almost all interviewees shared a similar observation about the way rules worked (or did not) in Turkey. In fact repeating sentiments of lack of rules in the country became a way to assert distinction from the rest of the society. For example, Filiz, who had moved to the United States during high school when her mother won the green card lottery and came to Turkey in her thirties, told us how lost she felt when she came back—a feeling more intense than most other interviewees expressed because she had left Turkey at a much younger age. She explained how she felt in the following words:

> There is something between these two cultures—a space that you can get lost in. I feel lost in that space because I do not know where I exactly belong. Am I a Turk or an American? I don't know. After I came back to Turkey, I found people acting in ways that would be unacceptable back in the States. Society does not seem to exist. Everything is unpredictable. Everyone breaks the rules. For example, they smoke cigarettes in places where they are not allowed to. You see; the rule is there. But no one gives a damn unless they know they will get punished. Politics is similar. In other words, social interactions are not based on shared rules here.

Interestingly, after she complained about this state of everyday affairs, she would switch and say something almost contradictory: "On the other hand, I like some of this unruly behavior. People are close, and one of the reasons that they feel close is because there are no rules, no predictability. They feel insecure alone, they need each other. Closeness is an insurance against unpredictability." As her switch in the middle of her description revealed, many interviewees had a somewhat conflicted attitude toward what they called the "Turkish culture." They criticized disrespect of rules, norms, and private space—a critique that showed itself when they emphasized how much they valued these norms in the United States. But they also felt that this unpredictability gave rise to close, intimate relations, and flexibility. This conflicting desire for both intimacy and privacy drove many people to sometimes express affinity with and, at other times, assert distance from what they called Turkish culture. Their dual citizenship and long-term residence in both countries gave them a way to juggle these contradictory impulses in their narratives, depending on what they needed to emphasize: When they wanted to stress their need for rules, predictability, and norms that guarantee respect for privacy, they underscored their affinity with the "American culture;" when they wanted to highlight their desire for intimate connections, they emphasized their Turkishness.

Mirror, Mirror on the Wall, Tell Me Who I Am!

Empirical evidence suggests that the significance attached to nation-state belonging has not declined. Regardless of their geographical mobility and access to different citizenships, people continue to use their citizenship statuses in their identity narratives in varying ways. The narratives of dual citizens reveal that the status of U.S. citizenship can create intersecting types of privilege outside the United States. It is these privileges that impact how people value and prioritize their citizenship statuses. Even when our interviewees used phrases such as cosmopolitan citizenship or global citizenship, they emphasized various internalized cultural practices attributed to being American citizens. These narratives also shed light on the paradoxes in these different sets of belongingness and the ongoing negotiations of identity and inequality.

What needs to be stressed here is that, during their stay in the United States, our interviewees felt neither completely American nor completely Turkish. They said that while they had acclimatized to American culture, especially through working there, they never felt fully American because they had not been born and raised there. For some it was their accents while for others it was their appearance. Contradicting the assertions of natural-born American citizens in the previous chapter, several shared with us stories of encounters in which they were asked where they were from, experiences that made them constantly remember that they were not from there. Whereas this signified a position of vulnerability in the United States, not fully and only belonging to Turkey could be a source of distinction.

This sense of not feeling completely from a place is also important for the meanings people ascribe to different citizenship ties. As the stories above show, they claimed to feel at home, for different reasons, in both countries. Both homes signified different material and symbolic opportunities when they occupied them. Thus each citizenship had its own set of meanings and instrumental values. Ultimately, however, there was still a hierarchy of meanings and values: Turkishness did come to connote a more intense cultural belonging, and the importance of U.S. citizenship was that it could provide benefits that its Turkish counterpart could not. The geographical mobility and flexibility in work and living preferences afforded by U.S. citizenship and its provision of security were important. These additional instrumental values were once again voiced when we asked the interviewees what their choice would be if they had to choose between U.S. and Turkish citizenship. Nearly all said that they would choose U.S. citizenship and give up Turkish citizenship if forced to do so. Ahmet, for example, compared the difference in power of the two passports in the larger world: "If I must choose, I would choose the American passport. I have many American friends here; many Americans work here. I can work here with an American passport. It is easy to do this in Turkey, but it will be difficult to live with a Turkish passport in the U.S." For others, this choice was not just about the ease of living in Turkey with a U.S. passport. It was the identity-preserving aspect of U.S. citizenship that they described: Several said that even if they gave up Turkish citizenship, they would remain Turkish. Turkishness was not a status that could be abandoned by breaking an institutional connection. Indeed, as we said earlier, those whose first citizenship was Turkish saw it as infused with cultural and emotional bonds. No matter what, Turkey could continue to be their home. However, their ability to assert Americanness required an institutional tie. Not only was their connection to America more fragile because it had been formed later, it was also one that needed the approval of the U.S. state much more intensely precisely because of the unequal powers of the two passports. In other words, to be able to say "I am American" was synonymous with being an American citizen legally, whereas being able to say "I am Turkish" did not require Turkish citizenship.

There were others who recollected stories about how this official connection felt almost like a betrayal of their Turkishness. Some like Arif, a young professional working for an international organization, felt the need to reclaim it through symbolic acts. He recalled visiting Atatürk's mausoleum in Ankara on his first trip to Turkey, right after receiving his green card.

> The day I got my green card, I promised myself that I would not forget my Turkishness. I promised myself that I would always feel close to Atatürk. I guess you get scared that you could lose your identity. What makes us the person that we are is our home, is our nation. Whether we love it or not, we are Turkish, in the end.

> Whether we like it or not, this is our identity. So what happened in my case was that right after I got my green card, [on my first trip to Turkey] I visited Atatürk's mausoleum.

Arif's American citizenship created a tension with his national identity that he had a hard time resolving. His dilemmas were not between a national justice and cosmopolitan morality, but between national belonging as an ideal and increasing his life chances.

Citizenship Priorities and Strategic Questions of Belonging

Postcolonial studies have written extensively on the workings of imperial power and how it distributes diverse subject positions with respect to allegiance, geographical proximity, ethnicity, race and gender, and the ways these produce contradictions, conditions of hybridity, and tension (Bhabha 1997; Chatterjee 1993; Colonna 1997; Mitchell 1988). Within citizenship studies, Isin has recently traced the genealogy of citizenship to the history of imperial states creating extraterritorial citizens and procuring protection for them. In this history, these extraterritorial groups also fashion themselves as citizens, making precarious claims of distinction and privilege on that basis. These interlinked processes extend the rule of the empire beyond its recognizable borders (Isin 2015). These Turkish Americans, whose identity negotiations and strategic calculations around multiple citizenships we have explored, display these conditions of hybridity. Their stories add a final layer to our discussions, drawing out the ways in which different citizenship statuses play out in tandem with one another. What we have documented here is the diffusion of American power, less into the institutional structures of another nation-state than into the everyday life chances, imaginaries, and desires of its inhabitants. The capacity the United States to bind these individuals as citizens even outside of the U.S. is founded on the power of U.S. models of production and culture that permeate national borders, not dissolve them (Panitch and Gindin 2004, 9–10). More important, the American empire, as our narratives reveal, does not entail a transfer of direct popular loyalty or patriotic attachment to the American state (Panitch and Gindin 2004, 30).

This was an unusual group of people, whose class origins and/or cultural dispositions enabled them to make credible claims being simultaneously integrated into the United States and Turkey. In Turkey, they belonged to the segment of the population that could identify themselves with terms such as cosmopolitan. This was primarily because they could claim affinity with what they called American cultural norms, distancing themselves from the contemporary evolution of the political system and hegemonic social norms in Turkey. In the United States, before they decided to return, their educational credentials and jobs made the return a choice, not an obligation. They carried back with them not only their cultural dispositions but also their official membership in the United States, added to their Turkish citizenship.

This raises new questions about the links between U.S. citizenship and the American empire. As we discussed in detail in Chapter 1, Turkey's political ties to the United States resonate with the country's dense cultural bonds and identification with the West throughout the twentieth century. Interestingly, these bonds have been also accompanied by rising political discourses of anti-Americanism and conspiracy theories. Our Turkish-American interviewees did not share such suspicions, but not necessarily because they supported U.S. foreign policies. It was more the outcome of a recognition that the United States is not a monolithic political agent. We constantly heard from our interviewees how it is impossible to equate the United States with its leaders, just as Turkish people cannot be equated with whomever is in government. They did not have overtly stylized, romanticized ideas about life in the United States either. They had lived there and knew the benefits as well as the costs of the choice. This discourse by people who could make credible claims of being both here and there introduced a more nuanced alternative to hegemonic anti-American rhetoric in Turkey.

People shared the idea that Turkey should remain part of the Western alliance, particularly because of its purported ties to values like democracy and human rights. Eschewing concepts like national loyalty, national culture, national identity, national interest, and national justice, this group instead stressed notions such as universality, universal human rights, and so on. When asked about their political identities, many said that the experience of living in a Western country had strengthened their commitment to these basic values. The American empire became the West in the words of its dual citizens, once again reminding us that discourses of the American dream, one of inclusiveness and multiculturalism, can travel to other lands (Grewal 2005).

However, there is a caveat: This cosmopolitanism is also linked to a relatively privileged status based on their unequal access to American citizenship. The hierarchies both within and between different nation-states, as we have discussed, granted them this privilege. Although our participants acknowledged themselves as cosmopolitans, the inequalities that made them cosmopolitans and the ways the American empire manifests itself were much less visible in their narratives. They emphasized the idea of being interconnected with fellow human beings and exalted the multiplicity of attachments, without dwelling as much on this attitude's classed origins. Elif Shafak (2017) has argued that people suspected of being "cosmopolites" are wrongly accused of being both rootless (not loving one's country) and heartless (not respecting one's ancestors). This argument misses the inequalities shaped around cosmopolitan identities, however. Our participants were neither rootless nor heartless, and were not so accused. Yet their cosmopolitan ideal was tightly linked to their class status and sharpening inequalities both at home and around the globe. That is exactly what we ask: What happens when the cosmopolitan ideal and attitude becomes enshrined with latent stories of privilege, at the intersection of the local and the global?

These narratives show that citizenship is not simply the name given to the ties people form with their own state, and the rights and responsibilities shaped by these ties. In a globalizing world, citizenship is also assessed in terms of the opportunities it provides to people beyond national borders. These people living within these new, crisscrossing borders described themselves as being both inside and outside (Altan-Olcay and Balta 2016). They are from both here and there. They are the subjects and objects of a moment carved out by fluid life opportunities, made possible by multiple citizenship statuses and not necessarily by the geographical boundaries of a single nation-state (Faist 2000; Kaya 2015). Because of their positions in existing inequalities in their home countries, they could obtain additional citizenships; and through them realign their identity narratives, build emotional bonds that transcend country borders, and utilize their dual passports to address diverse material concerns. Because they had this unequal opportunity, they lived in a relatively safe transnational zone. This crafted zone is also related to racialized global hierarchies and the geopolitical power relations that sustain them. Dual citizenship enhances opportunities both instrumentally and for refashioning subjectivities so that they are less significantly tied to one nation.

This isn't just any dual citizenship or any context either: This chapter shows how having U.S. citizenship outside the United States brings with it a set of symbolic meanings and strategic advantages. It does not only work as a guarantee of safe passage to what they perceive to be a stable, liberal democracy in times of political crisis, but it also works as an instrument of status mobility. Being a U.S. citizen in the United States does not mean much when everyone around you is also a U.S. citizen. Besides these people were also migrants who are constantly reminded of their un-Americanness through small encounters such as the constant question "Where are you from?" even after having lived in the United States for decades. However, when they relocated to Turkey, being a U.S. citizen brought more advantages. It was not just a question of institutional but also the cultural affinity they had developed with the United States that provided them resources that "ordinary" Turkish citizens do not have. In short, there is still a hierarchy in the transnational experiences of dual citizens whose primary citizenship is Turkish and those whose primary citizenship is American.

Bauböck has suggested that (2018) the instrumental and noninstrumental values of citizenship do not conflict but complement each other. People can feel a strong sense of belonging to different countries for diverse reasons while also attaching hierarchical values to them because of their instrumental benefits. While for Bauböck, such discrepancies do not signal that there is a general trade-off, we suggest here that the meanings and values people attach to citizenship are determined at the intersection of individual life experiences, cultural dispositions, and perceptions of macro-level risk. The narratives we follow show that individuals choose instrumental value over belonging and allegiance, and these two types of values complement each other only when they are not in conflict.

There is a further complication that results when being American or Turkish, or identifying oneself as a cosmopolitan citizen, cease to be politically neutral categories in a renationalizing political climate. Whether we are talking about Turkey or the United States, where every link to "the West" or "the Muslim East" is under scrutiny, we suggest that these instrumental and noninstrumental practices around citizenship regimes are harder to delineate from one another. In other words, when people make citizenship calculations, these are almost always explained along with existential anxieties, conflicts of belonging, and a heightened sense of insecurity. The calculations are never purely opportunistic but always reflect emotionally laden processes. What still needs to be emphasized is that they are possible only to the extent that people have U.S. citizenship in addition to their Turkish citizenship, reflecting the inequalities between citizenship statuses.

In the final pages of this book, we turn to the few years following our fieldwork. We explore further conditions of precariousness attached to different combinations of individual citizenship status and the ongoing struggles, strategies, and identifications that people develop around citizenship regimes within the ever-changing macropolitical circumstances in which they find themselves.

Conclusion

A Nation of Transnational Citizens

As this book was being written, the Turkish government's growing authoritarian tendencies in the second decade of the twenty-first century marked a sharp U-turn from the hopeful 1990s and early 2000s. The political system was becoming more centralized and the legal system's independence was thrown into doubt as it grew more punitive of the opposition without consistent due process. The Turkish government was also reexamining Turkey's alliance with the West. Political leaders were making proposals such as Eurasianism—turning toward China and Russia—and strengthening military cooperation with non-U.S. allies. The government's increasing repression of Turkish citizens in the aftermath of the 2016 coup attempt as well as its defiant attitude in jailing European and American citizens (*Financial Times* 19 October 2017) signaled to many that things were changing dramatically. In October 2017, for example, for a few months, the relations between the two states reached a new low when the U.S. government suspended all nonimmigrant visa services after a U.S. consulate employee in Istanbul was detained on terrorism charges and the Turkish government retaliated by doing the same (CNN 9 October 2017). Although the situation has improved since then, during the last days of 2017, op-eds abounded in major newspapers in the United States, questioning the alliance between the two countries (Cook 2017; Gordon 2017). Apparently, "the West" was also questioning where Turkey's allegiances lay.

It is not only Turkish politics or Turkish-U.S. relations that have been transformed radically, but also the political terrain of U.S. citizenship under the Trump presidency. What has characterized the Trump administration is conflict over who has a right to American citizenship. In a sense the Trump administration has been following the restrictive turn in the citizenship regulations of many European states in the last two decades. So far, by the early months of 2019, he has proposed a plan to end birthright citizenship for children whose parents are illegally in the U.S.; announced that he would make harder for legal immigrants to get visas or green cards if they ever used the social safety net; and introduced new measures to deny asylum to immigrants who enter country undocumented. There was a government shutdown when Congress did not approve the funding required to build a wall between the U.S. and Mexico, a major platform in Trump's electoral campaign. This episode was followed by an unprecedented declaration of national emergency, which Congress voted to block, but their resolution was vetoed.[1]

At the time of our writing, this growing gloom also meant a change for the groups that we had talked to. The fears of the groups whose stories we narrated in this book appear to be coming true, to a degree they could not have imagined. On the one hand, Turkey was closing in and on itself and for a growing number of people, the idea of change began to signify changing one's country. On the other hand, things in the United States did not look so bright either, given the political whirlwind, rise in anti-immigration rhetoric, and increasingly restrictive citizenship laws closing the doors to "outsiders" (not only in the United States but everywhere across the Global North). Citizenship rules have been transforming in such a way as to restrict immigration to the privileged of the world, with states competing to attract this global minority with wealth or sought-after skills and emphasizing in their anti-immigration rhetoric the will to keep out "the misery and the troubles of the world." In other words, the likelihood is high that the United States is no longer the welcoming, multicultural place envisaged by the American dream that many interviewees talked about.

Under these conditions, the strategy of exit by acquiring a second citizenhip becomes even more valued and utilized. Although the majority of the parents were still in Turkey, they were now more convinced of the rightness of the decision they had made in the name of their children. A few, who had already lived and worked in the United States for extended periods, found jobs in multinational companies located in the United States, while one founded a start-up company there, and the families moved. As we explained earlier, an impressive number of U.S. citizens left Turkey, especially those whose ties to Turkey were less strong. Among those who were married to Turkish citizens, a young woman was looking for ways to get her husband into the United States, which was not an easy endeavor, she told us; a story whose details once again revealed the hierarchy between the citizenships. As for the Turkish Americans, a few had also moved back. The majority who were still in Turkey stayed because, no matter how much mobility U.S. citizenship afforded them, starting anew presented overwhelming challenges, especially as people grew older. Nevertheless, there was still the comfort of their passports and a romanticized idea of evacuation by U.S. government choppers if things became intolerable.

Do these changes mean U.S. citizenship, useful as a form of prestige and status when Turkey was opening up, could become a serious disadvantage when borders are closing and citizenship regimes are renationalizing everywhere? While such a possibility would make anyone with U.S. citizenship in Turkey or anyone who is seen as connected to Western cultural and social circuits uneasy, this may not be the right question to ask. This book captured the life-worlds of three interrelated groups of people located in Turkey over the course of five years against a particular sociopolitical background, informed in the short term by radical shifts in Turkish domestic and foreign policies, following on the heels of similar trajectories in many parts of the world. Yet beyond them is a rich history of cultural debates about meanings of the West, the United States, and national identities, along with heated discussions about domestic and global inequalities, conditions of transnationality at the individual level, and the impact of official nationality status on them. These questions were asked by our interviewees as well as at the level of popular discourse because people's everyday experiences, anxieties, and hopes as well as the strategies they deploy to increase their life chances are ultimately shaped at the intersection of macro-level processes and the unequally distributed resources they command.

Hence, people still aspire to the status of U.S. citizenship. Others use whatever means they have at their disposal to make ancestral claims to obtain citizenship of countries in Eastern Europe as well as places like Israel and Spain. Those with financial means plan to buy estate in places like Portugal, Spain, Greece, and Malta to access free mobility in the EU. People migrate and take enormous risks to start life over again in various parts of the world. Thus, perhaps we should ask a more general question than one that focuses on the immediate changes we are witnessing: What can different citizenships do for people who feel threatened by macro-level changes beyond their control and who want to retain geographical and upward mobility, who want to ensure their children's future, and so on? If U.S.

citizenship, no matter what the connotations of U.S. foreign policy or the U.S. government at any historical moment, can still be a vehicle for leaving, for being mobile, for starting elsewhere—or, at the very least, for claiming differentiated identities, this is something to continue thinking about.

So perhaps it is a good idea to return to the original questions of the book: What does being a U.S. citizen signify *outside the United States* in contexts shaped by a history of its global power? What do the experiences and imaginaries around U.S. citizenship tell us about the unfolding of questions of the American empire today? Finally, and most important, how do we extrapolate from these experiences and expectations of U.S. citizenship to the meanings and values attached to national citizenship statuses in a world that is increasingly transnational, but also growing more unpredictable by the day? We contend, along with the literature on citizenship studies, that we need to study the impact of citizenship through the everyday practices of ordinary individuals. In this book, our goal was to make three assertions. First, we argued for the importance of tracing the meanings and values attributed to the institution of national citizenship in transnational spaces. We did this by following the narratives and imaginings that cluster around the American citizen outside of the United States. Second, in these narratives we showed that U.S. citizenship matters in unexpected ways for people who are not located inside the borders of the United States, and suggested that transnational imaginaries and practices around U.S. citizenship as status and identity are integral to the everyday workings of the American empire today. Finally, the citizenship narratives we heard simultaneously bore the imprint of rationality and anxiety, strategy and desire, attachment and ambivalence. These emotionally laden processes were shaped at the intersection of inequalities within and across nation-states. Thus, we have contended that the transnational implications of citizenship regimes shed light on the complex mutations of the category of citizenship itself. National citizenships continue to matter, shaping rescaled inequalities at the transnational level.

Throughout the book, people voiced several "languages" of citizenship. In these narratives, citizenship sometimes appeared as a purely legal status, echoing an instrumentalist view of citizenship. Some believed that they were U.S. citizens only because they were legally recognized as members of the U.S. political community—the status of citizenship translated into a language of rights to be protected by the U.S. government. Those who had dual citizenship or those who aspired to U.S. citizenship for their children constantly negotiated which citizenship would help them to manage future risks. Those who had U.S. citizenship from birth saw the advantages it provides once they moved out of the United States and often found themselves questioning what it means to be a part of a hegemonic power. All of the stories revealed that U.S. citizenship is closely associated with the power of the U.S. passport in a transnationalizing world: With this passport comes a kind of geographical mobility not available to the majority of the world's population. This passport is not only about mobility; it also increases one's individual ability to exit risky political contexts and transfer skills elsewhere when there is an economic crisis and/or labor market squeeze. Or it at least creates that possibility and eases anxieties, even when people do not actually act on them.

This is not a transnational citizenship, but it is a *citizenship with a transnational value.* Indeed, as we have argued throughout this book, for these groups the most important value of citizenship lies in the international mobility rights that come with it. Access to global mobility is always local and based on a person's citizenship status. Entry visas, passport controls, rights to abode and settlement, however, are always transborder processes and a direct consequence of hierarchies within the state system that cannot be regulated by the national legislation of any given state. This rising asymmetry between the extraterritorial nature of power relations and the continuing territoriality of life means that national citizenship acquires new meanings and values across borders. It creates incentives for the privileged citizens of not-so-privileged nations to negotiate their position within the international system by acquiring dual and sometimes even multiple citizenships. Some passports, as an interviewee put it, are more "prestigious" than others.

Ever since Benedict Anderson's writings on the forging of national identities (1983), the literature on citizenship has also focused on the concept of the desirable citizen. Who can be accepted as part of the political community? For the groups we interviewed, this question of belonging always loomed in the background: Did they belong in their countries of residence or birth, or both? How were they "recognized'? Where did they feel safe? The question was not always solely about their status as desirable citizens but also included debates on which *citizenship* could be more desirable in times of risk. In answer to this question, in addition to geographical mobility and exit options, their stories revealed that U.S. citizenship can also enable upward mobility outside the United States. Being recognized as a

U.S. citizen, being recognized as someone with ingrained knowledge of what is seen as admirable about the United States can translate into advantages outside of the United States, especially in the developing world. This book has documented the multiple ways people expected to and achieved upward mobility by moving to but also outside the United States. People who hold a U.S. passport not only have a reasonable chance of moving their existing privileges outside their home countries, but their U.S. citizenship can also become a marker of new sources of privilege in (as well as the ability to get into and get out of) the Global South. We already know that citizenship is always classed. It turns out that citizenship is classed outside the country of origin as well. The point is that, whatever the changes in macropolitical circumstances and the dynamic creativity these require on the part of individuals, citizenship statuses continue to be unequal in their ability to contribute to individuals' transnational opportunities.

These hierarchies between citizenship regimes appear to support current discussions in citizenship studies on the instrumental values of citizenship (and dual citizenship) and the strategic choices people make around them. Our contention has been that we need to look into the actual lived experiences of people who are described as making these strategic choices. People's thinking around citizenship involves calculations about instrumental values, but there is more to these individual practices than opportunism. National citizenship in these narratives is almost always more than one's legal status and is more akin to a signifier of particular cultural practices and values, a dense set of meanings that cannot be captured with assumptions of pure instrumentalism or focus on legal status. People often compared what they saw as different values and cultural practices in the two societies and negotiated their relationship to each through various languages of citizenship. These negotiations are part of an array of identity claims made possible by the fact that our interviewees had connections with U.S. citizenship but were living outside of the United States. Some claimed that their association with U.S. citizenship enabled them to transgress national forms of citizenship, critically distancing themselves from the U.S. government. Others, claiming an intimate experience of the West based on their U.S. citizenship status, could refashion their subjectivities and claim more credibly a status of being cosmopolitan. For some, their multiple belonging enabled them to emphasize local identities as opposed to national. The creativity with which people can make identity claims at the intersection of local, national, and transnational spaces thus appears to depend on their citizenship status. The status of U.S. citizenship becomes a marker of "globalized localisms" in ways that citizenships of only the most affluent countries can achieve.

American subjects outside of America become who they are in social realms and cultural contestations that are contextually specific but are always connected to the United States' unequal geopolitical power. We suggest that this is the enduring power of the so-called American empire, even under conditions where anti-Americanism is on the rise. American geopolitical power is currently being tested and its economic prospects are not what they once were. The American empire survives in the life-worlds of people who go about their ordinary lives distanced from the workings of governments but in contexts shaped by them. When U.S. citizenship outside the United States is valued and found meaningful for a variety of reasons, it is also the American dream that survives. These American citizens around the world are the markers of a new kind of empire, one that consists of individual strategies, desires, and ultimately conflicted subjectivities rather than recognizable political territories and hard power. This empire is manifested in the desires of pregnant women who travel thousands of miles to give birth to their children so that they can have U.S. citizenship. It lives on through the credibility of the identity claims dual citizens can make outside the United States. It resonates in the extension of the American dream elsewhere, in the words of American citizens who are both surprised and humbled by the opportunities they can attain.

The narratives of the people we talked to show us that they take America with them to the interior of their homes. This is not permeability of borders, as would be expected from an age of greater transnational mobility, or exclusionary borders within the nation-state, as migration studies show us. Rather, this is a different kind of border formation where physical passports expand the U.S. borders to include distant locations, to individual experiences of mobility and privilege, and identity narratives that juggle multiple national memberships. For these particular groups, U.S. citizenship means simultaneously locally specific privileges, their precariousness, and a sense of belonging that transcend national culture(s). Their stories reflect the transformation of membership in the American polity into a new kind of cultural and social capital. This is a different kind of imperial power, which manifests itself not directly in state-level relations but in the everyday lives, imaginaries, and desires of individuals, responding to these macropolitical contexts.

This brings us to our final point: This book has been based on the premise that individuals attempt to build strategies of survival and mobility under macropolitical and macroeconomic conditions over which they have little control. True enough, in a world of increased mobility, people's identities are no longer shaped solely by singular nation-state borders. Yet we emphasize that this does not mean national citizenship regimes do not matter. National citizenships are unequal and now these inequalities have been rescaled to transnational spaces. We suggest that we can capture these inequalities by looking at two dimensions: strategic values and symbolic meanings of national citizenship status outside countries of origin. The hierarchy of national citizenships and passports in a transnational terrain are shaped by both *strategic values* of geographic mobility, protection from political and economic risk, status and class mobility *and symbolic meanings* associated with identity and cultural affinity claims. Different national citizenships are valued in comparison with one another as a result of three kinds of strategic opportunities they can provide (or not). National citizenship status determines the degree to which the individual can escape political or economic risks as well as one's transnational geographical mobility, and it impacts the direction of one's class and status mobility outside the country of origin. The strategic value of any citizenship is never completely divorced from symbolic meanings people attribute to it. Thus, the symbolic value of any citizenship has to do with, first, the degree to which people who desire it assert cultural affinities with it, making official membership a source of claims for belonging. It also has to do with the popular identity narratives associated with any citizenship, which impact whether and the extent to (and places in) which citizens are recognized in terms of their governments' politics, or result in a situation where a mere showing of the passport can reduce unpleasant encounters.

One's national citizenship status is influential in the kind of identity claims people can make outside of their country of origin. National citizenship status is also paramount in people's ability to cross borders seamlessly and build transnational lives. It influences their ability to retain social positions or even anticipate upward mobility outside countries of origin. Thus, in reformulating citizenship in the context of the American empire, this book highlights the transnational values and meanings of national citizenship regimes. On the one hand, we are surrounded by individuals who seem to move freely across national borders. On the other hand, millions of immigrants face a proliferating array of legal and coercive restrictions on their movement. This apparent tension between the desire for freedom of movement and recognition and political and economic risks as well as the mass exclusion of immigrants is resolved through citizenship hierarchies. National citizenships not only organize inequalities within nation-states; they also perform similarly in transnational spaces. Citizenship is uniquely important in shaping inequalities and identity negotiations beyond nation-state borders. It is through these overlapping hierarchies that contemporary citizenship continues to shape our lives.

Notes

Chapter 1

1. See Institute of International Education statistics, which reveal that, until 2014, Turkey was consistently in the top ten. http://www.iie.org/Services/Project-Atlas/United-States/International-Students-In-US#.VxyHad6Je5Q.

2. What later became known as a regime of capitulations gave extraterritorial rights and privileges to Western capitalist powers while their continuity was guaranteed through successive treaties. See, for a discussion on the integration of the Ottoman economy into global capitalism and the effects of global capitalism on the Ottoman Empire: Pamuk (1987). For an earlier account of the effects of capitulations on Turkish-American relations, see Thayer (1923). Capitulations and their effects on the local economy are still an important part of nationalist/populist discourse in Turkey.

3. By the end of the nineteenth century, a new wealthy class had emerged in the United States from among investors in the newly booming industries of railroads, steel, coal, and oil. The first American investments in the Ottoman Empire mirrored the industries where wealth was consolidated in the United States (Phillips 2002, 43).

4. In the aftermath of the 1908 Young Turk revolution, when a group of men educated in the modern military institutions of the day organized a takeover of the government and reinstituted the Ottoman constitution, the newly established Committee of Union and Progress (CUP) in the Sublime Porte looked to American finance to balance the impact of French and German capital. Although their efforts did not succeed, their desire clearly indicated an interest in establishing ties with a neutral great power, which could also help with economic development (Ahmad 2011, 83).

5. Some of these works even argue that it is through American missionary activities that the Armenian question emerged in the Ottoman Empire. See Ergünöz (2007).

6. This decision was taken mainly to limit the war effort. However, the move was not without criticism, with some senators pressing the U.S. government to declare war against the Ottomans as well (Vander Lippe 1993, 38).

7. The list of American interests presented to European powers at the Lausanne conference included the maintenance of capitulations; the protection of American philanthropic, educational, and religious institutions; maintaining access for commercial enterprises; indemnity for losses suffered by Americans during the war; provisions for the protection of minorities; assurances of the freedom of the Bosporus Straits; and providing opportunities for archeological research (Vander Lippe 1993, 45).

8. First came an Anglo-Turkish security declaration, which was later formalized as a Mutual Assistance Treaty, between France, the UK, and Turkey. In March 1941, the United States and Turkey signed the Lend-Lease Agreement, which stated that the defense of Turkey was vital to the defense of the United States.

9. What felt particularly threatening were Soviet proposals to revise the Montreux agreement. Özkan (2017) argues that the perception of this Soviet territorial threat became the foundational myth of Turkish postwar foreign policy. Criss (2011) adds that the government's enthusiastic attitude towards the Western bloc was rooted in Turkey's security culture, which required avoidance of diplomatic and military isolation at all costs.

10. In February 1947, the British government advised the United States that it no longer had the capacity to back the Greek and the Turkish governments. This announcement signaled to the U.S. government that its support was necessary to protect these countries from Soviet invasion (Yılmaz 2012, 245).

11. The North Atlantic Treaty Organization (NATO) was established on 4 April 1949, but Turkey was not admitted as a founding member and its first application to join was denied. Although Turkey considered several other foreign options, such as neutrality or forming a Middle Eastern Alliance, the DP government was convinced that pursuing NATO membership was the best option, especially in countering the perceived Soviet threat (Brown 2011, 270). Thus, when the Korean War broke out in 1950, the DP government immediately saw it as an opportunity to prove that it was an important ally and enhance Turkey's prospects of NATO membership. Turkish public opinion was also in favor of the government's decision to send troops to the front since the public was largely united in their anticommunism (Brown 2011, 264). Accordingly, it dispatched 5,000 troops to help American-led troops fight North Korea in June 1950 (Tuğtan 2013). As expected, this decision helped Turkey's bid for NATO membership (Brown 2011, 273; Yılmaz 2011, 250). Since then, a popular historiography in Turkey has emerged that argues that the Turkish battalion's heroic fighting enabled the acceptance of its second NATO application in 1952 (Brockett 2004).

12. Unlike many European recipients, it was not a war-torn country experiencing a massive economic downturn or facing serious internal communist challenges (Kalkan and Uslaner 2011, 223).

13. In 1954, the U.S. Congress passed Public Law 480, otherwise known as the Agricultural Trade Development and Assistance Act. The act organized a program through which surplus U.S. grain could be sold to countries around the world and the countries, paid for in their local currencies. The proceeds from the sales would then be used to fund aid programs in the same countries (Mitchell 2002, 235). In Turkey, alongside several other countries in the Middle East, American educational institutions benefited from this funding throughout the 1950s and 1960s (Altan 2006a; Freely 2000).

14. On 14 July 1958, a military coup overthrew the Iraqi monarchy, which had been seen as a staunch Western ally. General Abdul Karim Qasim, leading the junta government, soon renounced the Baghdad Pact, initiated diplomatic relations with the Soviet Union, and announced a nonaligned position. As a result, in August 1959, the Baghdad Pact was renamed CENTO. (See Podeh 1995; Yaqub 2004).

15. In 1960, a U-2 spy plane, which was registered at İncirlik air base in Turkey, was shot down over Soviet airspace. The incident created tensions between the Soviet and Turkish governments, while the Turkish authorities realized that the U.S. government could use its

bases on the Turkish territory in a manner that jeopardized the country's national interests (Criss 1997 and 2002; Gunter 2005).

16. Güney (2011, 304) argues that, by early 1964, the main objective of U.S. foreign policy was to ensure that the conflict in Cyprus did not grow into a larger war. The U.S. government also tried to ensure that political disorder on the island would not determine U.S. bilateral relations with either Greece or Turkey.

1.7 As a result of the wide publicity about the Komer incident, the U.S. government dismissed him in May 1969, afraid of creating more dissent (Holmes 2014, 81).

1.8 The U.S. Sixth Fleet was formed in 1948 to support the Truman Doctrine. While the fleet was later assigned to NATO missions, it was initially part of U.S. unilateral naval diplomacy. The fleet became a public issue in 1956 during the Suez crisis because of its role in the defense of NATO's southern flank (Holmes 2014, 69). In fact, the Suez crisis was a major turning point for the emergence of the United States as a hegemonic power (McLaughin 2016).

19. See the annual data collected by Institute of International Education on their website: https://www.iie.org/Research-and-Insights/Open-Doors/Data/International-Students/Leading-Places-of-Origin (last accessed 14 October 2016).

20. For a discussion of Article 22/III of the 1964 Citizenship Law, see also Kadirbeyoğlu (2010, 4). This 1981 change directly targeted Turkish workers in Germany, who would otherwise have had to give up give up their Turkish citizenship if they decided to get German citizenship. Under this law they could now renounce their Turkish citizenship, obtain German citizenship, and then reacquire Turkish citizenship without any difficulties. As for the May 29 2009 Turkish Citizenship Act, No. 5901, Article 44-(1), see http://www.unhcr.org/refworld/docid/4a9d204d2.html (accessed September 12, 2012).

21. Indeed, in 2002, AKP announced that they aimed to persuade the EU to announce an official date to begin accession negotiations. This announcement initially established Erdoğan as a leader seeking to become a part of the West (Robins 2007, 292).

22. According to Grigoriadis (2010, 57), the Turkish government's refusal had a major consequence in that it lost its potential leverage in the postwar reconstruction of Iraq to Iraqi Kurds, which became a new point of contention in U.S.-Turkey relations.

23. According to Kadercan (2016), the popularity of anti-American sentiments is not new and, left to its own devices, this discourse would not necessarily result in a break in the U.S.-Turkish governments' alliance. She suggests that what would make a move in this direction possible is a conscious decision on the part of Turkish political leaders to end the alliance. Similarly, Blaydes and Linzer (2012, 227) argue that there is a causal relationship in various countries between the use of anti-American rhetoric by political leadership and popular expressions of anti-Americanism. Neither, however, necessarily leads to a major change in intergovernmental relations, which was the case in Turkey up until the 2010s.

24. KONDA Barometer, August 2016.

Chapter 2

This chapter uses previously published material. See Altan-Olcay and Balta 2014; Altan-Olcay and Balta 2016; Balta and Altan-Olcay 2016; Balta and Altan-Olcay 2017.

1. Although we initially aimed to interview both mothers and fathers, it quickly became clear that the decision to give birth in the United States was primarily maternal. It was also a maternal experience in that the fathers did not usually arrive in the United States until just

before the due date. In case of early deliveries, fathers even missed the birth of their children. Nevertheless, all the mothers in our interviews readily shared their own as well as their spouses' stories.

2. Estimation based on statistics on U.S.-born Turkish residents (between 2000 and 2012) received in 2012 from the Turkish General Directorate of Population and Citizenship via correspondence.

3. The data was downloaded from Centers for Disease Control and Prevention's website. https://www.cdc.gov/nchs/data/hus/2016/fig03.pdf.

4. Based on our interviews conducted in Istanbul in 2012–13 with birth tourism companies.

5. These twelve years correspond to the time the AKP government had been in power at the time of the interviews. In the five years following the interviews, interventions in the national education system have continued.

6. Before 2009, graduates of İmam Hatip schools were assigned a lower coefficient in the university entrance examinations, which meant that they received lower scores for answering the same number of questions as graduates of regular schools. This differential coefficient was invented as part of a stratified schooling system in which the graduates of various vocational schools were expected to join the labor market right after graduation and not go to university. This stratification meant, obviously, a status difference between different schools with the secular public and private schools at the top. Because the coefficient decreased the chances of university placement, this prospect dampened the popularity of İmam Hatip schools and limited their enrollment. However, in 2009, the AKP government removed the coefficient and equated religious and secular degrees (Kaya 2015, 477). In 2012, compulsory education, which was increased from eight to twelve years, was separated into three consecutive sections (four years of primary school, four years of middle school and then four years of high school, known as 4 + 4 + 4). This new system meant that, after four years of primary schooling common to all, students could be sent immediately to vocational schools, including religious ones (Kaya 2015). Even though the official declaration did not frame the changes in those terms, it effectively meant that the number of students enrolling in religious- track schools could be boosted. Consequently, these schools, originally intended to provide vocational training for government employment as preachers, were now becoming increasingly mainstream. A new practice has emerged of centrally transforming existing secular schools into religious-track schools and assigning students to these schools without parental consent (or making parents go through bureaucratic processes to opt out).

7. In this excerpt, when the interviewee is explaining her fear of the kind of school her child may end up in, she is referring to a wide network of schools in Turkey and abroad, established by a religious sect known as the Gülen movement. At the time of the interviews, the members of this network and members of AKP were allies, a situation that was dramatically reversed when Gülenists attempted a coup against the AKP government in July 2016. Since then the movement has been called the FETÖ terror organization; its schools and organizations have been shut down, and companies whose owners were known to be members of the network have been confiscated and scores of people have been put on trial.

8. Retrieved from Turkish Statistical Institute. 2017 Labor Force Statistics. Retrieved from https://biruni.tuik.gov.tr/medas/?kn=72&locale=en

9. "How Powerful Is Your Passport? Infographic," posted on June 22, 2014, http://progressivegeographies.com/2014/06/22/how-powerful-is-your-passport-infographic/ (last accessed 12 August 2014).

10. A region of Turkey popularly considered to have more traditional, conservative values.

11. April 23 and May 19 are national holidays, comemorating the establishment of republican Turkey's first parliament in 1923, and the day Mustafa Kemal Atatürk traveled to Samsun in 1919, a date which is depicted as the beginning of the national independence war. Şeker Bayramı is the Muslim holiday known as Eid-al-Fitr, expressed as either "Şeker Bayramı" or "Ramazan Bayramı."

Chapter 3

1. From April 2013 onward, according to the new Law on Foreigners and International Protection (Law no. 6458), foreigners who come to Turkey on a tourist visa are allowed to stay up to ninety days inside the country in any given one-hundred-eighty-day period.

2. Only to decline as part of a more general drop in the numbers of international tourists coming to Turkey since 2015.

3. Data is downloaded from (TURKSTAT 2017b) (data accessed on Nov 7 2017).

4. Açıkgöz says that this policy responds to official recognition of an expanding tourism industry and expectations of denser trade relations with neighboring countries. Accordingly, while citizens of eighty countries can enter Turkey without a visa due to bilateral visa exemption agreements, citizens of forty-five additional countries can obtain e-visas seamlessly—meaning nationals of one hundred twenty-five countries have ease of entry into Turkey without prolonged visa application processes (2015). At the time of writing, as the diplomatic relations between the two countries became strained, this visa procedure would change, for U.S. citizens as well, a development we outline in the final pages of the book.

5. See http://istanbulforeignersoffice.com/en/ and https://www.expatguideturkey.com/residence-permits/.

6. http://www.theguideistanbul.com/article/residence-permits-istanbul-all-you-need-know

7. Whereas 1,000 millionaires left Turkey in 2015, 6,000 left in 2016. These Turkish millionaires constituted 7.3 percent of the world's millionaires who changed their country of residence in 2016 (Sözcü 26 February 2017). There are around thirteen million millionaires in the world, and in 2015 Turkey boasted around 100,000 millionaires (*Hürriyet* 31 December 2015). These trends are also reflected elsewhere: In 2016, 50 percent of graduates of the most prestigious high schools applied for a college degree abroad (*Cumhuriyet* 21 August 2017). Scholars are also leaving Turkey in large numbers because of a continued government purge against academics (BBC 25 October 2016).

8. https://step.state.gov.

9. The Ferguson riots in the summer of 2014 were sparked by the shooting of Michael Brown, an unarmed black teenager, by a white police officer. There were protests in many cities. When the grand jury made the decision not to indict the police officer involved, there was another round of protests. The case became yet another example of endemic racism in police forces across the United States.

Chapter 4

1. For further discussion, see Balgamis and Karpat (2008).

2. While only a handful of states allowed dual citizenship in the 1980s, fifty-five did by 1998, and by 2001 the number was already ninety-three (Brondsted Sejersen 2008, 542).

3. Based on "Census 2010 SayTurk" campaign figures, which was organized by the Assembly of the Turkish American Associations and the U.S. Census Bureau to count people of Turkish origin.

4. Turkish immigrants in the United States are generally of middle-class origin, having come originally to the United States for education, skilled work, or vocational training. However, the numbers of unskilled or semiskilled workers are also on the rise. This has somewhat modified the general representation of this community as urbanized and belonging to higher income groups (Akcapar 2009a, 167).

5. This was the period that followed a decree issued by the Turkish military leadership on 28 February 1997 during a National Security Council meeting, warning of the rising Islamist threat. In the aftermath of this decree, the Islamist prime minister Necmettin Erbakan of the Welfare Party ended up resigning, and his coalition government came to an end.

Conclusion

1. See Deirdre Walsh, "Trump's National Emergency Stands as House Fails to Override Veto," 26 March 2019, NPR, https://www.npr.org/2019/03/26/706843365/trumps-national-emergency-stands-as-house-fails-to-override-veto.

Bibliography

Abu-Lughod, Lila. 2013. *Do Muslim Women Need Saving?* Cambridge, MA: Harvard University Press.

Acar, Feride, and Gülbanu Altunok. 2013. "The 'Politics of Intimate' at the Intersection of Neo-Liberalism and Neo-Conservatism in Contemporary Turkey." *Women's Studies International Forum* 41: 14–13.

Açıkgöz, Meral. 2015. "Turkey's Visa Policy: A Migration-Mobility Nexus." *Turkish Policy Quarterly* 14(2): 97–107.

Adaman, Fikret and Çaglar Keyder. 2006. *Poverty and Social Exclusion in the Slum Areas of Large Cities in Turkey.* Brussels: European Commission Employment, Social Affairs and Equal Opportunities.

Adas, Michael. 1989. *Machines as the Measure of Men: Science, Technology, and Ideologies of Western Dominance.* Ithaca: Cornell University Press.

Ahmad, Feroz. 1993. *The Making of Modern Turkey.* London: Routledge.

———. 2011. "Young Turk Relations with the United States, 1908–1918." In *American Turkish Encounters: Politics and Culture, 1830–1989.* Edited by Nur Bilge Criss, Selcuk Esenbel, Tony Greenwood, and Louis Mazzari, 83–99. Newcastle: Cambridge Scholars Publishing.

Akçapar, Şebnem. 2009a. "Turkish Associations in the United States: Towards Building a Transnational Identity." *Turkish Studies* 10(2): 165–193.

———. 2009b. "Turkish Brain Drain to the USA." In *Lands of Diverse Migration.* Edited by Ahmet Icduygu and Kemal Kirişci, 109–248. Istanbul: Istanbul Bilgi University.

Akçora, Ergünöz. 2007. *Van ve Çevresinde Ermeni İsyanları (1896–1916).* Istanbul: Türk Dünyası Araştırmaları Vakfı.

Aktaş, Umay. 2013. "Havuz Probleminden Daha Zor: 11 yılda Eğitim Sisteminde 13 Değişiklik." [More Difficult than a Math Problem: 13 Changes to the Education System in 11 Years]. *Radikal*, 3 June 2013. http://www.radikal.com.tr/turkiye/havuz-probleminden-daha-zor–11-yilda-egitim-sisteminde–13-degisiklik–1140795/.

Aleinikoff, T. Alexander. 2000. "Between Principles and Politics: U.S. Citizenship Policy." In *From Migrants to Citizens: Membership in a Changing World.* Edited by T. Alexander Aleinikoff and Douglas B. Klusmeyer, 119–172. Washington, DC: Carnegie Endowment.

Alnıaçık, Ayşe and Ayşen Üstübici. 2012. "Reflections from the Conference 'Turkey Debates its Social Policies': A Rights-Based Turn in Social Policy Making in Turkey?" *New Perspectives on Turkey* 47: 169–184.

Altan, Özlem. 2006a. *The American Third World: Transnational Elite Networks in the Middle East.* Unpublished doctoral dissertation. New York University.

———. 2006b. "Turkey: Sanctifying a Secular State." In *Teaching Islam: Textbooks and Religion in the Middle East.* Edited by Eleanor Abdella Doumato and Gregory Starrett, 197–214. Boulder, CO: Lynne Rienner.

Altan-Olcay, Özlem. 2008. "Defining 'America' from a Distance: Local Strategies of the Global in the Middle East." *Middle Eastern Studies* 44(1): 29–52.

———. 2009a. "Gendered Projects of National Identity Formation: The Case of Turkey." *National Identities* 11(2): 165–186.

———. 2009b. "Meanings of American Education in Beirut and Cairo." In *Liberty and Justice: America and the Middle East.* Edited by Patrick McGreevy and Nancy Batakji, 273–285. Beirut: American University of Beirut Press.

———. 2012. "Protest, Memory, and the Production of 'Civilized' Citizens: Two Cases from Turkey and Lebanon." *Citizenship Studies* 16(2): 135–151.

Altan-Olcay, Özlem and Evren Balta. 2014. "Market Embedded Transnationalism." In *Contemporary Turkey at a Glance.* Edited by Kristina Kamp, Ayhan Kaya, Fuat Keyman, and Özge Onursal, 139–155. Wiesbaden: Springer.

———. 2016. "Class and Passports: Transnational Strategies of Distinction in Turkey." *Sociology* 50(6): 1106–1122.

Anadolu Agency. 2015. "Turkey Home to 100,000 Millionaries." *Hürriyet,* 31 December 2015 http://www.hurriyetdailynews.com/turkey-home-to-100000-millionaires-93262.

Anderson, Benedict. 1932. *Imagined Communities: Reflections on the Origin and Spread of Nationalism.* London: Verso.

Anderson, Betty. 2009. "Making Men: Proselytizing at the Syrian Protestant College." In *Liberty and Justice: America and the Middle East.* Edited by Patrick McGreevy and Nancy Batakji, 261–272. Beirut: American University of Beirut Press.

———. 2011. *The American University of Beirut: Arab Nationalism and Liberal Education.* Austin: University of Texas Press.

Appadurai, Arjun. 1996. *Modernity at Large: Cultural Dimensions of Globalization.* Minneapolis: University of Minnesota Press.

Appiah, Kwame Anthony. 1997. "Cosmopolitan Patriots." *Critical Inquiry* 23(3): 617–639.

Arat, Yeşim. 2013. "Violence, Resistance, and Gezi Park." *International Journal of Middle East Studies* 45(4): 807–809.

Arat, Zehra. 1994. "Turkish Women and the Republican Construction of Tradition." In *Reconstructing Gender in the Middle East: Tradition, Identity, and Power.* Edited by Fatma Müge Göcek and Shiva Balaghi, 100–112. New York: Columbia University Press.

Armaoğlu, Fahir. 2000. "Atatürk Döneminde Türk-Amerikan İlişkileri." In *Atatürk Dönemi Türk Dış Politikası.* Edited by Berna Türkdoğan, 281–297. Ankara: Atatürk Araştırma Merkezi.

Arslan, Rengin. 2016. "Türkiye'den Akademisyen Göçü: Neden Gidiyorlar?" *BBC,* 25 October 2016, http://www.bbc.com/turkce/haberler-turkiye–37754038.

Atalay, Figen. 2017. "Gençler Kaçıyor." *Cumhuriyet,* 21 August 2017, http://www.cumhuriyet.com.tr/haber/egitim/808333/Gencler_kaciyor.html.

Ayata, Sencer. 2002. "The New Middle Class and the Joys of Suburbia." In *Fragments of Culture: The Everyday of Modern Turkey.* Edited by Deniz Kandiyoti and Ayşe Saktanber, 25–42. New Brunswick, NJ: Rutgers University Press.

Aydın, Mustafa. 2009. "Reconstructing Turkish-American Relations: Divergences versus Convergences." *New Perspectives on Turkey* 40: 125–146.

Aydın-Düzgit, Senem and Evren Balta. 2017. *Turkey After the July 15th Coup Attempt: When Elites Polarize over Polarization*. Istanbul Policy Center Publications. Accessed 1 May 2017. http://ipc.sabanciuniv.edu/wp-content/uploads/2017/04/Turkey-after-the-July–15-Coup-Attempt_Senem-Aydin-Duzgit_Evren-Balta.pdf.

Baban, Feyzi, Suzan Ilcan and Kim Rygiel. 2017. "Syrian Refugees in Turkey: Pathways to Precarity, Differential Inclusion, and Negotiated Citizenship Rights." *Journal of Ethnic and Migration Studies* 43(1): 41–57.

Babic, Annesa Ann. 2012. "Eastern Eye for Western Goods, Western Eyes for Eastern Markets: Consumer Goods, National Identity and US-Turkish Relations." In *The Transnational Turn in American Studies: Turkey and the United States*. Edited by Tanfer Emin Tunċ and Bahar Gürsel, 254–270. Bern: Peter Lang.

Bakker, Matt. 2010. "Mexican Migration, Transnationalism, and the Re-Scaling of Citizenship in North America." *Ethnic and Racial Studies* 34(1): 1–19.

Balgamış, Deniz and Kemal H. Karpat. 2008. *Turkish Migration to the United States: From Ottoman Times to the Present*. Madison: University of Wisconsin Press.

Bali, Aslı. 2010. "Unpacking Turkey's 'Court-Packing' Referendum." *MERIP Online*. 5 November 2010, http://www.merip.org/mero/mero110510.

Bali, Rifat N. 2002. *Tarz-ı Hayat'tan Life Style'a: Yeni Seçkinler, Yeni Mekanlar, Yeni Yaşamlar* [From Life Style to Life Style: New Elites, New Places, New Lives]. Istanbul: İletişim.

Balibar, Etienne. 2004. *We, the People of Europe? Reflections on Transnational Citizenship*. Princeton, N.J.: Princeton University Press.

Balot, Ryan. 2017. "Revisiting the Classical Ideal of Citizenship: A Dialectical Approach." In *The Oxford Handbook of Citizenship*. Edited by Ayelet Shachar, Rainer Bauböck, Irene Bloemraad, and Maarten Vink, 15–35. Oxford: Oxford University Press.

Balta, Evren. 2015. "The Syrian War and Turkey's Kurdish Conflict." In *Mapping GCC Foreign Policy: Resources, Recipients and Regional Effects*. Edited by Karen E. Young and Line Khatib, 4–19. Collected Papers Vol. 3. LSE Middle East Center Publications, pp. 4–19. http://www.lse.ac.uk/middleEastCentre/publications/Collected-Papers/MappingGCCFP.aspx.

———. 2016. "The Pendulum of Democracy: Turkey's Kurdish Conflict." In *The AKP and Turkish Foreign Policy in the Middle East*. Edited by Zeynep Kaya, 19–24. Vol. 5. LSE Middle East Center Publications. http://eprints.lse.ac.uk/66139/1/Kaya_AKPForeignPolicy_2016.p df.

Balta, Evren and Özlem Altan-Olcay. 2016. "Strategic Citizens of America: Transnational Inequalities and Transformation of Citizenship." *Ethnic and Racial Studies* 39(6): 939–957.

———. 2017. "Born in the USA: Citizenship Acquisition and Transnational Mothering in Turkey." *Gender, Place and Culture* 24(8): 1204–1223.

Balta Paker, Evren. 2005. "The Ceasefire This Time." *MERIP Online*. 31 August 2005 http://www.merip.org/mero/mero083105.

———. 2012a. *Küresel Güvenlik Kompleksi [The Global Security Complex]*. Istanbul: İletişim.

———. 2012b. "AKP's Approach to the Kurdish Problem: One Step Forward, One Step Backward." *Perspectives* 3(23): 12–16.

Balta Paker, Evren and Ismet Akça. 2012. "Beyond Military Tutelage: Analyzing Civil-Military Relations under the Justice and Development Party." In *Rethinking Security*. Edited by Ebru Sule Canan Sokullu, 77–93. Lanham, Lexington Books.

Barlas, Dilek and Şuhnaz Yılmaz. 2016. "Managing the Transition from Pax Britannica to Pax Americana: Turkey's Relations with Britain and the US in a Turbulent Era (1929–47)." *Turkish Studies* 17(3): 449–473.

Bauböck, Rainer. 1994. *Transnational Citizenship: Membership and Rights in International Migration*. Aldershot: Edward Elgar.

———. 2007. "Political Boundaries in a Multilevel World." In *Identities, Affiliations, and Allegiances*. Edited by Seyla Benhabib, Ian Shapiro and Danilo Petranovich, 113–135. Cambridge: Cambridge University.

———. 2010. "Studying Citizenship Constellations." *Journal of Ethnic and Migration Studies* 36(5): 847–859.

———. 2019. "Genuine Links and Useful Passports: Evaluating Strategic Uses of Citizenship." *Journal of Ethnic and Migration Studies* 45(6): 1015–1026.

Bauman, Zygmunt. 1998. *Globalisation: Human Consequences*. New York: Columbia University Press.

Bayraktar Aksel, Damla. 2019. *Home States and Homeland Politics: Interactions Between the Turkish State and its Emigrants in France and the United States*. London: Routledge.

Beck, Ulrich. 1992. *Risk Society: Towards a New Modernity*. London: Sage.

Bellin, Eva 2012. "Reconsidering the Robustness of Authoritarianism in the Middle East: Lessons from the Arab Spring." *Comparative Politics* 44(2): 127–149.

Belmonte, Laura A. 2013. *Selling the American Way: U.S. Propaganda and the Cold War*. Philadelphia: University of Pennsylvania Press.

Bender, Thomas, ed. 2002. *Rethinking American History in a Global Age*. Berkeley: University of California Press.

Bender, Thomas. 2006. *A Nation Among Nations: America's Place in World History*. New York: Hill and Wang.

Benhabib, Seyla. 2007. "Twilight of Sovereignty or the Emergence of Cosmopolitan Norms? Rethinking Citizenship in Volatile Times." In *Dual Citizenship in Global Perspective: From Unitary to Multiple Citizenship*. Edited by Thomas Faist and Peter Kivisto, 247–271. Basingstoke: Palgrave Macmillan.

Benson, Michaela and Karen O'Reilly. 2009. "Migration and the Search for a Better Way of Life: a Critical Exploration of Lifestyle Migration." *Sociological Review* 57(4): 608–625.

Berghahn, Volker R. 2001. *America and the Intellectual Cold Wars in Europe: Shepard Stone Between Philanthropy, Academy, and Diplomacy*. Princeton, N.J.: Princeton University Press.

Bhabha, Homi. 1997. "Of Mimicry and Man: Ambivalence of Colonial Discourse." In *Tensions of Empire: Colonial Cultures in a Bourgeois World*. Edited by Frederick Cooper and Ann Laura Stoler, 152–160. Berkeley: University of California Press.

Blaydes, Lisa and Drew A. Linzer. 2012. "Elite Competition, Religiosity, and Anti-Americanism in the Islamic World." *American Political Science Review* 106(2): 225–243.

Boller, Robert and Debora Halbert. 2015. "American Citizenship and Expatriatism: Identity and Politics outside the State." *Citizenship Studies* 19(3–4): 299–316.

Boratav, Korkut 1995. *İstanbul ve Anadolu'dan Sınıf Profilleri* [Profiles of Class from Istanbul and Anatolia]. Istanbul: Tarih Vakfı Yurt Yayınları.

Bosniak, Linda 2006. *The Citizen and the Alien: Dilemmas of Contemporary Membership*. Princeton: Princeton University Press.

Bottero, Wendy. 2004. "Class Identities and the Identity of Class." *Sociology* 38(5): 985–1003.

Bourdieu, Pierre. 1984. *Distinction: A Social Critique of the Judgment of Taste*. Cambridge: Harvard University Press.

———. 1986. "Forms of Capital." In *Handbook of Theory and Research for the Sociology of Education*. Edited by John Richardson, 241–258. Westport, CT: Greenwood.

———. 1987. "What Makes a Social Class?" *Berkeley Journal of Sociology* 32: 1–18.

———1989. "Social Space and Symbolic Power." *Sociological Theory* 7(1): 14–25.

Bozarslan, Hamit. 2015. "The Arab World Between 2011 and 2014: From Revolutionary Configurations to the State of Violence." In *Authoritarianism in the Middle East*. Edited by Jülide Karakoc Bakış, 67–91 New York: Palgrave Macmillan.

Bright, Charles and Michael Geyer. 2002. "Where in the World is America? The History of the United States in the Global Age." In *Rethinking American History in a Global Age*. Edited by Thomas Bender, 63–100. Berkeley: University of California Press.

Brockett, Gavin D. 2004. "The Legend of 'The Turk' in Korea: Popular Perceptions of the Korean War and Their Importance to a Turkish National Identity." *War and Society* 22(2): 109–142.

Brøndsted Sejersen, Tanja. 2008. "I Vow to Thee My Countries: The Expansion of Dual Citizenship in the 21st Century." *International Migration Review* 42(3): 523–549.

Brooks, Stephen G., G. John Ikenberry and William C. Wohlforth. 2012. "Don't Come Home, America: The Case Against Retrenchment." *International Security* 37(3): 7–51.

Brown, Cameron S. 2011. "The One Coalition They Craved to Join: Turkey in the Korean War." In *American Turkish Encounters: Politics and Culture, 1830–1989*. Edited by Nur Bilge Criss, Selcuk Esenbel, Tony Greenwood, and Louis Mazzari, 261–280. Newcastle: Cambridge Scholars Publishing.

Brown, Wendy. 2007. *Walled States, Waning Sovereignity*. Cambridge: MIT Press.

Brubaker, W. Rogers. 1989. "Membership without Citizenship: The Economic and Social Rights of Noncitizens." In *Immigration and Politics of Citizenship in Europe and North America*. Edited by W. Rogers Brubaker, 145–162. Lanham: University Press of America.

Çarkoglu, Ali. 2002. "Turkey's November 2002 Elections: A New Beginning?" *Middle East Review of International Affairs*. 6(4): 30–41.

Carling, Jorgen, and Marta B. Erdal. 2014. "Return Migration and Transnationalism: How Are the Two Connected?" *International Migration* 52(6): 2–12.

Carling, Jorgen, and Silje V. Pettersen. 2014. "Return Migration Intentions in the Integration–Transnationalism Matrix." *International Migration* 52(6): 13–30.

Castells, Manuel. 2000. *The Rise of the Network Society*. Oxford: Blackwell.

Castles, Stephen, Derya Özkul and Magdalena Cubas, eds. 2015. *Social Transformation and Migration: National and Local Experiences in South Korea, Turkey, Mexico and Australia*. London: Palgrave Macmillan.

Chakrabarty, Dipesh. 1997. "The Differences-Deferral of a Colonial Modernity: Public Debates on Domesticity in British Bengal." In *Tensions of Empire: Colonial Cultures in a Bourgeois World*. Edited by Frederick Cooper and Laura Ann Stoler, 373–405. Berkeley: University of California Press.

Chatterjee, Partha. 1989. "Colonialism, Nationalism, and Colonialized Women: The Contest in India." *American Ethnologist* 16(4): 622–633.

———. 1993. *The Nation and its Fragments: Colonial and Postcolonial Histories*. Princeton, N.J.: Princeton University Press.

Childress, Faith J. 2008. "Creating the 'New Woman' in Early Republican Turkey: The Contributions of the American Collegiate Institute and the American College for Girls." *Middle Eastern Studies* 44(4): 553–569.

Cindoğlu, Dilek and Didem Ünal. 2017. "Gender and Sexuality in the Authoritarian Discursive Strategies of 'New Turkey.'" *European Journal of Women's Studies* 24(1): 39–54.

Cinoğlu, Mustafa. 2006. "Private Education as a Policy Tool in Turkey." *International Education Journal* 7(5): 676–687.

Cole, Juan. 2014. "Democracy Exported, History Expunged: John Dewey's Trip to Turkey and the Challenge of Building 'Civilised' Nations for Democratic Life." *History of Education* 43(4): 504–523.

Colonna, Fanny. 1997. "Educating Conformity in French Colonial Algeria." In *Tensions of Empire: Colonial Cultures in a Bourgeois World.* Edited by Frederick Cooper and Laura Ann Stoler, 346–370. Berkeley: University of California Press.

Cook, Steven A. 2017. "The American Alliance with Turkey Was Built On a Myth." *Foreign Policy.* 12 October 2017, http://foreignpolicy.com/2017/10/12/the-american-alliance-with-turkey-was-built-on-a-myth/.

Cook-Martín, David. 2013. *The Scramble for Citizens: Dual Nationality and State Competition for Immigrants.* Palo Alto: Stanford University Press.

Cooper, Frederick and Laura Ann Stoler eds. 1997. *Tensions of Empire: Colonial Cultures in a Bourgeois World.* Berkeley: University of California Press.

Coşar, Simten and Metin Yeğenoğlu. 2011. "New Grounds for Patriarchy in Turkey? Gender Policy in the Age of AKP." *South European Society and Politics* 16(4): 555–573.

Costanzo, Joe and Amanda Klekowski von Koppenfels. 2013. "Counting the Uncountable: Overseas Americans." *Migration Information Source.* 17 May 2013. http://www.migrationpolicy.org/article/counting-uncountable-overseas-americans.

Criss, Nur Bilge. 1997. "Strategic Nuclear Missiles in Turkey: The Jupiter Affair, 1959–1963." *Journal of Strategic Studies* 20(3): 97–122.

———. 2002. "A Short History of anti-Americanism and Terrorism: The Turkish Case." *Journal of American History* 89(2): 472–484.

———. 2011. "The American Cold War Military Presence in Turkey." In *American Turkish Encounters: Politics and Culture, 1830–1989.* Edited by Nur Bilge Criss, Selcuk Esenbel, Tony Greenwood, and Louis Mazzari, 281–298. Newcastle: Cambridge Scholars Publishing.

Criss, Nur Bilge, Selcuk Esenbel, Tony Greenwood, and Louis Mazzari, eds. 2011. *American Turkish Encounters: Politics and Culture, 1830–1989.* Newcastle: Cambridge Scholars Publishing.

Croucher, Sheila. 2007. "'They Love Us Here:' American Migrants in Mexico." *Dissent,* Winter: 23–28.

———. 2012. "Privileged Mobility in an Age of Globality." *Societies.* 2: 1–13.

Danacıoğlu Temur, Esra. 2011." Early Missions and Eastern Christianity in the Ottoman Empire: Cross-Cultural Encounter and Religious Confrontation, 1820–1856." In *American Turkish Encounters: Politics and Culture, 1830–1989.* Edited by Nur Bilge Criss, Selcuk Esenbel, Tony Greenwood, and Louis Mazzari, 35–47. Newcastle: Cambridge Scholars Publishing.

Danış, Didem. 2011. "Changing Fortunes: Iraqi Refugees in Turkey." *International Journal of Contemporary Iraqi Studies* 5(2): 199–213.

Daniel, Robert L. 1967. "The United States and the Turkish Republic Before World War II: The Cultural Dimension." *Middle East Journal* 21(1): 52–63.

———. 1970. *American Philanthropy in the Near East, 1820–1960,* Athens: Ohio University Press.

Davison, Andrew 1998. *Secularism and Revivalism in Turkey: A Hermeneutic Reconsideration.* New Haven: Yale University Press.

de Koning, Anouk. 2006. "Café Latte and Caesar Salad: Cosmopolitan Belonging in Cairo's Coffee Shops." In *Cairo Cosmopolitan: Politics, Culture, and Urban Space in the New Globalized Middle East.* Edited by Diane Singerman and Paul Amar, 221–234. Cairo: American University of Cairo Press.

de Sousa Santos, Boaventura. 2006. "Globalizations." *Theory, Culture and Society* 23(2–3): 393–399.

Devine, Fiona, Mike Savage, John Scott, and Rosemary Crompton. 2005. *Rethinking Class: Culture, Identities and Life Style.* New York: Palgrave Macmillan.

Dezalay, Yves and Bryant Garth, eds. 2002. *Global Prescriptions: The Production, Exportation, and Importation of a New Legal Orthodoxy.* Ann Arbor: University of Michigan.

Dirks, Nicholas, ed. 1992. *Colonialism and Culture.* Ann Arbor: University of Michigan Press.

Dixon, David, Julie Murray and Julia Gelatti. 2006. "America's Emigrants: US Retirement Migration to Mexico and Panama." *Migration Information Source.* 1 September 2006 http://www.migrationpolicy.org/article/americas-emigrants-us-retirement-migration-mexico-and-panama.

Docquier, Frederic and Hillel Rapoport. 2007. "Skilled Migration: The Perspective of Developing Countries." IZA Discussion Papers, No. 2873.

Duara, Prasenjit. 2002. "Transnationalism and the Challenge to National Histories." In *Rethinking American History in a Global Age.* Edited by Thomas Bender, 25–46. Berkeley: University of California Press.

Edwards, Brian T. 2015. *After the American Century: The Ends of U.S. Culture in the Middle East.* New York: Columbia University Press.

Ekinsmyth, Carol. 2014. "Mothers' Business, Work/Life and the Politics of 'Mumpreneurship.'" *Gender, Place and Culture* 21(10): 1230–1248.

Elliott, Anthony and John Urry. 2010. *Mobile Lives.* London: Routledge.

El-Shakry, Marwa. 2007. "The Gospel of Science and American Evangelism in Late Ottoman Beirut." *Past and Present* 196: 173–214.

Emrence, Cem. 2008. "After Neoliberal Globalization: The Great Transformation of Turkey." *Comparative Sociology* 7: 51–67.

Er, H. Alpay, Fatma Korkut and Özlem Er. 2003. "US Involvement in the Development of Design in the Periphery: The Case History of Industrial Design Education in Turkey, 1950s–1970s." *Design Issues* 19(2): 17–34.

Erdem, Murat. 2011. "Perceptions of American Aid as Reflected in Political Cartoons Published in Turkish Humor Magazines 1945–1960." In *American Turkish Encounters: Politics and Culture, 1830–1989.* Edited by Nur Bilge Criss, Selcuk Esenbel, Tony Greenwood, and Louis Mazzari, 354–365. Newcastle: Cambridge Scholars Publishing.

Erel Umut. 2010. "Migrating Cultural Capital: Bourdieu in Migration Studies." *Sociology* 44(4): 642–660.

Erhan, Çağrı. 2001. *Türk Amerikan İlişkilerinin Tarihsel Kökenleri.* Ankara: İmge.

Erkmen, Deniz. 2015. "Houses on Wheels: National Attachment, Belonging, and Cosmopolitanism in Narratives of Transnational Professionals." *Studies in Ethnicity and Nationalism* 15(1): 26–47.

———. 2018. "Stepping into the Global: Turkish Professionals, Employment in Transnational Corporations, and Aspiration to Transnational Forms of Cultural Capital." *Current Sociology* 66(3): 412–430.

Esen, Berk and Şebnem Gumuscu. 2016. "Rising Competitive Authoritarianism in Turkey." *Third World Quarterly* 37(9): 1581–1606.

Esen, Engin. 2017. "Türk Milyonerler Kaçıyor." *Sözcü*, 26 February 2017, http://www.sozcu.com.tr/2017/ekonomi/turk-milyonerler-kaciyor–1700873/.

Faist, Thomas 2000. *The Volume and Dynamics of International Migration and Transnational Social Spaces.* Oxford: Oxford University Press.

———. 2009. "The Transnational Social Question: Social Rights and Citizenship in a Global Context." *International Sociology* 24(7): 7–35.

———. 2010. "Towards Transnational Studies: World Theories, Transnationalization and Changing Institutions." *Journal of Ethnic and Migration Studies* 36(10): 1665–1687.

———. 2016. "Cross-Border Migration and Social Inequalities." *Annual Review of Sociology* 42: 323–346.

Faist, Thomas, Jürgen Gerdes, and Beate Reaple. 2004. "Dual Citizenship as a Path Dependent Process." *International Migration Review* 38(3): 913–944.

Faist, Thomas and Peter Kivisto. 2010. *Beyond a Border: The Causes and Consequences of Contemporary Immigration.* London: Sage.

Faist, Thomas and Peter Kivisto, eds. 2007. *Dual Citizenship in Global Perspective: From Unitary to Multiple Citizenship.* Basingstoke: Palgrave Macmillan.

Falk, Richard. 1994. "The Making of Global Citizenship." In *The Condition of Citizenship.* Edited by Bart van Steenbergen, 127–140. London: Sage.

Faria, Caroline. 2014. "'I Want My Children to Know Sudan': Narrating the Long-Distance Intimacies of Diasporic Politics." *Annals of the Association of American Geographers* 104(5): 1052–1067.

Federal Bureau of Investigation (FBI). 2008. *What Happens When an American Is Harmed Overseas.* 3 June 2008. https://archives.fbi.gov/archives/news/stories/2008/june/international_060308.

Fisher Onar, Nora and Meltem Müftüler-Baç. 2011. "The Adultery and Headscarf Debates in Turkey: Fusing 'EU-niversal' and Alternative Modernities?" *Women's Studies International Forum* 34(5): 378–389.

Fitzgerald, David. 2004. "Beyond 'Transnationalism': Mexican Hometown Politics at an American Labour Union." *Ethnic and Racial Studies* 27(2): 228–247.

———. 2009. *A Nation of Emigrants: How Mexico Manages Its Migration.* Berkeley: University of California Press.

Freely, John. 2000. *A History of Robert College: The American College for Girls, and Boğaziçi University (Bosphorus University).* 2 vols. Istanbul: YKY.

Friedman, Jonathan. 2000. "American Again, or the New Age of Imperial Reason? Global Elite Formation, Its Identity and Ideological Discourses." *Theory, Culture and Society* 17: 139–146.

Fukuyama, Francis. 1989. "The End of History?" *National Interest* 16: 3–18.

Gilbertson, Greta and Audrey Singer. 2003. "The Emergence of Protective Citizenship in the USA: Naturalization Among Dominican Immigrants in the Post–1996 Welfare Reform Era." *Ethnic and Racial Studies* 26(1): 25–52.

Gilpin, Robert. 2000. *The Challenge of Global Capitalism: The World Economy in the 21st Century*. Princeton, NJ: Princeton University Press.

Glick Schiller, Nina. 1997. "The Situation of Transnational Studies." *Identities* 4(2): 155–166.

———. 1999. "Transmigrants and Nation-States: Something Old and Something New in the U.S. Immigrant Experience." In *The Handbook of International Migration: The American Experience*. Edited by Charles Hirschman, Philip Kasinitz, and Josh DeWind, 94–119. New York: Russell Sage Foundation.

Glick Schiller, Nina, Linda Basch, and Christina Szanton Blanc. 1995. "From Immigrant to Transmigrant: Theorizing Transnational Migration." *Anthropological Quarterly* 68(1): 48–63.

Glick Schiller, Nina and Noel B. Salazar. 2013. "Regimes of Mobility Across the Globe." *Journal of Ethnic and Migration Studies* 39(2): 183–200.

Goodman, Sara. 2014. *Immigration and Membership Politics in Western Europe*. New York: Cambridge University Press.

Gordon, Philip. 2017. "Turkey and the US face the end of a Promising Partnership." *Financial Times*. 10 October 2017 https://www.ft.com/content/d5fa0568-ad99–11e7–8076–0a4bdda92ca2?mhq5j = e6.

Gözen, Pinar. 2011. "The Cold War, Jazz, and Turkey." In *American Turkish Encounters: Politics and Culture, 1830–1989*. Edited by Nur Bilge Criss, Selcuk Esenbel, Tony Greenwood, and Louis Mazzari, 331–343. Newcastle: Cambridge Scholars Publishing.

Grant, Tyler. 2015. "Made in America: Medical Tourism and Birth Tourism Leading to a Larger Base of Transient Citizenship." *Virginia Journal of Social Policy and the Law* 22(1): 159–178.

Grewal, Inderpal. 2005. *Transnational America: Feminisms, Diasporas, Neoliberalisms*. Durham: Duke University Press.

———. 2006. "'Security Moms' in the Early-Twentieth Century United States: The Gender Security in Neoliberalism." *Women's Studies Quarterly* 34(1/2): 25–39.

Grigoriadis, I. N. 2010. "Friends No More? The Rise of Anti-American Nationalism in Turkey." *Middle East Journal* 64(1): 51–66.

Gross, Robert A. 2000. "The Transnational Turn: Rediscovering American Studies in a Wider World." *Journal of American Studies* 34(3): 373–393.

Gülalp, Haldun. 1999. "Political Islam in Turkey: The Rise and Fall of the Refah Party." *The Muslim World* 89(1): 22–41.

Gunter, Michael M. 2005. "The US-Turkish Alliance in Disarray." *World Affairs* 167(3): 113–123.

———. 2015. "Iraq, Syria, ISIS and the Kurds: Geostrategic Concerns for the US and Turkey." *Middle East Policy* 22(1): 102–111.

Güney, Aylin. 2008. "Anti-Americanism in Turkey: Past and Present." *Middle Eastern Studies* 44(3): 471–487.

———. 2011. "Revisiting the Origins of the Cyprus Conflict: The Impact of the Cold War and Turkish American Relations." In *American Turkish Encounters: Politics and Culture, 1830–1989*. Edited by Nur Bilge Criss, Selcuk Esenbel, Tony Greenwood, and Louis Mazzari, 299–314. Newcastle: Cambridge Scholars Publishing.

Gür, Asli. 2011. "Robert College, Laboratory for Religion, Shrine for Science: Transculturation of Evangelical College Model in Constantinople." In *American Turkish Encounters: Politics and Culture, 1830–1989.* Edited by Nur Bilge Criss, Selcuk Esenbel, Tony Greenwood, and Louis Mazzari, 48–60. Newcastle: Cambridge Scholars Publishing.

Gürel, Perin. 2015. "Turkey and the United States After World War I: National Memory, Local Categories, and Provincializing the Transnational." *American Quarterly* 67(2): 353–376.

———. 2017. *The Limits of Westernization: A Cultural History of America in Turkey.* New York: Columbia University Press.

Go, Julian, and George Lawson. 2017. "Introduction for a Global Historical Sociology." In *Global Historical Sociology.* Edited by Julian Go and George Lawson, 1–35. Cambridge: Cambridge University Press.

Gorman, Daniel. 2010. *Imperial Citizenship: Empire and the Question of Belonging.* Oxford University Press.

Hannerz, Ulf. 1996. *Transnational Connections: Culture, People, Places.* London: Routledge.

Hansen, Suzy. 2018. *Notes on a Foreign Country: An American Abroad in a post-American World.* New York: Farrar, Straus and Giroux.

Hansen, Thomas Blom and Finn Stepputat. 2001. *States of Imagination: Ethnographic Explorations of the Postcolonial State.* Durham: Duke University Press.

Harding, Sandra.1995. "Can Feminist Thought Make Economics More Objective?" *Feminist Economics.* 1(1): 7–32.

Hardwick, Susan W. 2010. "Fuzzy Transnationals? American Settlement, Identity, and Belonging in Canada." *American Review of Canadian Studies* 40(1): 86–103.

Hardwick, Susan W. and Ginger Mansfield. 2009. "Discourse, Identity, and 'Homeland as Other' at the Canadian-U.S. Borderlands." *Annals of the Association of American Geographers* 99(2): 406–422.

Harpaz, Yossi. 2013. "Rooted Cosmopolitans: Israelis with a European Passport – History, Property, Identity." *International Migration Review* 47(1): 166–206.

———. 2019. "Compensatory Citizenship: Dual Nationality as a Strategy of Global Upward Mobility." *Journal of Ethnic and Migration Studies* 45(6): 897–916.

Harpaz, Yossi, and Pablo Mateos. 2019. "Strategic Citizenship: Negotiating Membership in the Age of Dual Nationality." *Journal of Ethnic and Migration Studies* 45(6): 843–857.

Hays, Sharon. 1996. *The Cultural Contradictions of Motherhood.* New Haven: Yale University Press.

Heydemann, Steven, and Reinoud Leenders. 2013. *Middle East Authoritarianisms: Governance, Contestation, and Regime Resilience in Syria and Iran.* Palo Alto: Stanford University Press.

Hirschman, Albert O. 1970. *Exit, Voice, and Loyalty: Responses to Decline in Firms, Organizations, and States.* Cambridge: Harvard University Press.

Hirschman, Charles, Philip Kasinitz, and Josh DeWind, eds. 1999. *The Handbook of International Migration: The American Experience.* New York: Russell Sage Foundation.

Ho, Elaine Lynn-Ee. 2008. "'Flexible Citizenship' or Familial Ties that Bind? Singaporean Transmigrants in London." *International Migration* 46(4): 145–175.

———. 2009. "Constituting Citizenship Through the Emotions: Singaporean transmigrants in London." *Annals of the Association of American Geographers* 99(4): 788–804.

Hoffman, Mark N. 2013. *Rethinking the Politics of Immigration: Colonial Modes of Immigration Management and the Ambivalent Resilience of the Empire State* Unpublished Ph.D. dissertation. University of Minnesota.

Holmes, Amy A. 2014. *Social Unrest and American Military Bases in Turkey and Germany Since 1945*. New York: Cambridge University Press.

Huete, Raquel, Alejandro Mantecón, and Jesus Estévez. 2013. "Challenges in Lifestyle Migration Research: Reflections and Findings About the Spanish Crisis." *Mobilities*. *8*(3): 331–348.

Huntington, Samuel P. 1993. "The Clash of Civilizations?" *Foreign Affairs* 72(3): 22–49.

Icduygu, Ahmet and Damla Bayraktar Aksel. 2015a. *Turkey and International Migration, 2014–2015*. Report Prepared for the Annual Meeting of the OECD Expert Group on Migration, Paris, 12–14 October 2015: Istanbul.

———. 2015b. "Migration Realities and State Responses: Rethinking International Migration in Turkey." In *Social Transformation and Migration: National and Local Experiences in South Korea, Turkey, Mexico and Australia*. Edited by Stephen Castles, Derya Özkul and Magdalena Cubas, 115–132. London: Palgrave Macmillan.

Icduygu, Ahmet and Kemal Kirisci, eds. 2009. *Lands of Diverse Migration*. Istanbul: Istanbul Bilgi University.

Isin, Engin F. 2008. "Theorizing Acts of Citizenship." In *Acts of Citizenship*. Edited by Engin F. Isın and Greg M. Nielsen, 15–43. London: Zed Books, pp. 15–43.

———. 2015. *Citizenship After Orientalism: Transforming Political Theory*. New York: Palgrave Macmillan.

Isin, Engin F. and Greg M. Nielsen, eds. 2008. *Acts of Citizenship*. London: Zed Books.

Jackiewicz, Edward L., and Govdyak, Olga. 2015. "Diversity of Lifestyle: A View from Belize." *Yearbook of the Association of Pacific Coast Geographers* 77: 18–39.

Joppke, Christian. 2007. "Transformation of Citizenship: Status, Rights, Identity." *Citizenship Studies* 11(1): 37–48.

———. 2008. "Comparative Citizenship: A Restrictive Turn in Europe." *Law and Ethics of Human Rights* 2(1): 1–41.

———. 2010. *Citizenship and Immigration*. Cambridge: Polity Press.

———. 2019. "The Instrumental Turn of Citizenship." *Journal of Ethnic and Migration Studies* 45(6): 858–878.

Joppke, Christian and Eva Morawska, eds. 2003 *Toward Assimilation and Citizenship: Immigrants in Liberal Nation-State*. Basingstoke: Palgrave Macmillan.

Kadercan, Burak. 2016. "Turkey's Anti-Americanism Isn't New." *National Interest* 23 August 2016. http://nationalinterest.org/feature/turkeys-anti-americanism-isnt-new–17448.

Kadıoğlu, Ayşe. 1996. "The Paradox of Turkish Nationalism and the Construction of Official Identity." *Middle Eastern Studies* 32(2): 177–193.

Kalkan, Kerem Ozam, and Uslaner, Eric M. 2011. "American Public Support for Aid to Turkey After World War II." In *American Turkish Encounters: Politics and Culture, 1830–1989*. Edited by Nur Bilge Criss, Selcuk Esenbel, Tony Greenwood, and Louis Mazzari, 83–99. Newcastle: Cambridge Scholars Publishing.

Kalleberg, Arne L. 2009. "Precarious Work, Insecure Workers: Employment Relations in Transition." *American Sociological Review* 74(1): 1–22.

Kandiyoti, Deniz. 2015. "Gender Wars in Turkey: A Litmus Test for Democracy?" *Open Democracy*. 30 March 2015. https://www.opendemocracy.net/5050/deniz-kandiyoti/gender-wars-in-turkey-litmus-test-of-democracy.

Kaplan, Amy. 2009. "In the Name of Homeland Security." In *Liberty and Justice: America and the Middle East*. Edited by Patrick McGreevy and Nancy Batakji, 37–49. Beirut: American University of Beirut Press.

Karademir Hazır, Irmak. 2014. "Boundaries of Middle-Class Identities in Turkey." *Sociological Review* 62(4): 675–697.

Kardaş, Saban. 2011. "Turkish-American Relations in the 2000s: Revisiting the Basic Parameters of Partnership?" *Perceptions* 16(3): 25–52.

Karpat, Kemal. 2004. "The Turks in America: Historical Background: From Ottoman to Turkish Immigration." In *Studies on Turkish Politics and Society: Selected Articles and Essays.* New York: Brill.

Kaslı, Zeynep and Ayşe Parla. 2009. "Broken Lines of Il/legality and the Reproduction of State Sovereignty: The Impact of Visa Policies on Immigrants to Turkey from Bulgaria." *Alternatives: Global, Local, Political* 34(2): 203–227.

Katz-Gerro, Tally. 2002. "Highbrow Cultural Consumption and Class Cistinction in Italy, Israel, West Germany, Sweden, and the United States." *Social Forces* 81(1): 207–229.

Kaya, Ayhan. 2015. "Islamisation of Turkey Under the AKP Rule: Empowering Family, Faith and Charity." *South European Society and Politics* 20(1): 47–69.

———. 2016. "Ethno-Religious Narratives of Citizenship in Turkey: Fabricating Citizens Through National Education." *Research and Policy on Turkey* 1(2): 119–131.

Kaya, Ilhan. 2003. *Shifting Turkish American Identity Formations in the United States.* Unpublished doctoral dissertation. Florida State University, Tallahassee.

———. 2005. "Identity and Space: The Case of Turkish Americans." *Geographical Review* 95(3): 425–440.

———. 2009. "Identity across Generations: A Turkish American Case Study." *Middle East Journal* 63(4): 617–632.

Keck, Margaret E. and Katherine Sikkink. 1998. *Activists Beyond Borders: Advocacy Networks in International Politics.* Ithaca: Cornell University Press.

Kerslake, Celia, Kerem Öktem and Phillip Robins 2010. *Turkey's Engagement with Modernity: Conflict and Change in the Twentieth Century* Hampshire: Palgrave Macmillan.

Keskin Kozat, Burcak. 2011. "Reinterpreting Turkey's Marshall Plan: Of Machines, Experts, and Technical Knowledge." In *American Turkish Encounters: Politics and Culture, 1830–1989.* Edited by Nur Bilge Criss, Selcuk Esenbel, Tony Greenwood, and Louis Mazzari, 182–218. Newcastle: Cambridge Scholars Publishing.

Kessler, Glenn. 2015. " 'Birth Tourists' and 'Anchor Babies:' What Trump and Bush Got Right." *Washington Post.* https://www.washingtonpost.com/news/fact-checker/wp/2015/08/25/birth-tourists-and-anchor-babies-what-trump-and-bush-got-right/?noredirect=on&utm_term=.0627c4a91199 (last 12 accessed February 2019).

Keyder, Çağlar. 1987. *State and Class in Turkey.* London: Verso.

———. 2003. *Memalik-i Osmaniye'den Avrupa Birliği'ne.* Istanbul: İletişim Yayınları.

———, ed. 1999. *Istanbul: Between the Global and the Local.* New York: Rowman and Littlefield.

———. 2004. "The Turkish Bell Jar." *New Left Review* 28: 65–84.

Keyman, E. Fuat. 2007. "Modernity, Secularism and Islam: The Case of Turkey." *Theory, Culture and Society* 24(2): 215–234.

Keyman E. Fuat and Ahmet Icduygu. 2003. "Globalization, Immigration and Citizenship: The Case of Turkey." In *Globalization: Theory and Practice.* Edited by Eleonore Kofman and Gillin Young, 193–206. London: Continuum.

Kılıç, Azer. 2008. "The Gender Dimension of Social Policy Reform in Turkey: Towards Equal Citizenship?" *Social Policy and Administration* 42(5): 487–503.

King, Stephen J. 2003. *Liberalization against Democracy: Local Politics of Economic Reform in Tunisia*. Bloomington: Indiana University Press.

———. 2009. *The New Authoritarianism in the Middle East and North Africa*. Bloomington: Indiana University Press.

Kirişçi, Kemal. 2002. "Immigration and Asylum Issues in EU–Turkish Relations: Assessing EU's Impact on Turkish Policy and Practice." *Migration and the Externalities of European Integration*, edited by Sandra Lavenex and Emek M. Uçarer, 125–142. New York: Lexington Books.

———. 2003. "Turkey: A Transformation from Emigration to Immıgration." 1 November 2003 https://www.migrationpolicy.org/article/turkey-transformation-emigration-immigration.

Kivisto, Peter. 2003. "Social Spaces, Transnational Immigrant Communities, and the Politics of Incorporation." *Ethnicities* 3(1): 5–28.

Klekowski von Koppenfels, Aamanda. 2014. *Migrants or Expatriates? Americans in Europe*. New York: Palgrave Macmillan.

Kocabaşoğlu, Uygur. 1989. *Anadolu'daki Amerika: Kendi Belgeleriyle 19. Yüzyılda Osmanlı İmparatorluğu'ndaki Amerikan Misyoner Okulları* [America in Anatolia: American Missionary Schools in the 19th Century Ottoman Empire Through Their Own Documents]. Istanbul: Imge.

Koçak, Orhan. 2010. " 'Westernisation against the West': Cultural Politics in the Early Turkish Republic." In *Turkey's Engagement with Modernity: Conflict and Change in the Twentieth Century*. Edited by Celia Kerslake, Kerem Öktem, and Phillip Robins, 305–322. Basingstoke: Palgrave Macmillan.

Kofman, Eleonore and Gillin Young, eds. 2003. *Globalization: Theory and Practice*. London: Continuum.

Koşar-Altinyelken, Hulya, Kenan Çayır and Orhan Agirdag. 2015. "Introduction. Turkey at a Crossroads: Critical Debates and Issues in Education." *Comparative Education* 51(4): 473–483.

Krastev, Ivan. 2004. "The Anti-American Century?" *Journal of Democracy* 15(2): 5–16.

Kroes, Rob. 2002. "American Empire and Cultural Imperialism: A View from the Receiving End." In *Rethinking American History in a Global Age*. Edited by Thomas Bender, 295–313. Berkeley: University of California Press.

———. 2006. "Imaginary Americas in Europe's Public Space." In *The Americanization of Europe: Cultural Diplomacy and Anti-Americanism After* 1945. Edited by Alexander Stephan, 337–361. New York/Oxford: Berghahn Books.

Kuppinger, Petra. 2000. "Exclusive Greenery: New Gated Communities in Cairo." *City and Society* 16(2): 35–61.

Kuran, Aptullah. 2002. *Bir Kurucu Rektörün Anıları: Robert Kolej Yüksek Okulu'ndan Boğaziçi Üniversitesi'ne* [A Founding University President's Memoir: From Robert College to Boğaziçi University]. Istanbul: Boğaziçi Üniversitesi Yayınevi.

Kürkçü, Ertugrul. 1998. "Hala bir '68 Kuşağı' Var mı?" [Is there still a '68 Generation'?]. *Cogito* 14: 160–169.

La Porte, Amy. 2017. "United States and Turkey mutually suspend visa services." *CNN*, 9 October 2017, http://www.cnn.com/2017/10/08/world/us-turkey-halt-visa-service/index.html (last accessed 12 December 2018).

Lahire, Bernard. 2008. "The Individual and the Mixing of Genres: Cultural Dissonance and Self-Distinction" *Poetics* 36: 166–188.

Lamont, Michelle. 1992. *Money, Morals, Manners: The Culture of the French and American Upper-Middle Classes.* Illinois: University of Chicago.

Lamont, Michelle and Virág Molnar. 2002. "The Study of Boundaries in the Social Sciences." *Annual Review of Sociology* 28(1): 167–195.

Lan, Pei-Chia. 2014. "Compressed Modernity and Glocal Entanglement: The Contested Transformation of Parenting Discourses in Postwar Taiwan." *Current Sociology* 62 (4): 531–549.

Lawler, Stephanie. 2005a." Introduction: Class, Culture and Identity." *Sociology* 39(5): 797–806.

———. 2005b. "Disgusted Subjects: The Making of Middle-Class Identities." *Sociological Review* 53(3): 429–446.

Le Roux, Brigitte, Henry Rouanet, Mike Savage and Alan Warde. 2008. "Class and Cultural Division in the UK." *Sociology* 42(6): 1049–1071.

Leach, William. 2011. *Land of Desire: Merchants, Power, and the Rise of a New American Culture.* New York: Vintage.

Levitt, Peggy. 2003. "Keeping Feet in Both Worlds: Transnational Practices and Immigrant Incorporation in the United States." In *Toward Assimilation and Citizenship: Immigrants in Liberal Nation-State.* Edited by Christian Joppke and Ewa Morawska, 177–194. Basingstoke: Palgrave Macmillan.

Lewin, Tamar. 2015. "California Apartments Raided in Federal Investigation of Chinese 'Birth Tourism.'" *New York Times.* https://www.nytimes.com/2015/03/04/us/california-homes-raided-in-federal-crackdown-on-chinese-birth-tourism.html?_r=0 (last accessed 14 February 2019).

Little, Douglas. 2008. *American Orientalism: The United States and the Middle East since 1945.* Chapel Hill: University of North Carolina Press.

Lockman, Zachary. 2004. *Contending Visions of the Middle East: The History and Politics of Orientalism.* Cambridge: Cambridge University Press.

Ludden, David. 1992. "India's Development Regime." In *Colonialism and Culture.* Edited by Nicholas B. Dirks, 247–287. Ann Arbor: University of Michigan Press.

Lynch, Marc. 2014. *The Arab Uprisings Explained: New Contentious Politics in the Middle East.* New York: Columbia University Press.

Makdisi, Ussama. 2002. "'Anti-Americanism' in the Arab World: An Interpretation of a Brief History." *Journal of American History* 89(2): 538–557.

Mamdani, Mamdouh. 1996. *Citizen and Subject: Contemporary Africa and the Legacy of Late Colonialism.* Princeton: Princeton University Press.

Mardin, Şerif. 1997. *Din ve İdeoloji.* Istanbul: İletişim Yayınları.

Martin, Phillip L. 2017. "Election of Donald Trump and Migration." *Migration Letters* 14(1): 161–171.

Massey, Douglas S. 1995. "The New Immigration and Ethnicity in the United States." *Population and Development Review* 21(3): 631–652.

Mau, Steffen. 2010. "Mobility, Citizenship, Inequality, and the Liberal State: The Case of Visa Policies. *International Political Sociology* 4(4): 339–361.

Mazzari, Louis. 2011. "A Palazzo on the Boshporus: The American Embassy in Beyoğlu." In *American Turkish Encounters: Politics and Culture, 1830–1989.* Edited by Nur Bilge Criss,

Selcuk Esenbel, Tony Greenwood, and Louis Mazzari, 110–122. Newcastle: Cambridge Scholars Publishing.

McAlister, Melanie. 2001. *Epic Encounters: Culture, Media, and U.S. Interests in the Middle East, 1945–2000*. Berkeley: University of California Press.

Medina, Jennifer. 2011. "Arriving as Pregnant Tourists, Leaving with American Babies." *New York Times*. 28 March 2011. http://www.nytimes.com/2011/03/29/us/29babies.html?pagewanted=all&_r=0 (last accessed 1 October 2014).

Mendez, Luisa. 2008. "Middle Class Identities in a Neoliberal Age: Tensions Between Contested Authenticities." *Sociological Review* 56 (2): 220–237.

Meyersson, Erik and Dani Rodrik. 2014. "Erdogan's Coup: The True State of Turkish Democracy." *Foreign Affairs* 26 May 2014. https://www.foreignaffairs.com/articles/turkey/2014-05-26/erdogans-coup.

Migdal, Joel S. 2014. *Shifting Sands: The United States in the Middle East*. New York: Columbia University Press.

Milanovic, Branko. 2010. *The Haves and the Have-Nots: A Brief and Idiosyncratic History of Global Inequality*. New York: Basic Books.

Miller-Idriss, Cynthia and Elizabeth Hanauer. 2011. "Transnational Higher Education: Offshore Campuses in the Middle East." *Comparative Education* 47(2): 181–207.

Mitchell, Timothy. 1988. *Colonising Egypt*. Berkeley: University of California Press.

———. 2002. *Rule of Experts: Egypt, Techno-Politics, Modernity*. Berkeley: University of California Press.

Mortensen, Elin Berstad. 2014. "Not Just a Personal Decision: Moral Obligations and Collective Pressures on Return to Zimbabwe." *African Diaspora* 7(1): 15–37.

Mfti, Malik. 2011. "A Little America: The Emergence of Turkish Hegemony." *Middle East Brief* 51: 1–7.

Müftüler-Baç, Meltem. 2003. "The New Face of Turkey: The Domestic and Foreign Policy Implications of November 2002 Elections." *East European Quarterly* 37(4): 421–438.

Myers, Norman and Jennifer Kent. 2004. *The New Consumers: The Influence of Affluence on the Environment*. Washington, DC: Island.

Neofotistos, Vasiliki. 2009. "Bulgarian Passports, Macedonian Identity: The Invention of EU Citizenship in the Republic of Macedonia." *Anthropology Today* 25(4): 19–22.

Nguyen-Akbar, Mytoan. 2014. "The Tensions of Diasporic 'Return' Migration: How Class and Money create Distance in the Vietnamese Transnational Family." *Journal of Contemporary Ethnography* 43(2): 176–201.

Norton, Matthew. 2017. "Real Mystic Histories: Circulatory Networks and State-Centrism." In *Global Historical Sociology*. Edited by Julian Go and George Lawson, 37–58. Cambridge: Cambridge University Press.

O'Dougherty, Maureen. 2002. *Consumption Intensified: The Politics of Middle-Class Daily Life in Brazil*, Durham: Duke University.

Öncü, Ayse. 1999. "Istanbulites and Others: The Cultural Cosmology of Being Middle Class in the Era of Globalism." In *Istanbul: Between the Global and the Local*. Edited by Çaglar Keyder, 95–119. New York: Rowman and Littlefield.

Ong, Aihwa. 1999. *Flexible Citizenship: The Cultural Logics of Transnationality*. Durham: Duke University Press.

———. 2006. *Neoliberalism as Exception: Mutations in Citizenship and Sovereignty*. Durham: Duke University.

Öniş, Ziya. 2012. "The Triumph of Conservative Globalism: The Political Economy of the AKP Era." *Turkish Studies* 13(2): 135–152.

Öniş, Ziya and Suhnaz Yılmaz. 2016. "Turkey and Russia in a Shifting Global Order: Cooperation, Conflict and Asymmetric Interdependence in a Turbulent Region." *Third World Quarterly* 37(1): 71–95.

Örnek, Cangül. 2012. "From Analysis to Policy: Turkish Studies in the 1950s and the Diplomacy of Ideas." *Middle Eastern Studies* 48(6): 941–959.

Özcan, Gencer, Evren Balta and Burç Beşgül, eds. 2017. *Kuşku ile Komşuluk [Suspicious Neighbors].* Istanbul: İletişim.

Özek, Cetin. 1962. *Devlet ve Din* [Religion and State]. Istanbul: Ada Yayınları.

Özel, Soli. 2003. "After the Tsunami." *Journal of Democracy* 14(2): 80–94.

———. 2014. "A Moment of Elation: The Gezi Protests/Resistance and the Fading of the AKP Project." In *The Making of a Protest Movement in Turkey:# Occupygezi.* Edited by Umut Özkırımlı, 7–24. New York: Palgrave Macmillan.

Özer, Yonca. 2016. *Turkey and the European Union: Processes of Europeanisation.* London: Routledge.

Özkan, Behlül. 2015. "Turkey's Islamists: From Power-Sharing to Political Incumbency." *Turkish Policy Quarterly* 14(1): 71–83.

———. 2017. "1945 Türkiye-SSCB Krizi: Dış Politikada Kurucu Mitin İnşası" [1945 Crisis Between Turkey and the USSR: The Building of the Establishment Myth in Foreign Policy]. In *Kuşku ile Komuşuluk* [Suspicious Neighbors]. Edited by Gencer Özcan, Evren Balta, and Burç Beşgül, 55–79. Istanbul: İletişim.

Özkırımlı, Umut. 2014. *The Making of a Protest Movement in Turkey: #Occupygezi.* New York: Palgrave Macmillan.

Özoğlu, Hakan. 2011. "Admiral Mark Bristol and the Turkish Rebuplic." In *American Turkish Encounters: Politics and Culture, 1830–1989.* Edited by Nur Bilge Criss, Selcuk Esenbel, Tony Greenwood, and Louis Mazzari, 123–133. Newcastle: Cambridge Scholars Publishing.

Pakin, Esra. 2008. "American Studies in Turkey During the 'Cultural' Cold War." *Turkish Studies* 9(3): 507–524.

Pamuk, Sevket. 1987. *The Ottoman Empire and European Capitalism, 1820–1913: Trade, Investment and Production.* New York: Cambridge University Press.

Panitch, Leo and Sam Gindin. 2004. "Global Capitalism and American Empire." *Socialist Register* 40: 1–40.

Parla, Taha. 1992. *Türkiye'de Siyasi Kültürün Resmi Kaynakları: Kemalist Tek Parti İdeolojisi ve CHP'nin Altı Ok'u* [Official Sources of Political Culture in Turkey: Kemalist One Party Ideology and CHP's Six Arrows]. Istanbul: İletişim.

———. 1999. *Ziya Gökalp, Kemalizm ve Türkiye'de Korporatizm.* [Ziya Gökalp, Kemalism and Corporatism in Turkey]. Istanbul: İletişim.

Payne, Geoff and Malcolm Williams. 2005. "Generalization in Qualitative Research." *Sociology* 39(2): 295–314.

Pérez, Jr., Louis A. 2002. "We Are the World: Internationalizing the National, Nationalizing the International." *Journal of American History* 89(2): 558–566.

Peterson, Mark Allen. 2011. *Connected in Cairo: Growing up Cosmopolitan in the Modern Middle East.* Bloomington: Indiana University Press.

Pew Research Center. 2014. "Turks Divided on Erdogan and the Country's Direction: About Half Support Gezi Park Protests." 30 July 2014. http://www.pewglobal.org/2014/07/30/turks-divided-on-erdogan-and-the-countrys-direction/#negative-views-of-eu-u-s-and-nato (last accessed 15 January 2018).

Phillips, Kevin P. 2002. *Wealth and Democracy: A Political History of the American Rich.* New York: Broadway Books.

Pieterse, Jan Nederveen. 2004. "Neoliberal Empire." *Theory, Culture and Society* 21(3): 119–140.

Pieterse Jan Nederveen. 2006. "Beyond the American Bubble: Does Empire Matter?" *Third World Quarterly* 27(6): 987–1002.

Pink, Johanna. 2009. *Muslim Societies in the Age of Mass Consumption*. Newcastle: Cambridge Scholars Publishing.

Podeh, Elie. 1995. *The Quest for Hegemony in the Arab World: The Struggle over the Baghdad Pact.* Leiden: Brill.

Pogonyi, Szabolcs. 2011. "Dual Citizenship and Sovereignty." *Nationalities Papers* 39(5): 685–704.

———. 2019. "The Passport as Means of Identity Management: Making and Unmaking Ethnic Boundaries Through Citizenship." *Journal of Ethnic and Migration Studies* 45(6): 975–993.

Popina, Elena. 2018. "There is No Stopping the Russian Baby Boom in Miami." *Bloomberg News*. https://www.bloomberg.com/news/features/2018–12–16/there-s-no-stopping-the-russian-baby-boom-in-miami (last accessed 21 February 2019).

Portes, Alejandro. 1996. "Global Villagers: The Rise of Transnational Communities." *American Prospect* 25: 74–77.

———. 1999. "Toward a New World—The Origins and Effects of Transnational Activities." *Ethnic and Racial Studies* 22(2): 463–477.

Prashad, Vijay. 2012. *Arab Spring, Libyan Winter*. Edinburgh: AK Press.

Raw, Laurence. 2012. "Holywood's Turkish Films 1930–1960: A Nation Looks at Itself." In *The Transnational Turn in American Studies: Turkey and the United States*. Edited by Tanfer Emin Tunc and Bahar Gürsel, 191–209. Bern: Peter Lang.

Reay, Diane. 1997. "Feminist Theory, Habitus, and Social Class: Disrupting Notions of Classlessness." *Women's Studies International Forum* 20(2): 225–233.

Rees, Martha W. and Josephine Smart, eds. 2001. *Plural Globalities in Multiple Localities: New World Borders*. Lanham: University Press of America.

Reich, Jennifer A. 2014. "Neoliberal Mothering and Vaccine Refusal: Imagined Gated Communities and the Privilege of Choice." *Gender and Society* 28(5): 679–704.

Richardson, John, ed. 1986. *Handbook of Theory and Research for the Sociology of Education*. Westport: Greenwood.

Robins, Phillip. 2007. "Turkish Foreign Policy since 2002: Between a 'Post-Islamist' Government and a Kemalist State." *International Affairs* 83(2): 289–304.

Robinson, William I. and Jerry Harris. 2000. "Towards a Global Ruling Class? Globalization and the Transnational Capitalist Class." *Science and Society* 64(1): 11–54.

Rojas, Viviana, Paul LeBlanc and Thankam Sunil. 2014. "U.S. Retirement Migration to Mexico: Understanding Issues of Adaptation, Networking, and Social Integration." *International Migration and Integration* 15(2): 257–273.

Rosenberg, Emily S. 1982. *Spreading the American Dream: American Economic and Cultural Expansion, 1890–1945*. New York: Hill and Wang.

Rumelili, Bahar, E. Fuat Keyman and Bora Isyar. 2011. "Multilayered Citizenship in Extended European Orders: Kurds Acting as European Citizens." *Journal of Common Market Studies* 49(6): 1295–1316.

Saez, Emaanuel and Gabriel Zucman. 2016. "Wealth Inequality in the United States since 1913: Evidence from Capitalized Income Tax Data." *Quarterly Journal of Economics* 131(2): 519–578.

Said, Edward. [1979] 1994. *Orientalism*. New York: Vintage Books.

Sakallıoğlu, Ümit Cizre and Erinç Yaldan. 2000. "Politics, Society, and Financial Liberalization." *Development and Change* 31(2): 408–581.

Sarı Karademir, Burcu. 2012. "Turkey as a 'Willing Receiver' of American Soft Power: Hollywood Movies in Turkey During the Cold War." *Turkish Studies* 13(4): 633–645.

Saunders, Frances S. 2000. *The Cultural Cold War: The CIA and the World of Arts and Letters*. New York: New Press.

Savage, Mike. 2000. *Class Analysis and Social Transformation*. Oxford: Oxford University.

Savage, Mike, Gaynor Bagnall and Brian Longhurst. 2001. "Ordinary, Ambivalent and Defensive: Class Identities in the Northwest of England." *Sociology* 35(4): 875–892.

Sayer, Andrew. 2005. "Class, Moral Worth and Recognition." *Sociology* 39(5): 947–963.

Sever, Ayşegül. 1998. "The Compliant Ally? Turkey and the West in the Middle East 1954–58." *Middle Eastern Studies* 34(2): 73–90.

Schaeffer, Felicity Amaya. 2012. *Love and Empire: Cybermarriage and Citizenship Across the Americas*. New York: NYU Press.

Shachar, Ayelet. 2007. "The Worth of Citizenship in an Unequal World." *Theoretical Inquiries in Law* 8(2): 367–388.

———. 2009. *Birthright Lottery: Citizenship and Global Inequality*. Cambridge: Harvard University Press.

Shachar, Ayelet and Ran Hirschl. 2007. "Citizenship as Inherited Property." *Political Theory* 35(3): 253–287.

———. 2013. "Recruiting 'Super Talent': The New World of Selective Migration Regimes." *Indiana Journal of Global Legal Studies* 20(1): 71–107.

Shafak, Elif. 2017. "The Urgency of Cosmopolitan Ideal as Nationalism Surges." *Huffington Post*. 19 February 2014. https://www.huffingtonpost.com/elif-shafak/urgency-cosmopolitan-ideal-nationalism_b_4732212.html#.

Shamir, Ronen. 2005. "Without Borders? Notes on Globalization as a Mobility Regime." *Sociological Theory* 23(2): 197–217.

Sharp, Joanne P. 2001. *Condensing the Cold War: Reader's Digest and American Identity*. Minneapolis: University of Minnesota Press.

Sheehan, Matt. 2015. "Born in the USA: Why Chinese 'Birth Tourism' is Booming in California." *Huffington Post*. https://www.huffingtonpost.com/2015/05/01/china-us-birth-tourism_n_7187180.html (last accessed 14 February 2019).

Shirani, Fiona, Karen Henwood and Carrie Coltart. 2011. "Meeting the Challenges of Intensive Parenting Culture: Gender, Risk Management and the Moral Parent." *Sociology* 46(1): 25–40.

Sikkink, Katherine. 2002. "Transnational Advocacy Networks and Social Construction of Legal Rules." In *Global Prescriptions: The Production, Exportation, and Importation of a*

New Legal Orthodoxy. Edited by Yves Dezalay and Bryant Garth, 37–64. Ann Arbor: University of Michigan.

Simpson, Dwight J. 1965. "Development as a Process: The Menderes Phase in Turkey." *Middle East Journal* 19(2): 141–152.

Singerman, Diane and Paul Amar, eds. 2006. *Cairo Cosmopolitan: Politics, Culture, and Urban Space in the New Globalized Middle East*. Cairo: American University of Cairo Press.

Skeggs, Beverley. 1997. *Formations of Class and Gender: Becoming Respectable*. London and Thousand Oaks: Sage.

———. 2005. "The Making of Class and Gender Through Visualizing Moral Subject Formation." *Sociology* 39(5): 965–982.

Sklair, Leslie. 2001. *The Transnational Capitalist Class*. Oxford: Blackwell.

Smith, Michael Peter. 2003. "Transnationalism, the State, and the Extraterritorial Citizen." *Politics and Society* 31(4): 467–502.

———. 2007. "The Two Faces of Transnational Citizenship." *Ethnic and Racial Studies* 30(6): 1096–1116.

Smith, Neil and Isaiah Bowman. 1986. "Bowman's New World and the Council on Foreign Relations." *Geographical Review* 76(4): 438–460.

Soysal, Yasemin. 1994. *Limits of Citizenship and Postnational Membership in Europe*. Chicago: University of Chicago Press.

———. 2012. "Citizenship, Immigration, and the European Social Project: Rights and Obligations of Individuality." *British Journal of Sociology* 63(1): 1–21.

Spiro, Peter J. 2007. "Dual Citizenship: A Postnational View." In *Dual Citizenship in Global Perspective: From Unitary to Multiple Citizenship*. Edited by Thomas Faist and Peter Kivisto, 189–202. New York: Palgrave Macmillan.

———. 2008. *Beyond Citizenship: American Identity After Globalization*. Oxford: Oxford University Press.

———. 2016. *At Home in Two Countries: The Past and Future of Dual Citizenship*. New York: New York University Press.

———. 2019. "The Equality Paradox of Dual Citizenship." *Journal of Ethnic and Migration Studies* 45(6): 879–896.

Srivastrava, Mehlül. 2017. "Erdogan's Diplomatic Spats Leave a Trail of Turkish Disputes." *Financial Times*, 19 October 2017, https://www.ft.com/content/ac1727de-b326–11e7-aa26-bb002965bce8.

Staeheli, Lynn A. 2003. "Cities and Citizenship." *Urban Geography* 24 (2): 97 –102.

Staeheli, Lynn A., David J. Marshall and Naomi Maynard. 2016. "Circulations and the Entanglements of Citizenship Formation." *Annals of the American Association of Geographers* 106(2): 377–384.

Stephan, Alexander, ed. 2006. *The Americanization of Europe: Cultural Diplomacy and Anti-Americanism After 1945*. New York: Berghahn Books.

Stephens, Jacqueline. 2011. *States Without Nations: Citizenship for Mortals*. New York: Columbia University Press.

Sunil, T.S., Viviana Roja and Don Bradley. 2007. "United States' International Retirement Migration: The Reasons for Retiring to the Environs of Lake Chapala, Mexico." *Ageing and Society* 27(4): 489–510.

Tarhanlı, Istar. 1993. *Müslüman Toplum, "Laik" Devlet Türkiye'de Diyanet İşleri Başkanlığı*. Istanbul: Afa.

Taşpınar, Ömer. 2011. "The Rise of Turkish Gaullism: Getting Turkish-American Relations Right." *Insight Turkey* 13(1): 11–17.

Tekeli, Şirin. 1982. *Kadınlar ve Siyasal Toplumsal Hayat* [Women and Socio-Political Life]. Ankara: Birikim.

Thayer, Lucius Ellsworth. 1923. "The Capitulations of the Ottoman Empire and the Question of Their Abrogation as It Affects the United States." *American Journal of International Law* 17(2): 207–233.

Thelen, David. 1999. "The Nation and Beyond: Transnational Perspectives on United States History." *Journal of American History* 86 (2): 965–975.

Therrien, Catherine and Chloe Pellegrini. 2015. "French Migrants in Morocco: From a Desire for Elsewhereness to an Ambivalent Reality." *Journal of North African Studies* 20(4): 605–621.

Tintori, Guido. 2011. "The Transnational Political Prctices of 'Latin American Italians'." *International Migration* 49(3): 168–188.

Trask, Roger R. 1964. "The United States and Turkish Nationalism: Investments and Technical Aid During the Atatürk Era." *Business History Review* 38(1): 58–77.

Tsolidis, Georgina. 2011. "Memories of Home: Family in the Diaspora." *Journal of Comparative Family Studies* 43(3): 411–420.

Tugal, Cihan. 2013. "'Resistance Everywhere': The Gezi Revolt in Global Perspective." *New Perspectives on Turkey* 49: 157–172.

Tugtan, Mehmet Ali, ed. 2013. *Kore Savaşı: Uzak Savaşın Askerleri.* Istanbul: Bilgi University Publications.

"TÜİK: Türkiye'de yabancı uyruklu kişi sayısı 650 bin 308." *T24*, 2 February 2016, http://t24.com.tr/haber/tuik-turkiyede-yabanci-uyruklu-kisi-sayisi–650-bin–308,326566 (last accessed 12 February 2017).

Tummala-Narra, Pratyusha. 2004. "Mothering in a Foreign Land." *American Journal of Psychoanalysis* 64(2): 167–182.

Tunç, Tanfer Emin and Bahar Gürsel, eds. 2012. *The Transnational Turn in American Studies: Turkey and the United States.* Bern: Peter Lang.

Türkmen, Buket. 2009. "A Transformed Kemalist Islam or a New Islamic Civic Morality? A Study of 'Religious Culture and Morality' Textbooks in the Turkish High School Curricula." *Comparative Studies of South Asia, Africa and the Middle East* 29(3): 381–397.

Türkmen, Füsun. 2009. "Turkish-American Relations: A Challenging Transition." *Turkish Studies* 10(1): 109–129.

TURKSTAT. 2017a. *Adrese Dayalı Nüfus Kayıt Sistemi.* (Address Based Population Registration System). Retrieved from http://www.tuik.gov.tr/PreTablo.do?alt_id = 1059.

———. 2017b. *Turizm İstatistikleri.* (Tourism Statistics). Retrieved from http://www.tuik.gov.tr/PreTablo.do?alt_id = 1072.

Turner, Frederick Jackson.1961. *Frontier and Section: Selected Essays.* Englewood Cliffs: Prentice-Hall.

Tyrrell, Ian. 2007. *Transnational Nation: United States History in Global Perspective Since 1789.* Basingstoke: Palgrave Macmillan.

United Nations, Department of Economic and Social Affairs, Population Division. 2016. *International Migration Report, 2015* (ST/ESA/SER.A/384)

Urry, John. 2007. *Mobilities.* Cambridge: Polity Press.

Üsdiken, Behlül. 2011. "Transferring American Models for Education in Business and Public Administration to Turkey, 1950–1970." In *American Turkish Encounters: Politics and Culture, 1830–1989.* Edited by Nur Bilge Criss, Selcuk Esenbel, Tony Greenwood, and Louis Mazzari, 316–330. Newcastle: Cambridge Scholars Publishing.

Üstel, Füsun and Birol Caymaz. 2009. *Seçkinler ve Sosyal Mesafe* [Elites and Social Distance]. Istanbul: Bilgi University and Open Society Foundation.

Üstübici, Ayşen. 2018. *The Governance of International Migration.* Amsterdam: Amsterdam University Press.

Üstüner, Tuba and Douglas Holt. 2010. "Toward a Theory of Status Consumption in Less Industrialized Countries." *Journal of Consumer Research* 37(1): 37–56.

van der Pijl, Kees. 1998. *Transnational Classes and International Relations.* London: Routledge.

van Steenbergen, Bart, ed. 1994. *The Condition of Citizenship.* London: Sage.

Vander Lippe, John M. 1993. "The 'Other' Treaty of Lausanne: The American Public and the Official Debate on Turkish-American Relations." *Turkish Yearbook* 23: 31–38.

Vincent, Carol and Stephen Ball. 2007. " 'Making Up' the Middle-Class Child: Families, Activities and Class Dispositions." *Sociology* 41(6): 1061–1077.

Vitalis, Robert. 2007. *America's Kingdom: Myth-making on the Saudi Oil Frontier.* Palo Alto: Stanford University Press.

Von Eschen, Penny M. 2004. *Satchmo Blows Up the World: Jazz Ambassadors Play the Cold War.* Cambridge: Harvard University Press.

Vora, Neha. 2013. *Impossible Citizens: Dubai's Indian Diaspora.* Durham: Duke University Press.

Walker, Joshua. 2011. "World War II: The Foundation of the Modern Turkish-American Relationship 1939–1947." In *American Turkish Encounters: Politics and Culture, 1830–1989.* Edited by Nur Bilge Criss, Selcuk Esenbel, Tony Greenwood, and Louis Mazzari, 163–182. Newcastle: Cambridge Scholars Publishing.

Waltz, Kenneth N. 2000. "Structural Realism After the Cold War." *International Security* 25(1): 5–41.

Widmer, Ted. 2011. "The Long Journey of Cyrus Hamlin." In *American Turkish Encounters: Politics and Culture, 1830–1989.* Edited by Nur Bilge Criss, Selcuk Esenbel, Tony Greenwood, and Louis Mazzari, 61–74. Newcastle: Cambridge Scholars Publishing.

Wilson, Julie A. and Emily Chivers Yochim. 2015. "Mothering Through Precarity." *Cultural Studies* 29 (5–6): 669–686.

Wolff, Edward N. 2016. "Household Wealth Trends in the United States, 1962 to 2013: What Happened over the Great Recession?" *RSF: The Russell Sage Foundation Journal of the Social Sciences* 2(6): 24–43.

"Yabancılar ve Uluslararası Koruma Kanunu." *Resmi Gazete,* 11 April 2013, http://www.resmigazete.gov.tr/eskiler/2013/04/20130411-2.htm.

Yahirun, Jenjira J. 2014. "Take Me 'Home': Return Migration Among Germany's Older Immigrants." *International Migration* 52(4): 231–254.

Yaqub, Salim. 2004. *Containing Arab Nationalism: The Eisenhower Doctrine and the Middle East.* Chapel Hill: University of North Carolina Press.

Yazıcı, Berna. 2012. "The Return to the Family: Welfare, State, and Politics of the Family in Turkey." *Anthropological Quarterly* 85(1): 103–140.

Yetkiner, Cemal. 2011. "After Merchants, Before Ambassadors: Protestant Missionaries and Early American Experience in the Ottoman Empire, 1820–1860." In *American Turkish*

Encounters: Politics and Culture, 1830–1989. Edited by Nur Bilge Criss, Selcuk Esenbel, Tony Greenwood, and Louis Mazzari, 8–34. Newcastle: Cambridge Scholars Publishing.

Yılmaz, Hakan. 2011. "The Formation of the American-Turkish Alliance and Its Impact of Domestic-Political Developments in Turkey from 1940 to 1960." In *American Turkish Encounters: Politics and Culture, 1830–1989*. Edited by Nur Bilge Criss, Selcuk Esenbel, Tony Greenwood, and Louis Mazzari, 235–260. Newcastle: Cambridge Scholars Publishing.

Yılmaz, Şuhnaz. 2012. "Turkey's Quest for NATO Membership: The Institutionalization of the Turkish–American Alliance." *Southeast European and Black Sea Studies* 12(4): 481–495.

Yom, Sean L. 2015. *From Resilience to Revolution: How Foreign Interventions Destabilize the Middle East*. New York: Columbia University Press.

Yörük, Erdem and Murat Yüksel. 2014. "Class and Politics in Turkey's Gezi Protests." *New Left Review* 89: 103–123.

Young, Marilyn B. 2002. "The Age of Global Power. The History of the United States in the Global Age." In *Rethinking American History in a Global Age*. Edited by Thomas Bender, 274–294. Berkeley: University of California Press.

Yuval-Davis, Nira. 1997. *Gender and Nation*. London: Sage.

———. 2009. "Women, Globalization and Contemporary Politics of Belonging." *Gender, Technology and Development* 13(1): 1–19.

Zürcher, Erik Jan. 1998. "The Ottoman Empire and the Armistice of Moudros." In *At the Eleventh Hour: Reflections, Hopes, and Anxieties at the Closing of the Great War, 1918*. Edited by Hugh Cecil and Peter H. Liddle, 266–275. London: Leo Cooper.

———. 2004. *Turkey: A Modern History*. New York: I. B. Tauris.

Index

Acknowledgments

This book represents the labor of seven years and could not have been written without the incredible support of many institutions, colleagues, and friends. First, we are grateful to the 110 people who graciously agreed to meet with two strangers and share their life stories, anxieties, and aspirations for themselves and for their families. It is to their wonderful generosity that we owe this book—we hope we have done justice to them.

We would also like to thank the Turkish Scientific and Technological Research Council, whose two grants supported the two phases of this research (project numbers 111K574 and 113K639). As part of these grants, Betül Baki, Didem Seyis, and Büşra Ünlüönen were our brilliant research assistants. We owe a special thanks to Betül, who was with us from the start and whose meticulous work always kept us afloat. We would also like to thank Orhun Aras Köksal, Pelin Kılınçarslan, and Gizem Türkaslan, who came to our rescue when we needed extra help. Özlem has worked at Koç University and Evren at Yıldız Technical University and Özyeğin University, and we are grateful for the support we received from them. In 2018–19 we were both on sabbatical, Özlem at the Graduate Institute of International and Development Studies in Geneva and Evren at New York University in New York City, embarking on separate research projects but also working on our manuscript. We are grateful to Elisabeth Prügl, Claire Somerville, and Aslı Peker for making these sabbaticals amazing experiences and to the EU Marie Curie Individual Fellowship and Fulbright Scholarship, respectively, for making them possible.

We have presented our research in its different phases, in front of diverse audiences, since 2012. We are grateful to the organizers and participants of the Contemporary Turkish Studies at a Glance Conference at Bilgi University in Istanbul (2012); the British Sociological Association Conference in Birmingham (2013); the International Studies Association Conference in San Francisco (2013); the Middle Classes between the Lower and the Higher Conference at the Institut Français d'Études Anatoliennes, Istanbul (2014); Koç University Migration Research Center Conferences (2014 and 2015); the European Consortium for Political Research Annual Conference in Montreal (2014); the Middle Eastern Studies Conference in Washington, DC (2014); and the American Anthropological Association Conference in Denver (2015). The discussions we were part of in these settings were vital to our thinking. We have spent the better part of the last few years writing the book, and we probably have exposed several colleagues to more than they would like of the progress of our writing and thinking. We are immensely grateful to Ahmet Icduygu and Ayhan Kaya, who read different parts of what became this book, and to Ayşe Parla, Inderpal Grewal, and Yasemin Soysal, whose suggestions on the framing of the manuscript were invaluable. We are also grateful to Simon Watmough, who copyedited parts of an early version this manuscript. The research presented in Chapter 2 has been published in *Ethnic and Racial Studies*, *Gender, Place and Culture* and *Sociology*. We are thankful to the editors of these journals and the anonymous referees whose comments and suggestions sharpened our writing.

Soli Özel read the entire manuscript from cover to cover; it is hard to convey the combination of learning experience, inspiration, and entertainment his wonderful comments have instigated. We don't think we did justice to them, but we did our best. Jerry Spring has copyedited every single article that we have produced from this research as well as this book. He probably knows the material as well as we do by now, and we are immensely grateful to him for always making time for us and occasionally including little notes of encouragement when he really liked a piece (always received with much excitement). We would like to also thank Noreen O'Connor-Abel, from the University of Pennsylvania Press, for her careful reading of our text and to the two anonymous reviewers for their incredibly helpful suggestions and encouraging evaluation.

We met Peter Agree, our amazing editor, at one of the many international conferences that we were attending around the time we were also doing the research. There was no book in sight, but when we explained to him what we had in mind, his reaction was full-on encouragement. That did not subside one bit as we struggled through the research and then (really) took our time finishing the manuscript. We will always be indebted to him.

We know this book would not have been possible had it not been for the lives we share with our friends, spanning several cities and universities, and also going back to our graduate school days in New York. They know who they are. Özlem would like to thank Feriha, Orhan, and Sarp Altan and Oktay Olcay, and Evren would like to thank Elçin, Ece, Murat, Öner, Ela, Nimet and Selahattin, and for always being there and keeping us grounded.

And finally, Defne Paker and Efe Yağmur Olcay are the true inspirations for our book. Watching them grow up has probably been the most amazing part of writing together. We dedicate this book to them.

www.ingramcontent.com/pod-product-compliance
Lightning Source LLC
LaVergne TN
LVHW091517200926
848483LV00005B/437/J
* 9 7 8 0 8 1 2 2 5 2 1 5 6 *